100 Things You Need to Know: Best people practices for managers & HR

Volume 1

Robert W. Eichinger
Michael M. Lombardo
Dave Ulrich

Researcher: Kathleen Cannon

item number 01024

1st Printing December 2003

2nd Printing April 2004
3rd Printing May 2006
4th Printing November 2007
5th Printing September 2010
6th Printing September 2011

Published by Lominger International: A Korn/Ferry Company
Minneapolis, MN

BIOS

 Bob Eichinger is CEO and cofounder of Lominger Limited, Inc. (now Lominger International: A Korn/Ferry Company) and cocreator of The LEADERSHIP ARCHITECT® Suite of management, executive, and organizational development tools. During his 40-year career, he has worked inside companies such as PepsiCo and Pillsbury, and as a consultant in *Fortune 500* companies in the U.S., Europe, Japan, Canada, and Australia. Bob lectures extensively on the topic of executive and management development and has served on the Board of the Human Resource Planning Society. He has worked as a coach with more than 1,000 managers and executives. Bob's also authored, in collaboration with Mike Lombardo, *The Leadership Machine*. It outlines the steps necessary to develop effective and successful leaders and managers.

 Mike Lombardo was cofounder and director of research and product creation at Lominger Limited, Inc. (now Lominger International: A Korn/Ferry Company) and cocreator of The LEADERSHIP ARCHITECT® Suite. Mike was also director of research in leadership development at the Center for Creative Leadership for 15 years, where he coauthored *The Lessons of Experience*, a study of executive success and derailment that detailed which learnings from experience can teach the competencies needed to be successful. While at CCL, Mike also coauthored BENCHMARKS®, a 360 degree feedback instrument; coauthored the research on executive derailment revealing how personal flaws and overdone strengths caused otherwise effective executives to get into

career trouble; and the LOOKING GLASS® simulation. During his career, Mike has authored over 50 publications dealing with various issues of development and has won four national awards for research on managerial and executive development.

 Dave Ulrich has been listed by *BusinessWeek* as the top "guru" in management education and in HR by numerous publications. He has coauthored 14 books and over 100 articles, serves on the Board of Directors of Herman Miller, and has consulted with over half of the *Fortune 200*. Dave is a professor of business at the Ross School of Business, University of Michigan and Partner, the RBL Group (www.rbl.net).

Acknowledgements

First and foremost, we would like to thank the hundreds of researchers and authors who conceived of and conducted numerous groundbreaking research projects. Without them, this volume would not have been possible. Thanks to each of them for following their passion around each of our 100 topics. We acknowledge the limitations of these 100 topics and know that many more could have been included.

It's daunting enough to mount a research effort, and even more demanding to publish. As all of the researchers we cite know, publishing is a long and arduous journey of peer review, critique, and many rewrites before an article appears in journals or a book finally goes to press. It takes dedication, perseverance, and patience, and we are grateful to them.

Second, we would like to acknowledge the person who did most of the research review work. Kathleen Cannon worked for more than a year to scour and find representative articles and books to support our 100 topics. Many times, her discoveries changed the direction of a topic or changed the sureness of the answer. In addition to her adroit use of the Internet as a tool for sleuthing, her intellectual curiosity and interest in challenging us was extremely helpful.

Since we choose to self-publish, we would like to acknowledge the work of Lesley Kurke, our electronic publishing maven who worked with us over the multiple years this project took to complete. Her formatting ideas and expertise have added value to the work.

Bonnie Parks did her usual thorough job of making it appear we understand grammar and punctuation. She also corrected and hunted down citations for us, so if you search the Internet for one of the articles we cite, it will actually appear on your screen.

Lastly, we would like to thank our reviewers who kept us honest by challenging our findings. We want to especially thank Linda Hodge, Pat Pinto, Linda Rodman, Larry Clark, Rob Kaiser, James Penny, Cara Capretta Raymond, and Adrienne Johns for taking the time to review manuscripts and provide feedback.

Bob, Mike, and Dave

Who is this book for?

This book is intended for three populations:

1. **Any manager or supervisor of people.** The findings in this book point to how to better manage people.

2. **Any leader.** The findings in this book point to how organizational applications should be designed.

3. **Any HR professional.** The findings in this book form the foundation for best practices in Human Resources.

Robert W. Eichinger

Michael M. Lombardo

Dave Ulrich

INTRODUCTION

Over the past 10 years or so, there has been an explosion of research and commentary concerning the return on investment in people. The general form of the inquiry is: What is the return on the money we spend on people (HR) initiatives? If people are really our most important asset, do we really get a payoff for the money we spend on them?

The answer is yes. If we do things right.

There are seven vectors of inquiry on this issue. This book has been created to help increase the chances of getting a return on investment from the money we spend on people and people programs.

Vector 1: Can enterprise HR systems impact the bottom line?

People to follow: Huselid, Becker, Delany, Brockbank, Ulrich, Fitz-enz.

Many researchers are looking at whether the total collective HR system of policies, practices, and processes can impact the bottom line or impact achievement against goals in the case of nonprofits. They have studied whether the quality of the bundle of HR processes have an impact on revenue, profit, market values, and other financial indices. The answer is yes. And, the answer is, the impact can be big, particularly in the area of intangibles. There is much more to study, but the last 10 years have produced an impressive collection of findings.

Vector 2: Can smaller collections of HR practices and programs be traced all the way to the bottom line?

People to follow: Rucci, Kirn, Quinn, Spencer.

Many have studied less than full-enterprise-wide HR applications. Probably the best example of this line of research would be Tony Rucci's study of the retail sales outlet. Following the value chain of: If you create a compelling workplace for retail mangers and employees, they in turn will create a compelling place for customers to shop, who in turn will come more often and spend more, which will increase financial results, which will create a more compelling place to invest. The study documented that value chain and showed conclusively that a well-designed bundle of HR initiatives and applications can work and be traced directly to financial results.

Vector 3: Can single applications be measured in terms of return on investment?

People to follow: Spencer, Pfeffer.

Lyle Spencer has done a number of studies of single HR applications. Applications like better selection systems, better training and development, better coaching, better performance management, better team building, and the like. Across all of those HR practice areas, Lyle has shown that they each return a healthy payoff when done right. Pfeffer has demonstrated that a collection of six pay practices enhances firm financial performance. A lot of work is yet to be done, but it already looks like almost any HR application can be traced to the bottom line. The value chain can be demonstrated.

Vector 4: Is there a set of best practices?

People to follow: Pfeffer, Huselid, Becker, Delany, Spencer.

An effort is underway to see whether there is a specific set of best practices which, taken together, can be used to impact the bottom line. There is an emerging list of four to eight practices that are getting attention and have research behind them. Many question whether there is such a thing as a best practice, instead arguing for practices that best match the situations the firm is in. That view says there are several best practices in each application area. The key is the alignment of the practices with the business proposition. There is much more to come, but already results are intriguing.

Vector 5: Can the outcomes and results be tracked and measured?

People to follow: Kaplan, Norton, Huselid, Becker, Ulrich, Schuler, Boudreau, Flamholtz, Fitz-enz, Cabrera, Ramlall.

Many people are working on the metrics. How can the soft stuff of people be measured? Significant work has been done with the Balanced Scorecard, a combination of hard and soft measures. This has been extended into the HR Scorecard to measure the accomplishment of all of the above. There are endless suggestions of measures and metrics to track and measure the results and outcomes of applications and interventions. The end product will probably be a smaller demonstrated set of hard and soft measures that can be used to document the value chain.

Vector 6: What kind of an HR professional or community of HR professionals would it take to carry this off?

People to follow: Brockbank, Ulrich.

This line of inquiry asks whether we know what good HR people look like. What does it take to bring about the results alluded to above? The best series of studies done on that topic are from Wayne Brockbank, Dave Ulrich, and their colleagues at the University of Michigan. Over the years, they have studied thousands of HR professionals who were rated on effectiveness and personal characteristics by 27,000 customers

of HR. When the best are contrasted to the least, wh
the difference? In the 2003 run of the stu
differentiated between HR competencies that
business results and those that gained HR prof
respect. They found:

Impact of HR Competencies on:

	Personal Competence of HR Professional	Business Results
STRATEGIC CONTRIBUTION Culture Management Strategic Decision Making Fast Change Infrastructure Design	25%	43%
PERSONAL CREDIBILITY Effective Relationships Gets Results Personal Communication	33%	23%
HR DELIVERY Development Structure and HR Measurement Staffing Performance Management	22%	18%
BUSINESS KNOWLEDGE Value Chain Value Proposition Labor	12%	11%
HR TECHNOLOGY	8%	5%

They found that personal credibility had a large impact on the
perceived personal competence of the HR professional, but
strategic contribution had the largest impact on business
results. This makes sense. Personal credibility helps HR
professionals gain access to business meetings. But, the ability

⌐ contribute to the strategy (by shaping a culture, making change happen, focusing on strategic decisions, and building infrastructure) delivers strategic value. HR professionals need to be both credible and competent. Credibility gives them relationships of trust but competence ensures that they add value to the business. We will be hearing more on this as further studies confirm what we think is true about the best of the best HR professionals.

Vector 7: What kinds of leaders do you need to make all of this happen?

People to follow: McCall, Bennis, Kotter, Kouzes, Lombardo, Eichinger.

Under what kind of leadership would all of this happen? Visionary leadership. Empowering leadership. You would have to understand and appreciate the power of people. You have to trust your HR staff to deliver aligned best practices. You have to manage a team of performers. We think we know what these leaders look like, how you can find them and prepare them to lead.

Taken collectively, the seven vectors all come together at one point and show there is a lot of return on investment in people (ROIP) if you know what to do, have the leadership in place to sponsor it, and have the HR capability to execute it.

By consolidating what we know, we think this book will help nudge the needle forward. This book is about findings in the research relating generally to people and organizations. A best practice is one that's built on research and reality. It's doubtful a practice would work if it were not based upon good science. The content in this book addresses all of the vectors of ROIP.

The 100 Chapters

Each chapter contains a separate finding from one area of research important in understanding people and in managing them better. **Each chapter starts with a multiple-choice question with a single recommended answer that is more correct than all the others.** We decided to use multiple-choice questions to make it more fun and challenging. This way you can test yourself and see how many you get right the first time through.

The answer sheet included at the back of the book folds out so you can record your answers. A blank line follows each A–E choice to note the correct answer. If you extrapolate from the findings of Rynes et al. (2002) in their article entitled "HR Professionals' Beliefs About Effective Human Resource Practices: Correspondence Between Research and Practice," the average score should be about 57 correct, the lowest score should be about 26 correct, and the best score should be about 86 correct.

Chapter Coverage

The book is titled Volume 1. We intend further volumes as findings become available. We have made no attempt to have balance in the issues covered by the chapters. These are not necessarily the 100 best, most agreed to, or the most important findings. They simply are the first 100 we considered and found support for. Going forward, we will cover other important findings that lead to what best practices there should be.

What's so?

When turning the page, **you will find the correct answer at the top of the page.**

Next, we indicate on a five-point scale how sure we are of the answer at present. This is our judgment based on the number and consistency of studies to date. (See the end of this chapter for an explanation of the scale.) We would not argue with anyone who believes the real value on the scale should be up or down one scale point. Beyond that, we would differ.

Next comes a brief discussion about the answer.

After that, we present some research summaries. We have made no attempt to be complete, although we did try to select the best references available. The research summaries are a sample of what's available. Someone interested in looking further into the issue presented in the chapter should look at the references for one or more of the most recent research studies listed. These usually will reference most of the past research leading up to the date of the reference.

So what?

Next we present a brief *So what?* If the finding is true, what difference does it make? What should one do that's in line with the finding? What are the best practices that follow from the research?

Each chapter ends with the formal references, attributions, and citations.

What is the process?

Each chapter has a multiple-choice question with one correct answer. For each chapter, we indicate how sure we are of that answer. The **"How sure"** scale is a five-point scale. If challenged, we probably would not argue one point up or one point down from our sureness rating. Following is the five-point sureness scale we have used in the book.

How sure are we at this time?

1	2	3	4	**5**
Hint	Suggestive	Trending	Substantial	**Solid**

5. **SOLID:** Considerable research has been done and the answer is agreed to by almost all of the research done on this topic. The findings will not change in our lifetime.

4. **SUBSTANTIAL:** Enough research has been done to feel strongly about the answer, although further research might shade the answer slightly in one direction or the other.

3. **TRENDING:** Findings are mixed, with the noted answer being slightly favored over other possible answers.

2. **SUGGESTIVE:** Some research points to this answer, but other studies are either not supportive or do not exist. Further research might point in a different direction or not enough research has been done to form a definite view yet.

1. **HINT:** This answer is tentative pending additional research. Only a few studies have been done on this topic or what has been done is contradictory or inconclusive.

Table of Contents

TABLE OF CONTENTS

Chapter   **Page**

Chapter   Page

Table of Contents by Subject

Diversity (continued)   Page

EAP

E-Learning

Employee Development

Employee Motivation

Feedback

Gender

SUCCESS PREDICTION

1.

Are grades a proven predictor of performance as a manager?

SELECT ONE:

☐ A. Yes, if the management job is highly technical in nature.

☐ B. Yes, if the management job manages highly technical people.

☐ C. Only slightly.

☐ D. No, grades do not predict performance as a manager.

☐ E. Yes, for all but a few types of management jobs in manufacturing.

1.   **Are grades a proven predictor of performance as a manager?**

The correct answer is C: Only slightly.

How sure are we at this time?

1	2	3	4	5
Hint	Suggestive	Trending	Substantial	**Solid**

Discussion

Generally, grades in school have little or nothing to do with managerial performance, unless the job is highly intellectual in nature. Then, of course, intelligence would be a better predictor. The management job is one in which many attributes—interpersonal skills, emotional intelligence, drive, and tolerance for ambiguity—are called for, so no single variable will mean much.

Grades have been much studied and generally have not predicted much other than functional/technical skills, intelligence, and inner work standards—having one's own high work standards regardless of what's required by a supervisor or manager. They indicate some degree of technical proficiency, some intelligence, and some amount of drive to complete work. That's about all.

Selected Research

- In *The Bell Curve* by Herrnstein and Murray (1994), they report an overall relationship of .11 between college grades and general job performance, making it the sixth-best predictor of performance. In another study, Roth et al. (1996) reported a correlation of .14 with performance in business jobs (corrected validity of .33; type of job not specified).

- Howard's (1986) decades spanning meta-analysis of grades in school and what they relate and don't relate to for managerial performance revealed three significant findings: (1) No significant relationship was found between undergraduate grades and global success measures in business; (2) No relationship was found between grades and supervisory ratings of more specific qualities; and (3) Grades were largely irrelevant to later success for engineers. Although the overall feeling is that grades indicate intellectual abilities and technical proficiency, the idea that they have more than the slightest relationship to managing won't stand up to examination. It is much, much more the characteristics one brings to the job and what—and how—one learns than the grades earned in college.

- In McClelland's 1973 paper, he argued that traditional academic aptitude, school, and advanced credentials didn't predict how well people would perform on the job or whether they would succeed in life. He further said that competencies like empathy, self-discipline, and initiative distinguished the most successful from those who just got by (McClelland, 1973).

So what difference do these findings make?

- Grades correlate highly to intelligence or IQ. IQ does show a moderate correlation to level of achievement over a career. IQ does correlate to performance as an individual contributor or a manager, especially when the job is highly technical or the intellectual demands are high. So using grades as a selection criterion is somewhat like using intelligence plus commitment to get work done on time and up to specifications and expectations of professors.

- On the other hand, there are other variables like IQ, learning agility, numerous competencies, and EQ which have much stronger relationships to success as a manager.

- Don't overvalue grades or use grades to the exclusion of looking for the other two stronger predictors. The establishment of arbitrary GPA averages (cutoffs) is a bad practice with no science to back it up.

- Let grades be used to admit people into graduate schools, not managerial careers.

Some Key Sources

Herrnstein, R.J., & Murray, C. (1994). *The bell curve.* New York: Free Press.

Howard, A. (1986). College experiences and managerial performance. *Journal of Applied Psychology Monograph, 71* (3), 530–552.

McClelland, D.C. (1973). Testing for competence rather than intelligence. *American Psychologist, 46.*

Roth, P.L., BeVier, C.A., Switzer, F.S., & Schippmann, J.S. (1996). Meta-analyzing the relationship between grades and job performance. *Journal of Applied Psychology, 81,* 548–556.

RETENTION

2.

What's the major reason employees are looking to leave their present employer?

SELECT ONE:

☐ A. Getting away from a failing company.

☐ B. For more total (including incentive and bonus) money.

☐ C. Lack of career growth and development, often blocked by a bad boss.

☐ D. More suited geography or better location.

☐ E. For a better fit with their skills— discovering and banking on their strengths.

2.   What's the major reason employees are looking to leave their present employer?

The correct answer is C: Lack of career growth and development, often blocked by a bad boss.

How sure are we at this time?

1	2	3	4	**5**
Hint	Suggestive	Trending	Substantial	**Solid**

Discussion

It's not about money, or at least, not just money that attracts talented people or causes them to look elsewhere. Of course, there is a threshold for money where, if you are earning substantially less than you might elsewhere, you would be inclined to look around. While this threshold varies by person, most jobs pay within a salary range, so money is not the driving factor in leaving. Getting away from a "bad" boss, especially one who is seen as blocking advancement and achievement and not listening or delegating is the number one reason people look for opportunities elsewhere. Other reasons people move on are—give me a chance to advance, learn, grow; and notice me when I do that.

Selected Research

- A Society for Human Resource Management White Paper (2001) reviews research that demonstrates that one of the main reasons employees leave is because of the performance of their bosses. The authors cite several boss behaviors (lack of attention, recognition, and feedback, as well as "an inability to communicate up the organization") as reasons for leaving.

- Hogan et al. (1990) noted that organizational climate studies from the mid-1950s to the present routinely show that "60 to 75 percent of the employees in any organization—no matter when or where the survey was completed and no matter what occupational group was involved—report that the worst or most stressful aspect of their job is their immediate supervisor."

- Researchers at Robert Half International, Inc., in a sampling of the 1,000 largest employers in the United States, asked 150 top executives, half of them in HR, why good employees quit their jobs. Forty-one percent of executives surveyed said they quit their jobs because opportunities for advancement were limited. Twenty-five percent of those interviewed pointed to lack of recognition. Only 15 percent said money was the primary factor (Grossman, 1998).

- According to a study conducted by Watson Wyatt Worldwide, after examining the employment records of one million workers at 59 companies, the "average job tenure at midsize and large companies was 13.4 years during the period 1995 to 1997—up from 12.6 years from 1990 to 1992" (Grossman, 1998).

- McKinsey updated a 1997 study in which researchers surveyed 6,900 managers (including 4,500 senior managers and corporate officers) at 56 large and midsize U.S. companies. The update found that "89 percent of those surveyed thought it is more difficult to attract talented people now than it was three years ago, and 90 percent thought it is now more difficult to retain them." Just 7 percent of the survey's respondents strongly agreed that their companies had enough talented managers to pursue all or most promising business opportunities (Axelrod et al., 2001).

- Research by Bhagat et al. (1985) suggests that hindrance (negative or hassle) stress ("job demands that produce excessive or undesirable constraints on the individual, such as role ambiguity, conflict, and overload") influences the decision to search for a new job.

- Loden (1985) reports on a Gallup survey that showed that 71 percent of women interviewed stated they do not think they have had the same chance for promotions to top executives and that this belief leads them to identify less than White males do with their organizations and to look elsewhere more often.

- In a 1998 survey of IT workers, more than 80 percent of respondents said that receiving feedback, having individual development plans, and having access to nontechnical skills training would make them less likely to leave their companies. But fewer than 27 percent of respondents had an individual development plan, and only 41.6 percent of companies had programs to help IT workers develop nontechnical skills. And while 83.2 percent of respondents said they'd be more likely to stay with a company that offered 360 degree feedback, only 12.5 percent were currently receiving it (Joinson, 2001).

- Kaye and Jordon-Evans (1999) summarized the reasons most employees remain in their companies. The primary reasons they stay are because of career growth opportunities and exciting work challenges. Fair pay and benefits is 11 out of 11 items.

So what difference do these findings make?
- It's the soft stuff that generally retains talent. It's quality of supervision. It's systematic advancement and opportunities to learn and grow. It's recognition, listening, and delegation.

- Competition for talent (McKinsey). Demographic and social changes have played a growing role in this trend. In the United States and most other developed nations, the supply of 35- to 44-year olds is shrinking. And many of the best-trained people entering the workforce are not bound for large traditional companies, nor do they have the loyalties of the past. It is going to take better managers and better cultures to retain the best. While economic cycles may change the competition for talent, in up-and-down economic cycles, there is inevitable competition for the *right* talent.

- Losing talent (Loden). Current statistics on small, high-growth corporations suggest that, if selection systems are not perceived as rational and fair, ambitious managers might well look for—and take—jobs elsewhere. It appears those led by women are pacesetters in this category. For some, this suggests the importance of more aggressive development of executive skills in aspiring leaders from nontraditional groups, with mentoring being an oft-tried mechanism.

- Focus on retaining high performers (Grossman, Loden). Companies must truly deliver on their promises if they hope to retain talented people. They must demonstrate that they value and appreciate their people. Simply helping high potential people feel connected and vital to the future of the business can be a powerful retention tactic. Let them know they are wanted! One company decided in a downturn that instead of cutting off the bottom 10 percent, it would work aggressively to retain the top 20 percent by telling them they were valued, by giving them opportunities to progress, and by rewarding them. Twelve percent of the other 80 percent left, meeting their downsizing needs.

Some Key Sources

Axelrod, E.L., Handfield-Jones, H., & Welsh, T.A. (2001). The war for talent: Part two. *The McKinsey Quarterly*, Number 2.

Bhagat, R.S., McQuaid, S.J., Lindholm, H., & Segovia, J. (1985). Total life stress: A multi-method validation of the construct and its effects on organizationally valued outcomes and withdrawal behaviors. *Journal of Applied Psychology, 70,* 202–214.

Grossman, R.J. (1998, December). How recruiters woo high-demand candidates. *HR Magazine, 43.*

Hogan, R., Raskin, R., & Fazzini, D. (1990). The dark side of charisma. In K.E. Clark & M.B. Clark (Eds.), *Measures of leadership* (pp. 343–354). West Orange, NJ: Leadership Library of America.

Joinson, C. (2001, May). Employee sculpt thyself, with a little help. *HR Magazine, 46* (5).

Kaye, B., & Jordon-Evans, S. (1999). *Love 'em or lose 'em: Getting good people to stay.* San Francisco: Berrett-Koehler Publishers, Inc.

Loden, M. (1985). *Feminine leadership, or how to succeed in business without being one of the boys.* New York: Times Books.

Munzel, M., & Moore, J.E. (2001, November). *To retain key employees—Develop the boss.* White Paper for Society for Human Resource Management (SHRM). Appeared online October, 2002, at SHRMonline (Advanced search: Munzel).

EMPLOYEE MOTIVATION

What motivates people to work?

SELECT ONE:

☐ A. Pay and benefits compared to people their own age and experience.

☐ B. Pay and benefits in absolute amount; the higher the better.

☐ C. Pay and benefits compared to other possible opportunities.

☐ D. Absolute pay only; benefits generally don't figure in.

☐ E. Quality of jobs and tasks and quality of organization.

3.   What motivates people to work?

The correct answer is E: Quality of jobs and tasks and quality of organization.

How sure are we at this time?

1	2	3	4	**5**
Hint	Suggestive	Trending	Substantial	**Solid**

Discussion

The importance of quality of jobs and organization has been constant over the history of measuring it. The top motivators that turn on people to perform at their best never include pay in any form. The top motivators are usually things like job challenge, opportunities to use one's skills, and progress and quality of the organization in terms of things like quality of supervision and culture.

When pay is in a list of motivators, it is usually near the bottom, along with benefits. Pay may be a demotivator if it is not within a reasonable range, but it is not a motivator.

Selected Research

- According to the 1997 National Study of the Changing Workforce, employers who offer better quality jobs (the kind that offers autonomy, learning opportunities, meaning, and a chance to get ahead) have a demonstrated edge over their competition. They conclude that "the quality of workers' jobs and the supportiveness of their workplaces are the most powerful predictors of productivity—job satisfaction, commitment to their employers, and retention—which are generally competitive with the marketplace."

- Research by Bond et al. (1998) quotes the same study, noting that "Gen Xers are better educated, more racially diverse, work longer hours, and find their jobs more demanding than young workers (Boomers) of 20 years ago."

- According to research by Poe (2000) and the National Association of Colleges and Employers (NACE) (2001), when looking at Gen Xers and Baby Boomers, Gen Xers report higher job quality and job support today than Baby Boomers experienced 20 years ago. The study concludes that "job and workplace characteristics are far more important predictors of productivity than pay and benefits."

- In a global survey of 205 executives, Beer and Katz (2003) discovered that "the most important reason cited for instituting bonuses is that bonuses motivate. At the same time, however, executives believe incentives motivate or improve performance only slightly, if at all." The findings also indicated that incentive systems which make pay contingent on performance may be misguided, and they raise questions about current global trends that point toward the use of more executive incentives. Up until recently, the belief in monetary incentives has been more of a U.S. trend than European or Asian managerial beliefs. "The executives surveyed did not view either the potential positive effects or the potential negative effects of a performance bonus as particularly strong."

- Rewick and Lawler (1978) found pay was 12th on their list of motivating factors and benefits were 16th. The three things at the top of the list were: accomplishing something worthwhile, autonomy, and chances to learn new things.

So what difference do these findings make?

- The motivating factors aren't usually pay or benefits related, rather that workers are looking for job challenges and a supportive, family friendly workplace.

- Attracting, retaining, and motivating talent requires good job and organization design and high-quality bosses.

- Pay should be competitive.

Some Key Sources

Beer, M., & Katz, N. (2003). Do incentives work? The perceptions of a worldwide sample of senior executives. *Human Resource Planning. The Journal of the Human Resource Planning Society, 26* (3).

Bond, J., Galinsky, E., & Swanberg, J. (1998*). The 1997 National Study of the Changing Workforce.* Families and Work Institute: www.familiesandwork.org (Work-Life Research section).

Families and Work Institute. (1997). *Executive summary and synthesis of findings of the 1997 National Study of the Changing Workforce.* Retrieved July 16, 2003, from www.familiesandwork.org (Work-Life Research section).

National Association of Colleges and Employers (NACE). (2001). 2001 Graduating Student & Alumni Survey. (An annual study conducted by NACE.) *Journal of Career Planning & Employment.*

Poe, A.C. (2000, May). Face value. *HR Magazine.*

Rewick, P., & Lawler, E.E. (1978). What you really want from your job. *Psychology Today, 11* (12), 53–65.

4.

What is the relationship between IQ and creativity?

SELECT ONE:

☐ A. There is very little relationship between the two for people who are moderately intelligent and above.

☐ B. There is a strong relationship; you have to be bright to be creative.

☐ C. There is a strong relationship for technical creativity but less for the arts.

☐ D. There is a negative relationship; being too smart gets in the way of creativity.

☐ E. Creativity is actually part of the definition of intelligence so they are almost directly related.

4.   What is the relationship between IQ and creativity?

The correct answer is A: There is very little relationship between the two for people who are moderately intelligent and above.

How sure are we at this time?

1	2	3	4	**5**
Hint	Suggestive	Trending	Substantial	**Solid**

Discussion

There is no relationship between smarts or IQ and creativity beyond the threshold that is generally ensured by hiring college graduates (120 IQ). That means that although we may know your IQ, we can't estimate your creativity. Below that threshold, there is a relationship between intelligence and creativity. Therefore, it takes a threshold of intelligence to be creative and then beyond this it doesn't make a difference.

Selected Research

- According to research by Towers (1988), there is a definite relationship between measured intelligence and creative accomplishment for *groups* of people. Towers' research notes empirically-observable, optimum IQ for creative accomplishment. "Below this 120 IQ level, measured intelligence and creativity have a positive correlation. Above this level, there is no *systematic* relationship between IQ measurements and creativity for *individuals.*"

- Researchers Fuchs-Beauchamp et al. (1993) found that "intelligence and creativity have long been associated, although this relationship weakens with IQs higher than 120."

- Seminal research by Guilford and Christensen (1973) found a relationship between divergent thinking and intelligence but noted weaker relationships between the two after "one has passed some threshold level in basic cognitive capacity."

- In a study to determine the effects of creativity in English, mathematics, and art, McCabe (1991) rated students on the Torrance Test of Creative Thinking (TTCT) and correlated those scores with IQ, achieved grade, and teacher perceptions regarding each student. High creativity scores were associated with high math achievement in this study (McCabe, 1991).

- According to research by Minhas (1981) and later research by Sternberg and Kaufman (1998), traditional IQ tests are ineffective for identification of creativity.

- Vincent et al. (2002) studied the relationship between intelligence, expertise, and divergent thinking as they influence creative problem solving and performance and found that divergent thinking exerted unique effects on creative problem solving that could not be attributed to intelligence or expertise. Intelligence and expertise, however, also contributed to creative problem solving.

- Scratchley and Hakstian (2001) measured the relationship between creative management performance and constructs from the cognitive ability and personality domains. Although divergent thinking and openness correlated significantly with key creative-management criteria, general intelligence correlated only marginally with the criteria, and when divergent thinking was statistically removed, not at all.

So what difference do these findings make?

- Both IQ/intelligence and creativity are important for current performance and future potential and need to be assessed separately because of the low relationship between the two at the moderate to higher IQ levels. Most professionals and managers who have college degrees are at sufficiently high IQ levels for creativity to be a relatively independent characteristic.

- Before hiring for either IQ or creativity, it is important to know the demands of the particular job.

Some Key Sources

Fuchs-Beauchamp, K.D., Karnes, M.B., & Johnson, L.J. (1993). Creativity and intelligence in preschoolers. *Gifted Child Quarterly, 73* (3), 113–117.

Guilford, J.P., & Christensen, P.R. (1973). The one-way relation between creative potential and IQ. *Journal of Creative Behavior, 7*, 247–252.

McCabe, M.P. (1991). Influence of creativity on academic performance. *Journal of Creative Behavior, 25* (2), 116–122.

Minhas, L.S. (1981). A factor analytic study of psychometric and projective indices of creativity and those of intelligence and personality. *Personality Study & Group Behaviour, 1* (2), 29–38.

Scratchley, L.S., & Hakstian, A.R. (2001, October 1). The measurement and prediction of managerial creativity. *Creativity Research Journal, 13* (3–4), 367–384(18).

Sternberg, R.J., & Kaufman, J.C. (1998). Human abilities. *Annual Review of Psychology, 49*, 479–502.

Towers, G M. (1988, August/October). IQ, creativity and the twisted pear, or why the sidekick gets the girl. Reprinted from *Lucid*, Vol. VIII, No. 4/5 (#42/43), Aug./Oct. 1988. *Lucid* is the newsletter of the Mensa "Truth SIG" (Search the Web: Mensa Truth Sig). Retrieved from http://www.foursigma.org/intel/hiqsocs/megasoc/noes149/iq&pear.html

Vincent, A.S., Decker, B.P., & Mumford, M.D. (2002, April 1). Divergent thinking, intelligence, and expertise: A test of alternative models. *Creativity Research Journal, 14* (2), 163–178(16).

DIVERSITY

5.

What is the fastest growing minority in the United States?

SELECT ONE:

☐ A. African Americans.

☐ B. Latin Americans.

☐ C. Asian Americans.

☐ D. Arab Americans.

☐ E. European Americans.

5

5.   **What is the fastest growing minority in the United States?**

The correct answer is B: Latin Americans.

How sure are we at this time

1	2	3	4	**5**
Hint	Suggestive	Trending	Substantial	**Solid**

Discussion
The census has shown that the Latin American minority population is the fastest growing in the United States, with Asian being number two.

Selected Research
* Census 2000 (Census Bureau 2000) reports that Hispanics are the fastest growing minority in the United States. They are now 12.5 percent of the total population. Census estimates show that between July 1, 1990 and July 1, 1999, the Hispanic population grew 38.8 percent to 31.3 million.

* The Hispanic population has more than doubled in size since 1980. In 1980 there were 14.6 million Hispanics in the United States. From 1980 to 1990 they grew by 7.7 million people, or 53 percent, to 22.3 million, and in the next decade the growth rate was even higher. During the 1990s, the Hispanic population increased by 13.0 million people, or 58 percent, reaching a population of 35.3 million at the century's close. Overall, the Hispanic population grew by 20.7 million people from 1980 to 2000. High levels of immigration contributed to this rapid growth, coupled with relatively high fertility levels. The much more rapid growth of the Hispanic population

relative to the non-Hispanic population increased the Hispanic share of the total population in both decades. In 1980 Hispanics constituted 6.4 percent of the total population. By 1990 their share had increased to 9.0 percent, and during the 1990s their share increased by an additional 3.5 percentage points, so that by 2000, Hispanics represented 12.5 percent of the U.S. population, nearly twice the proportion than just 20 years earlier (Hobbs & Stoops, 2002).

So what difference do these findings make?

- Part of getting better at managing diversity in both the customer base and employee population is understanding different ethnic and cultural communities. The data suggest that organizations should orient and train managers to be sensitive to the Latin American and Asian American communities. They need to understand their cultural history, special holidays, ingrained rituals, life priorities, etc. From a language standpoint and in targeted areas, learning some conversational Spanish might be an intelligent move.

- Helping the marketing and sales communities understand and target marketing to the various cultures and ethnic groups served would be an intelligent business strategy.

- Putting the two together would mean having the employee base match the customer base so Latin American employees could help the organization address the Latin American population, and the same would be true for the other ethnic minorities.

Some Key Sources
Hobbs, F., & Stoops, N. (2002, November). Demographic trends of the 20th century. *Census 2000 Special Report.*

U.S. Census Bureau. (2000). U.S. Department of Commerce 2000 Census Results. Online at http://www.census.gov

PERFORMANCE APPRAISAL

6.

How do high performers rate themselves compared with the ratings of others?

SELECT ONE:

☐ A. Rate themselves higher than others rate them.

☐ B. Rate themselves the same as others rate them.

☐ C. Rate themselves lower than others do.

☐ D. Rate themselves lower than others do and lower than low performers.

☐ E. Rate themselves at the same level as low performers.

6

6.   How do high performers rate themselves compared with the ratings of others?

The correct answer is D: Rate themselves lower than others do and lower than low performers.

How sure are we at this time?

1	2	3	4	**5**
Hint	Suggestive	Trending	Substantial	**Solid**

Discussion

In study after study, higher performers rate themselves lower than others rate them, and low performers rate themselves higher than others. The low performers fail to recognize their relative incompetence in a skill, possibly because they don't know what good performance would look like and since they have never done it at a high level. High performers, on the other hand, are more self-critical and have higher expectations of themselves. Another source of higher performers giving themselves lower self-ratings might be the overestimation of how good other people are. It's a matter of calibration compared to others. High performers may not know how good they are.

Overrating is more correlated with poor performance and termination, and underrating is more correlated with better performance. This occurs for managers and executives as well as employees.

Selected Research

- Several researchers found that top performers tend to underestimate their abilities relative to people with whom they compare themselves (Ehrlinger et al., 2003; Haun et al.,

2000; Hodges et al., 2001; Kruger & Dunning, 1999). At the same time, while top performers usually have a good sense of how well they perform in absolute terms (e.g., on a test), they consistently tend to overestimate how well others do on the same test (Fussell & Krauss, 1992).

- Dunning et al. (2003) report that many poor performers are unaware of their poor performance primarily because of their preconceived notions about their skills. They argue that this lack of awareness can "lead people to make judgments about their performance that have little to do with actual accomplishment." They report findings of one study that reveal an overestimate of performance with bottom performers by almost 30 percent. They define this inability to evaluate their own performance as "incompetence means that people cannot successfully complete the task of metacognition, referring to the ability to evaluate responses as correct or incorrect."

- Goleman (1990) found that on 360 degree competence assessments, average performers typically overestimate their strengths, whereas star performers rarely do; if anything, the stars tended to underestimate their abilities, an indicator of high internal standards.

- Research by Fleenor et al. (1996) concludes that those who overrate themselves are perceived as lower in effectiveness, noting that the evidence is clear that "self-ratings tell us little about leader effectiveness," and that there is a kind of manager who routinely overevaluates his or her performance and that tendency is associated with poor leadership.

- In terms of actual promotion (as well as performance), the higher the self-rating compared with those of other groups, the more likely a person is to be terminated (Lombardo & Eichinger, 2003). Those who are terminated rate themselves higher (as do their direct reports). Bosses and peers rated them much lower (a full standard deviation on average). Those who are unchanged rate more similarly to their rater groups. And those who are promoted rate themselves lower than do any rater group. The same trend holds for career stallers. Those terminated rate themselves lower (more favorable) on career stalling behaviors; those promoted rate themselves higher (less favorable).

So what difference do these findings make?

- Self-ratings are suspect in a number of ways. Lower performers overrate (the bottom 20 percent think they are in the top 50 percent) and higher performers underrate.

- Low performers who overrate and high performers who underrate need to be treated differently in appraisal settings.

- Programs (courses, career planning, job placement, etc.) based upon unaided self-assessment or self-selection are therefore questionable.

- Self-assessment should be supported by ratings and evaluations from other groups and constituencies (bosses, peers, customers, direct reports, and HR professionals).

- How a person rates himself or herself compared to how others collectively rate them is one indicator or predictor of future success. Look for indicators that the person consistently overrates or underrates himself.

- 360 degree feedback is a must. Overestimators can learn to modify their ratings after receiving feedback that their self-view is inflated.

Some Key Sources

Dunning, D., Johnson, K., Ehrlinger, J., & Kruger, J. (2003, June). Why people fail to recognize their own incompetence. *Current Directions in Psychological Science, 12* (3), 83.

Ehrlinger, J., Johnson, K., Banner, M., Dunning, D., & Kruger, D. (2003). *Why the unskilled are unaware. Further explorations of (absent) self-insight among the incompetence.* Unpublished manuscript, Cornell University, Ithaca, NY.

Fleenor, J.W., McCauley, C.D., & Brutus, S. (1996). Self-other agreement and leader effectiveness. *The Leadership Quarterly, 7* (4), 487–506.

Fussell, S.R., & Krauss, R.M. (1992). Coordination of knowledge in communication: Effects of speakers' assumptions about what others know. *Journal of Personality and Social Psychology, 62,* 378–391.

Goleman, D. (1998, November/December). What makes a leader? *Harvard Business Review.*

Haun, D.E., Zeringue, A., Leach, A., & Foley, A. (2000). Assessing the competence of specimen processing personnel. *Laboratory Medicine, 31,* 633–637.

Hodges, B., Regehr, G., & Martin, D. (2001). Difficulties in recognizing one's own incompetence: Novice physicians who are unskilled and unaware of it. *Academic Medicine, 76,* S87–S89.

Lombardo, M., & Eichinger, R. (2003). *The LEADERSHIP ARCHITECT® norms and validity report.* Minneapolis: Lominger Limited, Inc.

DEVELOPMENT

7.

As it stands in the nature/nurture debate, the percent influence on adult personality, skills, and traits is approximately:

SELECT ONE:

☐ A. All nurture. People are born a blank slate and a person's upbringing and life experiences create the whole adult person.

☐ B. Mostly nurture. Although there are a few things that get influenced or determined by the jumble of your DNA at birth, the vast majority of who you get to be is influenced by upbringing and life experiences.

☐ C. About half and half. There is an equal influence from your DNA, your upbringing, and life experiences, although the effects vary widely depending upon which trait you're examining.

☐ D. Mostly nature. The jumble of your DNA determines a lot of who you end up to be because most behavior has its origin in your body structure and chemistry. Nurture shades nature but not by that much.

☐ E. All nature. People are born with pre-dispositions toward certain behaviors and behavior patterns, and there is not much that nurture can do to change it.

7.   **As it stands in the nature/nurture debate, the percent influence on adult personality, skills, and traits is approximately:**

The correct answer is C: About half and half. There is an equal influence from your DNA, your upbringing, and life experiences, although the effects vary widely depending upon which trait you're examining.

How sure are we at this time?

1	2	3	**4**	5
Hint	Suggestive	Trending	**Substantial**	Solid

Discussion
Most researchers agree that both heredity (makeup) and the environment influence behavior. What they don't agree on is how to disentangle the specific biological determinants from environmental ones. In other words, you can't assign individuals a predetermined biological makeup, nor can you keep environmental influences constant. From the research we do have, it looks safe to say that there is a significant influence from your physical makeup (structure, chemistry, circuitry) on various traits, characteristics, and even personality. On the other hand, there is probably as much influence from your environment and upbringing. So at the moment, it's a draw— fifty-fifty.

Selected Research
- According to Bouchard et al. (1990), there were two surprising outcomes in the Minnesota Study of Twins Reared Apart: (1) Genetic factors account for a large part of behavioral variability, and (2) Being reared apart in the

same environment has only a negligible effect on the development of similar psychological traits.

- Researchers in another study found that heritability generally accounts for 40 to 50 percent of the variance in personality characteristics when measurements are made in adulthood (McGue et al., 1993).

- Results of a meta-analysis by Harris (1998) revealed that "reared-together siblings are alike in personality only to the degree that they are alike genetically," adding that "the genes they share can entirely account for any resemblances between them." The correlation of personality traits (as estimated by scores on personality tests) is only about .50 for identical twins reared in the same home.

- According to Harris (1995), referring to the Twins studies, correlation values from monozygotic and dizygotic twin studies have been used to calculate the contribution of heredity to personality. In virtually every area of human psychological development that we would ordinarily associate with personality, including those that impact strongly on our social interactions, it has been found that, on average, about 50 percent of the variation among individuals is related to genetic differences (Harris, 1995). (The Minnesota researchers actually believe this figure may be closer to 70 percent because the personality tests used, when applied to the same individual on different days, show a correlation of only about 0.8. So if an 0.8 correlation is taken as potentially representative of complete genetic identity, then the correlations for all of the twin pairs in these tests would actually be higher than the raw scores suggest.)

So what difference do these findings make?
- While 50 percent of who we are might be locked in, 50 percent isn't. Strong counter-environmental influences can override genetic predispositions. The nature/nurture

ratio differs widely depending upon what characteristics you are looking at. Some things like IQ or emotional composition or adventuresomeness have a heavy makeup component, whereas other characteristics have less. When recruiting, look first for those characteristics with the heaviest nature portion because those would be the hardest to train and develop if missing.

• But it's dangerous to assume something isn't developable until you know it isn't. People make too many generalizations about what is developable and what isn't. Even intelligence can be honed and enhanced to a small degree, and IQ tests show that with mentally active people, their scores increase slightly across a lifetime. Other than extremely stubborn traits, most behaviors important to success at work are at least somewhat developable.

Some Key Sources

Bouchard, T.J., Jr., Lykken, D.T., McGue, M., Segal, N.L., & Tellegen, A. (1990, October 12). Sources of human psychological differences: The Minnesota study of twins reared apart. *Science Magazine, 250.*

Harris, J.R. (1995, July). Where is the child's environment? A group socialization theory of development. *Psychological Review, 102* (3), 458–489.

Harris, J.R. (1998). *The nurture assumption: Why children turn out the way they do.* New York: The Free Press.

McGue, M., Bouchard, T.J., Jr., Iacono, W.G., & Lykken, D.T. (1993). Behavioral genetics of cognitive ability: A life-span perspective. In R. Plomin & G.E. McClearn (Eds.), *Nature, nurture, and psychology* (pp. 59–76). Washington, DC: American Psychological Association.

MEASUREMENT

8.

How high does a statistical correlation in the social sciences have to be before it has any practical meaning (e.g., between a test score and performance)?

SELECT ONE:

☐ A. All it has to be is statistically significant; all statistically significant results have practical meaning.

☐ B. It has to be statistically significant and at or above .20.

☐ C. It has to be statistically significant and at or above .30.

☐ D. It has to be statistically significant and at or above .40.

☐ E. It has to be statistically significant and at or above .50.

8. How high does a statistical correlation in the social sciences have to be before it has any practical meaning (e.g., between a test score and performance)?

The correct answer is C: It has to be statistically significant and at or above .30.

How sure are we at this time?

1	2	3	4	**5**
Hint	Suggestive	Trending	Substantial	**Solid**

Discussion

The usual standard in the social sciences is .30 and above. In the widely accepted text on statistical interpretation (Cohen, 1988), .50 is described as large, .30 as moderate, and .10 as small. Although this number might appear low, since many people interpret it as a percent relationship, this is not what it represents. A correlation shows the relationship of two measures—to interpret it as a percent, it must be squared. This yields 9 percent for a correlation of .30, making it look even more meaningless. But this is not the case. Say you want to hire those who are more like the top 50 percent of your managers. You are willing to hire only 1 in 10 qualified candidates, using a predictor test with a correlation of .30 with the performance level of the top 50 percent of your managers. Seventy-one percent should be satisfactory. This is 21 percent better than you are getting now. Another way to look at the practical significance is to ask yourself how much of a discount would entice you to buy something you hadn't quite budgeted for? Ten percent might do it, but 4 percent probably wouldn't.

But, there are a few cases where 4 percent would be just as meaningful. Say you have a correlation of .20 between productivity and some skills-training module. This yields a 4 percent of the variance result. If 1 percent productivity is worth a million dollars, that would undoubtedly be enough to get your attention! So pay the most attention to practical impact, not a number.

The other, more common, case is that many criterion measures (such as performance ratings) are severely range restricted: 5 percent get below average, 70 percent get average, and 25 percent are rated as great. In this case, nothing will correlate much with performance because there is no variance to correlate with. If you have this problem, and most organizations do, use a correction for range restriction formula to get a more accurate view of the likely correlation if the criterion were more normally distributed. Or, work hard to get more spread in your measure of performance.

A correlation measures the strength of relationship between two variables. The strength is measured in a range from -1 to +1. The closer to +1 or -1, the stronger the relationship. The closer to zero, the weaker the relationship. A correlation of +1 would mean two variables vary exactly together. For example, the height of an object measured in both inches and centimeters. As one variable (height in inches) goes up, the other variable (height in centimeters) goes up an equal amount. As another example, the correlation between height and weight is positive and somewhere between 0 and +1, perhaps around .65. In general, the taller you are, the more you will weigh. Thus, the correlation is positive. But it is not always true for every person, so the strength of the relationship is not +1.

A negative relationship occurs when one variable goes up and the other goes down. For example, cigarette smoking and life expectancy have a negative relationship. The more cigarettes you smoke, the shorter your life expectancy.

Selected Research

- Thompson (1994) argues that two analyses need to be emphasized over statistical significance testing: (1) Effect sizes should be calculated and interpreted in all analyses (to evaluate the proportion of variance explained in the analysis, or standardized differences in statistics); and (2) "The replicability of results must be empirically investigated, either through actual replication of the study or by using methods such as cross-validation, the jackknife, or the bootstrap."

- In his book *Successful Intelligence*, Sternberg (1996) puts it this way: "Every student of elementary statistics soon learns that correlation does not imply causation. In other words, the fact that one variable is related to another variable does not mean that the first variable causes the second variable. The second variable may cause the first or both may be related to some third variable, which causes both of them" (p. 227). He adds that addressing causality needs to include reliability and validity (face, content, criterion, and construct).

- Thompson (1994b) notes that using the correct sample size is critical in achieving statistically valid results. "The exact sample size changes based on statistic used, desired confidence level, and desired power (how likely you wish it to be that you will find what you are looking for)."

- A special issue of the *Journal of Experimental Education* (1993) notes, "It is an unfortunate circumstance that statistical methods used to test the null hypothesis are commonly called tests of statistical significance. Equally unfortunate is the tendency to make statements of the type, 'The difference between the experimental and control group was significant at the .05 level,' or the correlation between the two variables was significant at the .05 level. The word 'significant' misleads professional practitioners and the lay public into thinking that the research results are important for this reason. In fact, even researchers and research journal editors might be swayed into thinking that a research result is important because it is statistically significant, or the converse: that a research result is not important because it is not statistically significant."

So what difference do these findings make?

- In normal circumstances, follow the standard (Cohen, 1988) where .50 is a large correlation, .30 is moderate, and .10 is small. Normal is defined as a fairly small sample (say, 30 to 200) with good spread of ratings in both the predictor (e.g., competency ratings) and the criterion (e.g., performance ratings).

- When evaluating whether a study or finding have any meaning in real life, look beyond the statement of statistical significance and the size of the correlation to the practical difference the finding makes in trying to predict something. Be wary when a study has a large sample and the statistics are "significant" but the correlations are very low. This occurs in some large-scale, national studies with lots of respondents.

- Don't dismiss the practical significance of small correlations, however. A correlation of .30 can yield impressive real-world results. Imagine that you could add 9 percent difference in a firm's financial return. Nine percent and lower can mean a lot!

- If your criterion measure(s) is range restricted, then you have two choices. Either apply a range restriction formula to get closer to the true relationship or work harder to spread out the criterion measure. Nothing will correlate much with a performance rating system where 85 to 95 percent of people score average or above.

Some Key Sources

Cohen, J. (1988). *Statistical power analysis for the social sciences* (2nd ed.). New Jersey: Lawrence Erlbaum.

Journal of Experimental Education. (1993). *The role of statistical significance testing in contemporary analytic practice: Alternatives with comments from journal editors* [Special issue]. Washington, DC: Heldref Publications.

Sternberg, R.J. (1996). *Successful intelligence: How practical and creative intelligence determine success in life.* New York: Simon & Schuster.

Thompson, B. (1994, February). *The concept of statistical significance testing.* Washington, DC: ERIC Clearinghouse on Assessment and Evaluation, ERIC/AE Digest.

Thompson, B. (1994b). The pivotal role of replication in psychological research: Empirically evaluating the replicability of sample results. *Journal of Personality, 62* (2), 157–176.

LEARNING AGILITY

9.

Do people differ in how much they learn from experience?

SELECT ONE:

☐ A. Given that they go through the same experiences, they differ very little.

☐ B. Except for people who have obvious learning blockages (i.e., they are arrogant), most people benefit about equally from experience.

☐ C. There are marked differences in how much people learn from experience.

☐ D. The more intelligent you are, the more you learn.

☐ E. People who have received the highest grades in the past learn the most from experience.

9

9.   **Do people differ in how much they learn from experience?**

The correct answer is C: There are marked differences in how much people learn from experience.

How sure are we at this time?

1	2	3	4	5
Hint	Suggestive	Trending	Substantial	**Solid**

Discussion

Some people learn much more from experience than others. Some learn more new perspectives and behaviors from life and work and some less. For example, studies show that successful executives had a strong and similar pattern of learning from key job assignments.

Low-performing executives seem to have much more difficulty learning from experience...tending to form preconceived and general notions of, for example, how to develop others.

The derailed executives, all of whom had been successful for many years before derailing and who had gone through many of the same key assignments as the successful executives, had virtually no pattern of learning from jobs. Their learning appeared to be virtually random. Derailed executives quit learning, thought they were infallible, became legends in their own minds, or couldn't make the transition to a different job or way of behaving. They relied on what had gotten them to where they were, ironically, becoming victimized by their past successes. They got locked into standard ways of thinking and acting that didn't really meet the new demands. They also underestimated the newness of the demands, seeing them as just another version of what they had done before (Lombardo & Eichinger, 2002).

So, people differ widely on what they learn from life and work experience.

Selected Research

- In the CCL studies (McCall et al., 1988), successful executives had a strong and similar pattern of learning from key job assignments. Though successful and unsuccessful managers had many of the same experiences, the "right stuff" of the successful executives in the study seemed to be an ability to "make the most of your experience" (p. 122). In a companion study (McCall & Lombardo, 1983), one of the key reasons cited for derailment was being blocked to new learning.

- In studies that have dealt with success and derailment, failure to learn to do something differently in order to make key transitions has figured prominently in the results. Additionally, lack of self-awareness and a tendency to overrate oneself have been found to be crippling. In contrast, successful people learned more new behavior and were more self-aware (Lombardo & Eichinger, 2000; Shipper & Dillard, 2000).

- Research from Yale by Robert Sternberg states that scores on a measure of learning from experience were unrelated to IQ scores and that the best predictor of level attained was a measure of learning from experience (Sternberg et al., 1995).

- In numerous studies of successful leaders, researchers at the Center for Creative Leadership (CCL) in Greensboro, NC, have determined that developmental learning occurs primarily through work experiences, less in formal training programs, and that successful corporations emphasize job challenge for developing managers (McCauley et al., 1994).

- In a study which related learning agility, IQ, and Big Five personality measures to job performance and measures of promotability, learning agility was by far the most related to performance. According to Connolly and Viswesvaran (2002), the other measures added very little to the regression equations.

- Lombardo and Eichinger (2003) found that the best predictors of actual promotion were competencies measuring learning agility and drive for results (achievement motivation).

So what difference do these findings make?

- Since scores on measures of learning from experience are not very related to IQ and grades, this means that when a company hires graduates with a 3.8 grade point average from the top schools, how well they will learn new behavior over time is unknown. Additional assessment must be done on how they learn.

- Learning new behavior, skills, and attitudes is tougher than factual or technical learning. Fewer people do this well.

- The essence of learning from experience is learning from experiences you have—having challenging jobs and tasks where you either perform against the need or fail. Even if you do hire people who learn well from experience, they have to have the right experiences.

- There is a cycle or pattern to individuals who learn. They make choices, tie choices to consequences, and take corrective action. Nonlearners don't try new things (take choices), cannot connect choices to consequences, and fail to seek feedback that leads to corrective action.

- Of all the things you measure people on, how well they learn from experience is probably the one most important for predicting future performance and potential. There are several well-established measures of acquiring new learning/behaviors.

Some Key Sources

Connolly, J.A., & Viswesvaran, C. (2002, April). *Assessing the construct validity of a measure of learning agility.* A presentation at the Seventeenth Annual Conference of the Society for Industrial and Organizational Psychology, Toronto, Canada.

Lombardo, M., & Eichinger, R. (2000). High potentials as high learners. *Human Resource Management, 39* (4), 321–330.

Lombardo, M., & Eichinger, R. (2004). *The leadership machine.* Minneapolis: Lominger Limited, Inc.

Lombardo, M., & Eichinger, R. (2003). *The LEADERSHIP ARCHITECT® norms and validity report.* Minneapolis: Lominger Limited, Inc.

McCall, M.W., & Lombardo, M. (1983). What makes a top executive? *Psychology Today, 17* (2), 26–31.

McCall, M.W., Lombardo, M., & Morrison, A. (1988). *The lessons of experience: How successful executives develop on the job.* Lexington, MA: Lexington Books.

McCauley, C.D., Ruderman, M.N., Ohlott, P.J., & Morrow, J.E. (1994). Assessing the developmental components of managerial jobs. *Journal of Applied Psychology, 79,* 544–560.

Shipper, F., & Dillard, J. (2000). A study of impending derailment and recovery of middle managers across career stages. *Human Resource Management, 39* (4), 331–347.

Sternberg, R.J., Wagner, R.K., Williams, W.M., & Horvath, J.A. (1995). Testing common sense. *American Psychologist, 50* (11), 912–927.

10.

Is there any evidence that well-designed and executed Human Resource practices have any impact on organizational performance?

SELECT ONE:

☐ A. The evidence is scant.

☐ B. The evidence is equivocal—sometimes yes, sometimes no.

☐ C. The evidence is generally positive.

☐ D. The evidence is impressive.

☐ E. Couldn't actually be measured.

10

10. **Is there any evidence that well-designed and executed Human Resource practices have any impact on organizational performance?**

The correct answer is D: The evidence is impressive.

How sure are we at this time:
1	2	3	4	**5**
Hint	Suggestive	Trending	Substantial	**Solid**

Discussion
There is strong evidence that what are called High Performance HR Practices, such as employee recruitment and selection procedures, incentive compensation, performance management systems, and extensive employee involvement and training can improve many outcome measures, such as productivity, product quality, and innovative work practices.

In addition to bottom-line impact, studies show a correlation between these High Performance HR Practices and job satisfaction, employee recruitment, and retention.

Selected Research
- In the award-winning Mark Huselid study of about 1,000 publicly held U.S. firms, a one standard deviation increase in these high performing HR applications produced: $27,000 more in sales per employee, $18,600 in market value per employee, $41,000 in shareholder value per employee, $3,800 more in profit per employee, and a 7 percent decline in turnover (Huselid, 1995).

- An analysis of nearly 3,000 firms showed a strong relationship between high performance HR systems and shareholder value. Becker et al. (2001) found that a 35 percent increase in this index is associated with a 10 to 20 percent increase in shareholder value.

- A study of nearly 200 banks found that "differences in HR practices are associated with large differences in financial performance...financial performance was estimated to be approximately 30 percent higher for banks one standard deviation above the mean than it was for those banks at the mean" (Pfeffer, 1998).

- McKinsey's War for Talent 2000 survey of 410 corporate officers at 35 large U.S. companies showed that a high performer generates 40 percent more in increased productivity in operations roles, 49 percent higher increased profit in general management roles, and 67 percent more in increased revenue in sales roles (McKinsey's War for Talent 2000 survey in Axelrod et al., 2001).

- The National Study of the Changing Workforce found that "the quality of workers' jobs and the supportiveness of their workplaces are the most powerful predictors of productivity—job satisfaction, commitment to their employers, and retention. Job and workplace characteristics are far more important predictors than pay and benefits, which are generally competitive with the marketplace" (Bond et al., 1998). This is supported by numbers from a study of retail workers by Rucci (1998) where creating a compelling place to work led to increased sales on the floor.

- A study by MacDuffie (1995) found that innovative human resource practices are likely to contribute to improved economic performance when three conditions are met: (1) Employees possess knowledge and skills that managers lack; (2) Employees are motivated to apply this skill and knowledge through discretionary effort; and (3) The firm's business or production strategy can only be achieved when employees contribute such discretionary effort.

So what difference do these findings make?

- The evidence of sound HR practices and their impact is impressive. Research has consistently found that use of effective human resource management practices enhances firm performance...and the effects are large and managerially important.

- The effects of investment in HR and business impact follow a traditional "S" curve. Firms that have little or no HR and begin sound HR practices will have a jump in performance. Firms in the middle range of HR practices (those that do some things well and some not so well) will not see dramatic business results. Firms at the high end of sound HR practices (those that do most HR practices well) have another jump in business impact. This implies that if you are going to invest in HR for business success, it is important to go all the way and invest in many good HR practices, not one at a time.

- HR professionals who talk to business leaders should be able to talk about business results (e.g., financial performance or acquiring capabilities), not just HR activities (e.g., we did 40 hours of training).

- HR professionals need to become familiar with the research results over the last 10 years and begin to apply the technology.

Some Key Sources

Axelrod, E.L., Handfield-Jones, H., & Welsh, T.A. (2001). The war for talent: Part two. *The McKinsey Quarterly,* Number 2.

Becker, B., Huselid, M., & Ulrich, D. (2001). *The HR Scorecard: Linking people, strategy and performance.* Boston: Harvard Business School Press.

Bond, J., Galinsky, E., & Swanberg, J. (1998). *The 1997 National Study of the Changing Workforce.* Families and Work Institute: www.familiesandwork.org (Work-Life Research section).

Huselid, M. (1995). The impact of human resource management practices on turnover, productivity, and corporate financial performance. *Academy of Management Journal, 38* (3), 635–672.

MacDuffie, J.P. (1995). Human resource bundles and manufacturing performance: Organizational logic and flexible production systems in the world auto industry. *Industrial and Labor Relations Review, 48,* 199.

Pfeffer, J. (1998). *The human equation. Building profits by putting people first.* Boston: Harvard Business School Press.

Rucci, A.J., Kirn, S.P., & Quinn, R.T. (1998, January/February). The employee-customer-profit chain at Sears. *Harvard Business Review.*

FEEDBACK

11.

Which of the following Is the most true about managers/supervisors in delivering negative feedback/criticism to direct reports?

SELECT ONE:

- ☐ A. Most managers/supervisors find it hard and uncomfortable.

- ☐ B. Most managers/supervisors find it hard but most do it.

- ☐ C. Most managers/supervisors find it uncomfortable but not hard.

- ☐ D. Most managers/supervisors find it easy but uncomfortable.

- ☐ E. Most managers/supervisors give adequate negative feedback easily.

11. **Which of the following is the most true about managers/supervisors in delivering negative feedback/criticism to direct reports?**

The correct answer is A: Most managers/ supervisors find it hard and uncomfortable.

How sure are we at this time?

1	2	3	**4**	5
Hint	Suggestive	Trending	**Substantial**	Solid

Discussion

Most managers aren't very adept at developing people for the long-term (usually bottom or worst 10 in terms of competencies). They're not much better at giving critical feedback (again, among the bottom 10 skills). Peers and colleagues aren't any better either when it comes to timely face-to-face critical feedback. After all, peers and colleagues are made up of the same people (managers and executives).

Selected Research

- Research shows that high potentials—especially executives—get less feedback. They are more likely to be told how wonderfully they are doing; specific feedback or even formal performance appraisals can be rare (Kaplan et al., 1991).

- O'Reilly (1983) found that "the supportiveness of a feedback source affects how frequently it is used. So do accessibility, credibility, and the potential affective sign of the information sought."

- Murphy and Cleveland (1991) noted that the evaluation of a manager's performance depends, in part, on the relationships that the person has established with his or her subordinates.

- Lombardo and Eichinger (2003) have found repeatedly over the years that the competency, confronting problem direct reports (giving negative and critical feedback), ranks 63rd out of a library of 67 typical competencies, and developing direct reports is dead last (67th out of 67).

So what difference do these findings make?

- Face-to-face feedback can be improved by focusing on agreed-upon competencies necessary to reach work goals. This makes it easier to discuss and improve, since people generally believe that competencies are developable, and if developed, will lead to higher performance. Low performers consistently overrate themselves, so having them track their own performance helps them gain a more accurate view of their contribution.

- There should never be feedback just for its own value. There is no evidence that accurate negative data hurts people or that positive feedback helps them. In an analysis of numerous studies, feedback improved average performance. However, in one-third of the cases, it decreased performance. Any feedback intervention must be accompanied with goal setting. Tied to a goal or purpose, feedback helps people improve. Tied to nothing, it can backfire (Kluger & DiNisi, 1996).

- 360 degree feedback can help. Giving anonymous feedback is easier than face-to-face. That is, the same people who are reluctant to deliver critical feedback face-to-face will do it on a confidential 360 degree questionnaire or when being anonymously interviewed. This may be because giving critical feedback anonymously invites us to be more honest. To knowingly give an inflated rating is, in effect, lying to ourselves and, more importantly, to the people who are trying to work on their development.

- Leaders who have feedback to give to subordinates should just do it! It does not get easier over time. Employee problems generally do not go away. How feedback is given matters a great deal, e.g., being specific, clear, and supportive, but it matters more that it is given.

Some Key Sources

Kaplan, R.E., Drath, W.H., & Kofodimos, J.R. (1991). *Beyond ambition*. San Francisco: Jossey-Bass.

Kluger, A.N., & DiNisi, A. (1996). The effects of feedback interventions on performance: A historical review, a meta-analysis, and a preliminary intervention theory. *Psychological Bulletin, 119*, 254–284.

Lombardo, M., & Eichinger, R. (2003). *The LEADERSHIP ARCHITECT® norms and validity report*. Minneapolis: Lominger Limited, Inc.

Murphy, K.R., & Cleveland, J.N. (1991). *Performance appraisal*. Boston: Allyn & Bacon.

O'Reilly, C.A., III. (1983). The use of information in organizational decision-making: A model and some propositions. In L.L. Cummings & B.M. Staw (Eds.), *Research in organizational behavior* (Vol. 5, pp. 109–139). Greenwich, CT: JAI Press.

CAREER DEVELOPMENT

12.

As you move from individual contributor to supervisor to manager to director to executive, which of the following is most correct?

SELECT ONE:

☐ A. The need for technical skills increases at each step up.

☐ B. Interpersonal skills decrease in importance because you are managing mostly through others who have to have the interpersonal skills.

☐ C. The intellectual challenges increase so you have to be smarter as you move up the chain.

☐ D. The conceptual challenges increase so you have to be more flexible and open to new learning and making decisions under increasing levels of uncertainty.

☐ E. The managerial challenges increase so you have to be better at EQ each step up the ladder.

12. **As you move from individual contributor to supervisor to manager to director to executive, which of the following is most correct?**

The correct answer is D: The conceptual challenges increase so you have to be more flexible and open to new learning and making decisions under increasing levels of uncertainty.

How sure are we at this time?

1	2	3	**4**	5
Hint	Suggestive	Trending	**Substantial**	Solid

Discussion

While all the answers other than A contain some truth, as people move up the hierarchy, jobs become progressively more complex—more processes to manage, more innovations to nurture, and many more unknowns. The problems become increasingly nontechnical, unstructured, and unanticipated.

Selected Research

• Research by Katz and Kahn (1978) demonstrates that "while tactical and technical, interpersonal, and conceptual skills are required at any level of leadership, conceptual skills and flexibility overshadow all other skills necessary at upper levels of management."

• Howard and Bray (1988) found that the ability to deal with ambiguity had the highest correlation with long-term success in the AT&T management progress studies.

• Lombardo and Eichinger (2003) found that, for managers and executives, competencies like creativity, innovation management, and dealing with ambiguity become strong predictors of promotion.

- One of the basic principles of Jaques' Stratified Systems Theory (SST) is that "leadership performance requirements change at higher organizational levels." Research by Zaccaro (1996) concludes that "at higher organizational levels, problem types and decision choices become more ambiguous, less structured, and more differentiated."

- In their decade-long research, Jacobs and Jaques (1990) found that the conceptual demands on leaders become more complex as they move into more senior leadership roles.

- Stamp (1988) used the CPA (Career Path Appreciation procedure that captures a person's "capability," defined on four dimensions that was developed by Jaques) with several samples of executives and showed strong correlations (in the low .70s) of scores on the CPA and the eventual organizational level to which the executive was promoted.

- Personality tests also seem to have more validity as one moves into more responsible managerial levels. Research by Schmidt et al. (1992) found evidence of personality factors as predictors of managerial success.

So what difference do these findings make?
- The key skills as one moves up in the organization tend to be conceptual flexibility, dealing with complexity and ambiguity, and learning agility; plus all of the other more typical skills needed to manage others and to manage organizations. These are skills that can be acquired if they are defined, practiced, and monitored.

- Develop skills a level early before the stakes get too high. For discussion on how to develop people, see Lombardo and Eichinger (2002) and McCall (1998).

Some Key Sources

Howard, A., & Bray, D. (1988). *Managerial lives in transition: Advancing age and changing times.* New York: Guilford Press.

Jacobs, T.O., & Jaques, E. (1990). Military executive leadership. In K.E. Clark & M.B. Clark (Eds.), *Measures of leadership* (pp. 285–295). West Orange, NJ: Leadership Library of America.

Katz, D., & Kahn, R.L. (1978). *The social psychology of organizations* (2nd ed.). New York: Wiley.

Lombardo, M., & Eichinger, R. (2004). *The leadership machine.* Minneapolis: Lominger Limited, Inc.

Lombardo, M., & Eichinger, R. (2003). *The LEADERSHIP ARCHITECT® norms and validity report.* Minneapolis: Lominger Limited, Inc.

Schmidt, F.L., Ones, D.S., & Hunter, J.E. (1992). Personnel selection. *Annual Review of Psychology, 43,* 627–670.

Stamp, G. (1988). *Longitudinal research into methods of assessing managerial potential.* Alexandria, VA: U.S. Army Research Institute for the Behavioral and Social Sciences.

Zaccaro, S.J. (1996). *Models and theories of executive leadership: A conceptual/empirical review and integration.* Alexandria, VA: U.S. Army Research Institute for the Behavioral and Social Sciences.

13.

Writing about and talking about your issues, limitations, and weaknesses:

SELECT ONE:

13

☐ A. Actually can decrease the severity of the problems and start you on the road to fixing them.

☐ B. Actually makes things worse because it just reminds you of the long list of things you have to work on.

☐ C. Has no documentable impact on how you feel nor on progress fixing the problems.

☐ D. Only has a benefit if it involves talking about the problems with a person skilled at helping.

☐ E. Can help a person feel better but has no actual benefit to helping fix or solve the problems.

13. **Writing about and talking about your issues, limitations, and weaknesses:**

The correct answer is A: Actually can decrease the severity of the problems and start you on the road to fixing them.

How sure are we at this time?

1	2	**3**	4	5
Hint	Suggestive	**Trending**	Substantial	Solid

Discussion

The original theory in the first studies of writing as a form of therapy was based on the idea that not talking about important psychological events is a form of inhibition. Inhibited people seem to exhibit more health problems than those who are less inhibited due to the physical damage caused by holding emotions and feelings back. In *Opening Up: The Healing Power of Expressing Emotions* by James Pennebaker, he says, "Confession, whether by writing or talking, can neutralize many of the problems of inhibition."

Pennebaker also learned that a criminal's heart rate and breathing was much slower after a confession than before, implying that inhibiting behavior, or holding back, has an effect (assumed to be damaging) on health. In other studies on lie detection, actively holding back showed instances of higher blood pressure, heart rate, and skin conductance. Most practitioners and writers in the area of emotional disclosure endorse Pennebaker's results and refer to him as one of the pioneers of expressive writing intervention.

Studies have also shown that prolonged emotional stress can increase the incidence of many illnesses. One of the important predictors is the way in which individuals handle traumatic experiences. Breaking the trauma into smaller pieces by writing about it seems to give the writer a sense of increased control and understanding of the issue and enables him/her to better manage the situation, not unlike Freud's talking therapy. "Translating important psychological events into words is uniquely human. Therapists and religious leaders have known this intuitively for generations" (Pennebaker, 1997).

These findings can be extended to the workplace. What does one do with the feedback from performance discussions and 360s? Celebrate the good news, yes, but what about the bad news? Just discovering and talking with a facilitator, boss, friend, or mentor should have a positive effect on feeling better and might even lead to some progress on the issues.

Selected Research

- Sigmund Freud discusses inhibition in his book *Inhibitions, Symptoms and Anxiety*, saying, "One can quite well call a normal restriction of a function an inhibition of it." He further states that an inhibition in work is when a "subject feels a decrease in his pleasure in it or becomes less able to do it well; or he has certain reactions to it, like fatigue, giddiness, or sickness, if he is obliged to go on with it."

- Pennebaker, Kiecolt-Glaser, and Glaser (1988) showed that failure to confront traumatic events, resulting in being forced to live with unresolved issues or actively holding back emotions, can become manifested in disease, but those who confront these situations show improvement in health. Subjects who wrote about topics that they had previously held back from telling others showed the greatest health improvements.

- Joshua Smyth et al. (1999) showed that writing is good for emotional and physical health. He showed that expressive writing reduced pain and increased motion in arthritis patients and increased lung capacity for asthmatics for

47 percent of the group that wrote about their traumas. During the three-day writing exercise, some participants exhibited stressful, negative short-term effects from the process, but long-term effects seemed to be beneficial.

- Pennebaker (1990) and Spera, a psychologist with an outplacement company, conducted a study on men who were laid off from their jobs and were unable to find work after four months. Half of the study group was asked to write about their thoughts and feelings about the layoff for 30 minutes a day for five consecutive days. The other half of the group wrote about how they used their time. A third group did not write at all and just served as a comparison group. Twenty-seven percent of the group that wrote about the layoff and the associated emotions landed jobs and only 5 percent of the time-management group and the comparison group were able to find employment. A few months later the percentages increased to 53 percent for the thoughts and feelings group and 18 percent for the other groups. The men in all three groups went on the same number of interviews. The study showed that those who had come to terms with the layoff and had processed their anger through writing seemed to fare better in interviews, appeared less hostile, and came across as more promising candidates.

- Many additional practitioners and researchers advocate journaling and feedback sessions using structured expressive writing to get both physical and emotional benefits (Lange et al., 2002; Adams, 1990).

So what difference do these findings make?
- Writing about or talking with someone about something you have been worrying about or avoiding, something that is affecting your life in an unhealthy way, can improve physical and mental health.

• Providing people feedback on their issues and weaknesses and then having them talk it out with someone who is qualified to coach or mentor can have a positive effect on feelings and even physical health. The short-term stress of dealing with conflict is offset by the long-term results.

Some Key Sources

Adams, K. (1990). *Journal to the self.* New York: Warner Books.

Dienstfrey, H. (1999). Disclosure and health: An interview with James W. Pennebaker. *Advances in Mind-Body Medicine 15*, 161–194. © John E. Fetzer Institute.

Glaser, R., Kiecolt-Glaser, J.K., Pennebaker, J.W. (1988). Disclosure of traumas and immune function: Health implications for psychotherapy. *Journal of Consulting and Clinical Psychology, 56* (2), 239–245.

Lange, A., Mirjam, S., Bart, S., & Van De Ven, J-P. (2002). Interapy: A model for therapeutic writing through the Internet. In S.J. Lepore & J. Smyth (Eds.), *The writing cure: How expressive writing promotes health and emotional well-being.* Washington, DC: American Psychological Association.

Lepore, S.J., & Smyth, J. (Eds.). (2002). *The writing cure: How expressive writing promotes health and emotional well-being.* Washington, DC: American Psychological Association.

Pennebaker, J.W. (1990). *Opening up: The healing power of expressing emotions.* New York: Scribner.

Pennebaker, J.W. (1997). Writing about experiences as a therapeutic process. *Psychological Science, 8,* 162–165

Pennebaker, J.W. (1995). *Emotion, disclosure & health.* Washington, DC: American Psychological Association.

Slomski, G. (2001). *Gale Encyclopedia of Alternative Medicine.* Gale Group.

Smyth, J.M., Stone, A.A., Hurewitz, A., & Kaell, A. (1999). Effects of writing about stressful experiences on symptom reduction in patients with asthma or rheumatoid arthritis: A randomized trial. *Journal of the American Medical Association, 281,* 1304–1309.

14.

What can be said about the underlying structure of the brain and it's ability to change over time?

SELECT ONE:

14

☐ A. The brain's structure is established at birth and almost no fundamental changes occur past that point.

☐ B. Through a combination of genetics and early infant and childhood experiences, the brain grows and changes up to about the age of 10 and then stabilizes into a relatively static structure.

☐ C. Through a combination of genetics and early infant and childhood experiences, the brain grows and changes up to about the age of 20 and then stabilizes into a relatively static structure.

☐ D. Although the brain's structure is primarily determined by genetics and early life experiences, small changes can continue up until about the age of 50, after which few changes take place.

☐ E. Although the brain's structure is primarily determined by genetics and early life experiences, significant changes can continue throughout life; the more active and new-learning oriented the person is, the more changes that occur.

14. **What can be said about the underlying structure of the brain and it's ability to change over time?**

   The correct answer is E: Although the brain's structure is primarily determined by genetics and early life experiences, significant changes can continue throughout life; the more active and new-learning oriented the person is, the more changes that occur.

How sure are we at this time?

1	2	3	**4**	5
Hint	Suggestive	Trending	**Substantial**	Solid

Discussion

There is a significant impact on the brain from prebirth genetics, pre- and postnatal experiences, and early life experiences. Early life experiences can have a dramatic impact on the structure and the capabilities of the brain extending into adult behavior. That said, experience alters the brain's structure and capabilities throughout life. The more significant the experiences, the more significant the change. Evidence also shows that seemingly similar experiences can alter neuronal circuits in different ways. In studies of aging and brain function, the adage "use it or lose it" turns out to be true. Older people who stay mentally active lose less brain function. In some cases, searching out and engaging in new and unique challenges might even increase brain function in older people. In the context of organizational behavior, this would argue for life-long learning and the continuous improvement of the brain's capacity to function by learning new and unique things and exposing oneself to new and different challenges.

Selected Research

- Research (Kolb, Gibb, & Robinson, 2003) has shown that the brain and nervous system are capable of change—often noted as change in behavior or psychological function. Although psychologists have assumed that the nervous system and the brain are sensitive to experience during development, it's only in recent years that they've begun to appreciate the potential for "plastic changes in the adult brain." Kolb et al. conclude that "if neural networks are changed by some experience, there should be an accompanying change in the functions those neurons mediate." Their research identified two changes: the first in the modification of current circuits, and the second in the addition of new circuits based upon adult experiences. They further note that many things affect brain circuitry throughout life; these include experiences, drugs, hormone changes, diet, disease, stress, and injury to the brain.

- Kramer and Willis (2003) note that the related decline in cognitive skills can sometimes be reduced through experience, cognitive training, and other interventions such as fitness training.

- Hultsch et al. (1999) showed participation in cognitively demanding everyday activities buffers cognitive decline in later life. Research results showed that those with higher levels of intellectual activity, or those who showed less decline in intellectual activities, also showed less decline in cognition.

- Wilson et al. (2002) had similar findings. They found that more frequent participation in cognitively stimulating activities is associated with a reduced risk of Alzheimer's disease (AD). On a scale measuring cognitive activity, a one-point increase in cognitive activity corresponded with a 33 percent reduction in the risk of AD.

- Following a study of older persons from geographically defined communities, Wang et al. (2002) confirm an association between cognitive activity and a reduced incidence of Alzheimer's disease.

- Research by Dr. Mary Haan (2002), who studied 6,000 volunteers aged 65 or older for seven years, found that 70 percent of the volunteers "had no change in a test that measures mental acuity during the course of the study." She notes that the people who did score lower over time most likely did so for several reasons: They had the genetic marker for Alzheimer's disease or other risk factors like heart disease, high blood pressure, high cholesterol, and diabetes. She also found that educational level of the volunteers affected the risk of cognitive decline, noting that "those with 9 to 11 years of education had some change, but the most rapid decline in cognition was associated with those who had less than 9 years of education."

- Wilson and Bennett (2003) report findings that suggest "frequent participation in cognitively stimulating activities may reduce risk of Alzheimer's disease in old age." A four-year study of older residents of a community found that those who had more education had a lower incidence of Alzheimer's disease. However, when increased cognitive activity was added to the analysis, the educational attainment status became statistically insignificant.

- Research by Stern et al. (1994) reports evidence from their research that found that "people with higher educational and occupational attainment tend to have a lower risk of developing Alzheimer's disease than do people with lower educational and occupational attainment."

- Evans et al. (1997) hypothesize that the reason research has shown that those with higher education backgrounds and greater occupational success have a lower incidence of Alzheimer's is that both of these achievements point to "frequency of participation in cognitively stimulating activities." So again, it is use it or...?

So what difference do these findings make?

* Changes in the nervous system and the brain can and do occur throughout life. Learning-active people will improve their nervous system and brain to improve performance throughout life.

* Cynics and some "select, don't develop" types claim people don't change significantly after adolescence. Some even cite "evidence" from brain research. Such claims are most likely false.

* Hiring older employees may be a good source of talent. Older employees may not work as quickly as younger employees, but they are often more accurate and service oriented.

* In the nature/nurture debate, it is about fifty-fifty. Some people have predispositions (nature) that limit what they can do, but most have opportunities (nurture) that far exceed their limitations.

Some Key Sources

Evans, D.A., Hebert, L.E., Beckett, L.A., Scherr, P.A., Albert, M.A., Chown, M.J., Pilgrim, D.M., & Taylor, J.O. (1997). Education and other measures of socioeconomic status and risk of incident Alzheimer's disease in a defined population of older persons. *Archives of Neurology, 54,* 1399–1405.

Haan, M.N., Jagust, W.J., Galasko, D., & Kaye, J. (2002) Effect of extrapyramidal signs and lewy bodies on survival in patients with Alzheimer disease. *Archives of Neurology, 59,* 588–593.

Hultsch, D.F., Hertzog, C., Small, B.J., & Dixon, R.A. (1999). Use it or lose it: Engaged lifestyle as a buffer of cognitive decline in aging? *Psychology and Aging, 14,* 245–263.

Kolb, B., Gibb, R., & Robinson, T.E. (2003, February). Brain plasticity and behavior. *Current Directions in Psychological Science, 12* (1).

Kramer, A.F., & Willis, S.L. (2003). Enhancing the cognitive vitality of older adults. *Current Directions in Psychological Science, 11* (5), 173–177.

Stern, Y., Gurland, B., Tatemichi, T.K., Tang, M.X., Wilder, D., & Mayeux, R. (1994). Influence of education and occupation on the incidence of Alzheimer's disease. *Journal of the American Medical Association, 271,* 1004–1010.

Wang, H.H., Karp, A., Winblad, B., & Fratiglioni, L. (2002). Late-life engagement in social and leisure activities is associated with a decreased risk of dementia: A longitudinal study from the Kungsholmen Project. *American Journal of Epidemiology, 155,* 1081–1087.

Wilson, R.S., & Bennett, D.A. (2003, June). Cognitive activity and risk of Alzheimer's disease. *Current Directions in Psychological Science, 12* (3), 87.

Wilson, R.S., Mendes de Leon, C.F., Barnes, L.L., Schneider, J.A., Bienias, J.L., Evans, D.A., & Bennett, D.A. (2002, February 13). Participation in cognitively stimulating activities and risk of incident Alzheimer's disease. *Journal of the American Medical Association, 287* (6), 742–748.

DIVERSITY

15.

Is there still bias against African Americans in business organizations?

SELECT ONE:

☐ A. Yes, but it is getting much better in a hurry.

☐ B. No, it is now about equal on all important measures.

☐ C. Yes, and it is very slowly decreasing.

☐ D. There is no way to really tell.

☐ E. Yes, and it is increasing.

15

15. Is there still bias against African Americans in business organizations?

The correct answer is C: Yes, and it is very slowly decreasing.

How sure are we at this time?

1	2	3	**4**	5
Hint	Suggestive	Trending	**Substantial**	Solid

Discussion

There is still bias and the struggle continues. Some progress is being made. African American women are making more progress than their male counterparts.

Selected Research

- Research by Schneider (1987) concludes that, as organizations are formed, there is an "increased tendency toward homogeneity—in education, personality, and demographic factors like race, sex, and age. The problem might be the lack of clear definition of executive effectiveness. If executives use criteria like 'top-management material,' senior management will be made up of people in the CEO's image, which is currently White male."

- Research by Mueller et al. (1989) found that minorities are held to higher standards than White males.

- Work by Kanter (1987) refers to the exclusion of minorities from senior management as "homosocial reproduction"; managers develop and promote individuals who resemble them. She argues that "working with and promoting individuals like themselves creates a sort of psychological comfort and serves to keep out dissimilar individuals, such as other nationalities, other industries, or even other organizations with dissimilar corporate values."

- Research by Hakel (1992) concludes that "until that [executive] suite itself becomes more diverse (in such areas as demography, career histories, and functional areas of expertise), the leadership at lower ranks in the organization is likely to move at only a glacial pace towards diversity." Concerted effort to expand diversity at the executive level will probably only happen when executives themselves have some kind of powerful personal experiences with diversity.

- In an unpublished study, the Center for Creative Leadership looked at the experiences of African American male and female managers and executives (compared with a Caucasian sample). All the following are statistically significant: Caucasians had more challenging assignments than African Americans; Caucasian men had more challenging assignments than African American men; Caucasian men learned more lessons about managing the work than either African American males or females of both races; African American men had more challenging assignments than African American women; and, like women, African Americans were less likely to have start-ups and fix-its and were also less likely to have experienced the all-purpose developer projects; African Americans report more learning dealing with their racial identity and cynicism and less about managing direct reports and developing their skills (Lessons of a Diverse Workforce, 2000).

So what difference do these findings make?
- With the shrinking of the available talent pool and increasing pressure from all sides, it's critical for companies to move in the direction of diversity, especially in the executive suite. The challenge companies face requires

looking beyond what is comfortable (choosing and surrounding themselves with others who look and act like them) and, at the same time, providing opportunities to develop the identified competencies in minority and disadvantaged populations.

• This is just one of many biases that have to be worked on constantly in order to make any progress. Executives need to accept that people from different backgrounds see the world differently from them. One company did a survey and among the executive team they had a 90 percent score on "we treat people of different backgrounds with respect." The executives thought they had mastered the problem until they were shown that among Black single women, the score was in the 30 percent range. These executives did not know what they did not know. They needed to associate with people different from them to find out what was really going on.

• It's jobs, jobs, jobs. Challenging jobs are the engine of personal growth. Without them, all your diversity efforts will amount to nothing.

Some Key Sources

Center for Creative Leadership. (2000, June). *Lessons of a diverse workforce project*. Working report.

Hakel, M.D. (1992, November). *Meta view, too*. Paper presented at the Executive Selection Conference, Center for Creative Leadership, Greensboro, NC.

Kanter, R.M. (1987). Men and women of the corporation. *Management Review, 76,* 14–16.

Mueller, C.W., Parcel, T.L., & Tanaka, K. (1989). Particularism in authority outcomes of Black and White supervisors. *Social Science Research, 18,* 1–20.

Schneider, B. (1987). The people make the place. *Personnel Psychology, 40,* 437–451.

CAREER DEVELOPMENT

16.

The best mix of developmental remedies to help someone build critical skills to become an effective manager or executive is:

SELECT ONE:

☐ A. 70% Jobs/Tasks; 20% Bosses/Coaches/ Mentors, 10% Self-Development, Courses.

☐ B. 50% Jobs/Tasks; 25% Bosses/Coaches/ Mentors; 25% Self-Development, Courses.

☐ C. 33% Jobs/Tasks; 33% Bosses/Coaches/ Mentors; 33% Self-Development, Courses.

☐ D. 25% Jobs/Tasks; 25% Bosses/Coaches/ Mentors; 50% Self-Development, Courses.

☐ E. 10% Jobs/Tasks; 20% Bosses/Coaches/ Mentors; 70% Self-Development, Courses.

16. The best mix of developmental remedies to help someone build critical skills to become an effective manager or executive is:

The correct answer is A: 70% Jobs/Tasks; 20% Bosses/Coaches/ Mentors; 10% Self-Development, Courses.

How sure are we at this time?

1	2	3	**4**	5
Hint	Suggestive	Trending	**Substantial**	Solid

Discussion

In long-term studies of how successful and effective managers and executives get to be that way, it's consistently: jobs, people, and then self-help and courseware. The proportion of lessons learned—from what source—is roughly 70 percent from tough jobs; 20 percent from people, mostly bosses; and 10 percent from courseware. On-the-job training is still the best teacher of the mission critical skills for managers and executives.

Selected Research

- The first empirical evidence of how much on-the-job development adds to success came from the initial report on the long-term AT&T studies (Bray et al., 1974).

- In CCL's long-term studies (McCall, Lombardo, & Morrison, 1988; Morrison, White, & VanVelsor, 1987, rev. 1992), the powerful jobs that create learning were "major shifts in challenges." Jobs were the primary source of most learning for men. Women had somewhat less learning from jobs, but this is viewed as a result of having less developmental jobs. Many studies conducted around the world have reinforced these initial findings (McCauley et al., 1994; McCauley & Brutus, 1998)

- Mumford et al. (2000) and Lyness and Thompson (2000) show how skills develop through experience. In the latter article, the authors demonstrate how level and compensation are related to breadth of experience, and developmental assignments are strongly related to career success.

- Evidence for the effectiveness of courses can be found in Spencer (2001), Morrow et al. (1997), and Burke and Day (1986).

So what difference do these findings make?

- The most potent development tool or remedy is what we call Assignmentology—who goes in what job when and for what development? People who are learners who go through a series of challenging job assignments are the ones who end up legacy leaders. Toughness and diversity of challenges seem to be the keys. For an extensive discussion of Assignmentology and on-the-job development, see Lombardo and Eichinger (2002).

- Coursework should be designed to include as much real learning as possible through team assignments, action learning, live case studies, and the like.

Some Key Sources

Bray, D.W., Campbell, R.J., & Grant, D.L. (1974). *Formative years in business: A long-term AT&T study of managerial lives.* New York: Wiley.

Burke, M.J., & Day, R.R. (1986). A cumulative study of the effectiveness of managerial training. *Journal of Applied Psychology, 71* (2), 232–245.

Lombardo, M., & Eichinger, R. (2004). *The leadership machine.* Minneapolis: Lominger Limited, Inc.

Lyness, K.S., & Thompson, D.E. (2000). Climbing the corporate ladder: Do male and female executives follow the same route? *Journal of Applied Psychology, 85* (1), 86–101.

McCall, M.W., Lombardo, M., & Morrison, A. (1988). *The lessons of experience: How successful executives develop on the job.* Lexington, MA: Lexington Books.

McCauley, C.D., & Brutus, S. (1998). *Management development through job experiences: An annotated bibliography.* Greensboro, NC: Center for Creative Leadership.

McCauley, C.D., Ruderman, M.N., Ohlott, P.J., & Morrow, J.E. (1994). Assessing the developmental components of managerial jobs. *Journal of Applied Psychology, 79,* 544–560.

Morrison, A., White, R., & VanVelsor, E. (1987, rev. 1992). *Breaking the glass ceiling: Can women reach the top of America's largest corporations?* Reading, MA: Addison-Wesley.

Morrow, C., Jarrett, M., & Rupinski, M. (1997). An investigation of the effect and economic utility of corporate-wide training. *Personnel Psychology, 50* (1), 91–120.

Mumford, M.D., Marks, M.A., Connelly, M.S., Zaccaro, S.J., & Reiter-Palmon, R. (2000). Development of leadership skills: Experience and timing. *The Leadership Quarterly, 11* (1), 87–114.

Spencer, L. (2001). The economic value of emotional intelligence competencies and EIC-based HR programs. In D. Goleman & C. Cherniss (Eds.), *The emotionally intelligent workplace: How to select for, measure, and improve emotional intelligence in individuals, groups, and organizations.* San Francisco: Jossey-Bass.

PERFORMANCE APPRAISAL

17.

Who is the least accurate judge of job performance?

SELECT ONE:

☐ A. Boss.

☐ B. Peers.

☐ C. Direct Reports.

☐ D. Self.

☐ E. Customers.

17

17. Who is the least accurate judge of job performance?

The correct answer is D: Self.

How sure are we at this time?

1	2	3	**4**	5
Hint	Suggestive	Trending	**Substantial**	Solid

Discussion

Self is generally the worst judge of performance in management and professional jobs. This may not be as true for technical and nonexempt jobs where clear, commonly recognized, and objective measures of performance exist. Self-ratings on competencies are often unrelated to job success (actual performance). Whether a person rates himself or herself high or low is unrelated to performance dimensions. On the other hand, the ratings of all the other groups generally show significant relationships with actual performance.

Self-ratings are most accurate on strengths, least accurate on weaknesses, and least accurate on interpersonal skills and the impressions we leave on people (EQ). Coincidentally, most of the skills missing in managers and executives were those very same skills about which people are least accurate.

Selected Research

- According to several studies by Murphy and Cleveland (1995), "all rater groups (bosses, peers, direct reports, customers) agreed more with each other than any agreed with self-ratings." They report that "all rater groups (bosses, in- and out-of-unit peers, direct reports, customers) consistently show significant relationships between their ratings and the performance of the person rated."

- The correlation between self-ratings and ratings of performance is .00 (Lombardo & Eichinger, 2003). "Boss, direct reports, and peer ratings all correlate with performance, especially those of boss."

- In one study (Vance et al., 1988), managers who were rated on three dimensions by superiors, peers, and the managers themselves, convergence was greater for superior and peer ratings than for either of these with self-ratings. Their results show that self, supervisors, and peers can be equally valid as sources of performance information, although performance of some tasks may be more validly evaluated by one source than another.

- One study on biases in self-perception found that, in individuals' recollections of their behavior, they tend to remember engaging in more positive behaviors and fewer negative behaviors than actually occurred (Gosling, 1998).

So what difference do these findings make?

- Relying on self-ratings for job improvement and career development would not be a sound practice. Almost anyone else's ratings would be more accurate. So when you need to produce data for a person to use to plan for and work on their career, look to raters from multiple sources (360).

- We may know our intentions and values and some of our behavior, but a lot of what we do is on autopilot. We often judge ourselves by our intentions and others judge us by our behaviors. Other people are more accurate, because they are more likely to see our behavior from a fresh point of view and because our behavior has an impact on them. If self-assessment were more accurate, there wouldn't be a feedback problem. Everyone would know where they stood on the things that matter, and those who were career-minded would do something about the competencies where they didn't measure up. Unfortunately, this isn't the case. We can't create a winning competitive-edge strategy based on self-assessment. At least not by itself. Self-assessment is a well-meaning practice that doesn't work very well alone. So in order to manage our own career effectively, we have to accept that our self-view is not adequate, and we need to supplement it with information from knowledgeable others.

Some Key Sources

Gosling, S.D., John, O.P., Craik, K.H., & Robins, R.W. (1998). Do people know how they behave? Self-reported act frequencies compared with on-line codings by observers. *Journal of Personality and Social Psychology, 74,* 1337–1349.

Lombardo, M., & Eichinger, R. (2003). *The LEADERSHIP ARCHITECT® norms and validity report.* Minneapolis: Lominger Limited, Inc.

Murphy, K.R., & Cleveland, J.N. (1995). *Understanding performance appraisal.* Thousand Oaks, CA: Sage.

Vance, R.J., MacCallum, R.C., Coovert, M.D., & Hedge, J.W. (1988). Construct validity of multiple job performance measures using confirmatory factor analysis. *Journal of Applied Psychology, 73* (1), 74–80.

JOB TENURE

18.

The average tenure of managers and executives is:

SELECT ONE:

☐ A. Holding steady.

☐ B. Increasing because of the tight economy (2003); no place to go.

☐ C. Decreasing steadily over the past 10 years.

☐ D. Decreasing for large companies, increasing for smaller companies.

☐ E. Decreasing for small companies, increasing for larger companies.

18

18. The average tenure of managers and executives is:

The correct answer is C: Decreasing steadily over the past 10 years.

How sure are we at this time?

1	2	3	**4**	5
Hint	Suggestive	Trending	**Substantial**	Solid

Discussion

In the U.S. currently, with an escalating war for talent, companies are finding increased "job-hopping" and shorter average tenure. This is especially true of high-demand IT professionals, high potential professionals, and CEOs. Fewer and fewer people are ending their career with the company they started with.

Selected Research

- Andrews (2001) examined CEO turnover at *Fortune 200* companies from 1980 to 1996 and found that "CEOs appointed after 1985 are three times more likely to be fired than CEOs who were appointed before 1985." He also noted that 34 percent of *Fortune 100* companies have replaced their CEOs since 1995. When an outside hire replaced a fired CEO, company performance rose by more than 4 percent during the three-year period following the change. However, when an outsider replaced a retiring CEO, the study registered an almost 6 percent drop in performance.

- According to Koretz (1997), between 1991 and 1996, the median job tenure for men 25–64 years of age fell by an average of approximately 19 percent, with older workers most affected: males 55–64 years of age had a 29 percent drop in tenure and males 45–54 years of age had a 25 percent drop.

- Research by Grossman (1998) notes that half of those who graduated in the 1971 1990 period left their first jobs within three to five years, and among those who graduated from 1991 to 1993, more than two-thirds did. In some professions (e.g., accounting and auditing), typical tenure ranges from three to six months.

- Data from research by Kransdorrf (1997) found that, while in the early 1970s a manager worked for one or two companies in his or her entire career, "U.S. managers today are more likely to hold seven to ten jobs in their lifetime, with the average tenure for the managers dropping continuously."

- Among information technology managers, the turnover rate is 15.5 percent for 12 months (Cone, 1996).

- Young workers typically demonstrate their quest for a good career match by frequent job moves. According to Feller (1996), "as many as 50 to 60 percent of all new hires leave their jobs within the first seven months" (p. 95).

- According to the Bureau of Labor Statistics, 10 percent of the workforce switches jobs every year (Henkoff, 1996).

- Because it is costly to hire and train new workers, some employers believe that a worker must remain with a company for at least four years to allow the company to recover hiring costs alone (Blyth, 1996).

- Comeau-Kirchner (1999) suggests additional incentives, besides higher pay and competitive benefits, are needed to retain high potential professionals. These incentives include career development, training programs, promotions, better corporate communications, flexible staffing, and stock options.

- Research by Andrews (2001) shows that "to improve a company's performance, an outsider should be brought in following a forced departure."

So what difference do these findings make?

- Moving for career advancement and opportunity is increasing, as well as failures of people who get into the top few jobs.

- Sharper hiring processes, more accurate succession planning, and retention planning for key performers is an increasing requirement to stay competitive.

- Leaders should be aware of new sources of job candidates, particularly those from other companies. This means that HR professionals should have networks that identify high talent from other companies.

- When bringing in mid-career employees, socialization needs to occur quickly and aggressively. This socialization deals not only with the administrative procedures for work (e.g., how to get paid, do benefits, find your office), but also with the culture and relationships in the new company.

Some Key Sources

Andrews, K.Z. (2001, Winter). The performance impact of new CEOs. When a CEO departs, choosing the best successor depends on why the incumbent left. *MIT Sloan Management Review, 42* (2).

Blyth, J. (1996, April 15). The mobility trap. *Newsweek, 127* (16), 20.

Comeau-Kirchner, C. (1999). Reducing turnover is a tough job. *Management Review, 88* (9).

Cone, E. (1996). Nice money, if you can get it. *Information Week, 592* (64).

Feller, R., & Walz, G. (Eds.). (1996). *Career transitions in turbulent times: Exploring work, learning, and careers* (ED 398 519). Greensboro, NC: ERIC Clearinghouse on Counseling and Student Services.

Grossman, R.J. (1998, December). How recruiters woo high-demand candidates. *HR Magazine, 43,* 122–130.

Henkoff, R. (1996, January 15). So you want to change your job. *Fortune, 133* (1), 52–56.

Koretz, G. (1997, January 27). Job mobility, American-style. *BusinessWeek Online,* 3511, 20. http://www.businessweek.com/archives/1997/b3511037.arc.htm#B3511037

Kransdorrf, A. (1997). Fight organizational memory lapse. *Workforce, 76,* 34–39.

360 DEGREE FEEDBACK

19.

Which of the following best describes the relationship between accuracy of people's ratings (e.g., on a 360 degree questionnaire) and how public the results are?

SELECT ONE:

☐ A. The more public the data, the less accurate the ratings.

☐ B. People's ratings don't change because they will be made public.

☐ C. People's ratings get more accurate when they know others will see the ratings.

☐ D. When raters know that their individual ratings can be identified by the person being rated, their ratings get more accurate.

☐ E. Accuracy of ratings decreases when there are a lot of raters.

19

19. **Which of the following best describes the relationship between accuracy of people's ratings (e.g., on a 360 degree questionnaire) and how public the results are?**

The correct answer is A: The more public the data, the less accurate the ratings.

How sure are we at this time?

1	2	**3**	4	5
Hint	Suggestive	**Trending**	Substantial	Solid

Discussion

The findings to date indicate that the more public the ratings, the less accurate the ratings become. When people know that their individual ratings can be identified by the learner, the boss, or the organization, their ratings become less accurate. People don't want to give honest feedback when the feedback is negative and will be tied to them.

Selected Research

*   Lombardo and Eichinger (2003) found accuracy decreases when the ratings become more public and identifiable. The 360 process they use (VOICES®) allows each rater to select their level of confidentiality. Raters can choose to have the learner see their results directly, only with one other rater, or only with two other raters. So they can choose no confidentiality, a little, or maximum. Lombardo and Eichinger found that when raters said that they don't care if the learner sees their individual ratings, the correlation with independent ratings of performance was .09 and not significant. When raters selected "my rating will be combined with one other rater," the correlation was .27. When they selected "see my ratings only in groups of

three" (the maximum anonymity), the correlation was .30. So accuracy increased as confidentiality and anonymity increased. When raters said "it doesn't matter if the learner sees my ratings," the average score went up, the variance (spread of ratings over the scale) decreased, and the ratings had no relationship to performance ratings. So when ratings are made public, they bland out and go up.

• Research by Chappelow (1998) argues that the effective use of 360 degree feedback for either development or appraisal purposes depends on being able to create an environment that is respectful of the individual's need for privacy. He notes that when raters' responses aren't anonymous or if individuals don't feel enough safeguards have been put in place to protect their anonymity, raters may fear retribution and be less than candid in their responses or not respond at all.

• Antonioni's (1994) study of upward feedback (ratings of the supervisor by direct reports only) found that direct reports whose ratings were not anonymous rated their managers significantly higher than direct reports whose ratings were anonymous.

• Research by Bracken et al. (2001) found that providing feedback providers (raters) with a guarantee of anonymity (or the perception of anonymity) maximizes honesty, candor, and response rates. They note that the perception of rater anonymity can be as important as the guarantee of actual anonymity and can affect feedback honesty. They also note that "there are some legal opinions regarding the ability to guarantee anonymity in all circumstances." Sometimes, according to the researchers, it's the technologies themselves that are "not perceived to guarantee anonymity" (e.g., internally processed). A Timmreck & Bracken study (1997) revealed that any technology must be capable of protecting the data (questionnaires and reports) from access by unauthorized parties, and that feedback policies and procedures need to clearly state who can see the reported results and under what circumstances. They argue further that reliability and anonymity require the specification of minimum group size (no less than three except for self-scores, supervisor scores, and any other agreed-upon one-on-one relationship).

So what difference do these findings make?

- To get the most accurate ratings on a 360 questionnaire, confidentiality and anonymity are essential.

- The more public the results, the less accurate the results will be. So if the boss sees it or the organization gets a copy or if learners are required to share the results with their boss, accuracy will be compromised.

- One company started their 360 feedback by giving the data only to the employee; in the second round of 360 (10 to 12 months later), the employee and the HR manager saw the data, but it did not go into a permanent file and was not used for performance appraisal; in the third round, the data became part of the performance appraisal process and was tied to rewards. This enabled the employee to use the data to make improvements. In all rounds, the assessors were confidential.

Some Key Sources

Antonioni, D. (1994). The effects of feedback accountability on upward appraisal ratings. *Personnel Psychology, 47,* 349–356.

Bracken, D.W., Timmreck, C.W., & Church, A.H. (Eds.). (2001). *The handbook of multisource feedback: The comprehensive resource for designing and implementing MSF processes.* San Francisco: Jossey-Bass.

Chappelow, C. (1998). 360 Degree feedback in individual development. In C.D. McCauley, R. Moxley, & F VanVelsor (Eds.), *The Center for Creative Leadership's handbook of leadership development.* San Francisco: Jossey-Bass.

Lombardo, M., & Eichinger, R. (2003). *The LEADERSHIP ARCHITECT® norms and validity report.* Minneapolis: Lominger Limited, Inc.

Timmreck, C.W., & Bracken, D.W. (1997). Multisource feedback: A study of its use in decision making. *Employment Relations Today, 24* (1), 21–27.

GENDER

20.

When it comes to how boys and girls learn, research has shown that:

SELECT ONE:

☐ A. Boys and girls learn differently but the difference has no practical value.

☐ B. Brains are brains; there are no differences between the brains of boys and girls.

☐ C. Boys and girls learn differently but it is due totally to upbringing and culture and not brains; the differences go away over time.

☐ D. Boys and girls learn differently and the differences matter.

☐ E. Boys and girls differ in athletic abilities but not in how they learn.

20

20. **When it comes to how boys and girls learn, research has shown that:**

The correct answer is D: Boys and girls learn differently and the differences matter.

How sure are we at this time?

1	2	3	**4**	5
Hint	Suggestive	Trending	**Substantial**	Solid

Discussion

Recent advances in brain imaging research, which examines what the brain is actually doing while the subject is active, has confirmed that there are significant differences between how the average boy learns and how the average girl learns. The differences are significant enough to call for differences in how they are educated in primary and secondary education. The differences narrow but some continue through life. In studies of how executives learn the lessons of leadership, there continues to be a difference between how men and women learn.

Selected Research

• Michael Gurian, author of *Boys and Girls Learn Differently*, cautions educators to keep up with the latest brain research about developmental differences, noting that brain research in the past decade reveals that boys are "usually superior spatial thinkers and possess the ability to see things in three dimensions...and drawn to play that involves intense movement and an element of make-believe violence." In terms of education, instead of forcing boys to conform to a teaching style that simply doesn't work for them, schools would be better off teaching them how to harness this energy in a more productive and healthy way.

- Research at the Center for Creative Leadership by VanVelsor and Hughes-James (1990) concludes that "women tend to learn more from other people in the company than their male counterparts." They say further that there are significant differences in the way that women and men develop on the job. Their report presents evidence taken from a comparison study of experiences that both male and female executives consider developmental.

- In her *BusinessWeek* (2003) article, Michelle Conlin quotes the codirector of ERIC Clearinghouse on Elementary and Early Childhood Education, Lilian Katz, as saying that "the 'earliness' push, in which schools are pressured to show kids achieving the same standards by the same age or risk losing funding, is also far more damaging to boys." She adds that early developmental difficulties can "plant a distaste for school as early as the first grade."

- Research by Eagly et al. (1995) reports no overall difference in male/female skill levels but points out that men do better in stereotypically masculine jobs and vice versa.

- William Pollack, a psychologist at Harvard Medical School, reviews two decades of research along with conclusions about how we can better address developmental needs of boys in his book, *Real Boys* (1999). His book explores what he refers to as this generation's "silent crisis"; describing many of today's boys as "sad, lonely, and confused, although they may appear tough, cheerful, and confident." He challenges some of the conventional expectations about masculinity that encourage parents to treat boys as little men, "raising them through a toughening process that drives their true emotions underground."

So what difference do these findings make?

- It's popular and politically correct to say and act as if there are no differences between boys and girls and men and women, but there are. Some of the differences make little or no difference in the world of work, but some do. There is nothing wrong with tailoring learning opportunities differently to take special advantages of how different categories of people usually learn. We would think nothing of designing a learning experience for someone with special needs, but we would hesitate doing so when the split is on gender.

- When managing the careers of future leaders of our organizations, the research would support slightly differential treatment based upon gender. Typical men and women learn differently and from different sources. Women in general learn more from people and men more from direct job experience.

Some Key Sources

Conlin, M. (2003, May 26). The new gender gap. *BusinessWeek*, p. 75–84.

Eagly, A., Karau, S.J., & Makhijani, M.G. (1995). Gender and the effectiveness of leaders: A meta-analysis. *Psychological Bulletin, 117* (1), 125–145.

Gurian, M. (2001). *Boys and girls learn differently*. San Francisco: Jossey-Bass.

Pollack, W.J. (1999). *Real boys: Rescuing our sons from the myths of boyhood*. New York: Holt/Owl Publishing.

VanVelsor, E., & Hughes-James, M.W. (1990). *Gender differences in the development of managers: How women managers learn from experience* (Report No. 145). Greensboro, NC: Center for Creative Leadership.

RECRUITING AND HIRING

21.

Do applicants have any preferences among the various selection techniques and tools organizations use?

SELECT ONE:

☐ A. Not really. They just want to get an offer.

☐ B. They prefer good old-fashioned face-to-face interviewing to any other method.

☐ C. They prefer methods that are job related and not personal.

☐ D. They like any method that has been shown to be valid and reliable.

☐ E. They prefer multiple tools and methods because they think they have a better chance.

21. **Do applicants have any preferences among the various selection techniques and tools organizations use?**

    The correct answer is C: They prefer methods that are job related and not personal.

How sure are we at this time?

1	2	**3**	4	5
Hint	Suggestive	**Trending**	Substantial	Solid

Discussion

Applicants seem to have a basic sense of fairness where they think that job-related measures and tools should be used to see if they are the best qualified for the job opening. They are less favorable to tools and methods that seem more personal, like personality tests, which to them represents an invasion of personal privacy.

Selected Research

- Rynes and Connerley (1993) report that procedures with a "strong relationship to job content" are favored by applicants and perceived as more fair and "less invasive than procedures that lack job relatedness."

- Schultz (1996) developed hard biodata, soft biodata, and personality items to measure three personal constructs— dependability, demeanor, and ambition—and found that "subjects had a strong preference for the model that separated the personality and soft biodata items in one factor and the hard biodata items in another distinct factor."

- Some research shows that applicants do not react favorably to personality tests. In Rosse et al. (1991), job applicants perceived personality tests as having "low face validity, low predictive validity, and low job relatedness."

- Organizations may suffer when individuals react negatively to selection or other personnel procedures. Smither and his colleagues (1993) gave two practical reasons for organizations to be concerned with applicants' reactions. "First, the effects that applicants' reactions have on organizational attractiveness can indirectly influence pursuit or acceptance of a job offer. Second, applicants' reactions may be related to both the likelihood of litigation and how successfully a selection procedure can be defended."

- Mael et al. (1996) evaluated biodata items for their perceived invasiveness from three perspectives: (1) substantive topics seen as invasive, (2) attributes that typify invasive items, and (3) individual differences in the tendency to perceive items as invasive. Results show that individuals with more education and positive attitudes toward biodata and organizational selection measures viewed fewer items as invasive.

So what difference do these findings make?

- Applicants prefer having the screening method match the job and separating various aspects of the questions so they're identifiable. HR professionals should regularly audit their procedures from a customer (new employee) standpoint. How do your applicants view your procedures?

- There are a number of methods to query and test applicants that evaluate their job experience more than their personality. Role plays, small group projects, in-basket exercises, realistic job previews, simulations, situational questions, etc. can be used to determine fit of applicant for job.

Some Key Sources

Mael, F.A., Connerley, M., & Morath, R.A. (1996, Fall). None of your business: Parameters of biodata invasiveness. *Personnel Psychology, 49* (3), 613–650.

Rosse, J.G., Miller, J.L., & Barnes, L.K. (1991). Combining personality and cognitive ability predictors for hiring service-oriented employees. *Journal of Business and Psychology, 5* (4), 431–446.

Rynes, S.L., & Connerley, M.L. (1993). Applicant reactions to alternative selection procedures. *Journal of Business & Psychology, 7* (3), 261–279.

Schultz, K.S. (1996, Spring). Distinguishing personality and biodata items using confirmatory factor analysis of multitrait-multimethod matrices. *Journal of Business and Psychology, 10* (3), 263–288.

Smither, J.W., Reilly, R.R., Millsap, R.E., Pearlman, K., & Stoffey, R.W. (1993). Applicant reactions to selection procedures. *Personnel Psychology, 46,* 49–76.

FEEDBACK

22.

When people seek positive feedback only, what is the effect on others?

SELECT ONE:

☐ A. Others often think the person lacks self-confidence.

☐ B. Others expect the person to be defensive if they respond with any negative feedback and therefore don't give any.

☐ C. Others think less positively of the person.

☐ D. Others respond by actually increasing negative feedback to counter the request.

☐ E. It has no measurable impact on others.

22. When people seek positive feedback only, what is the effect on others?

The correct answer is C: Others think less positively of the person.

How sure are we at this time?

1	2	3	**4**	5
Hint	Suggestive	Trending	**Substantial**	Solid

Discussion

Seeking positive feedback can lower opinions of our effectiveness and is often unlikely to yield much new information. People who are obviously seeking good news appear insecure or unable to take constructive advice. Couple that with the natural tendency to withhold bad news, and people can easily get an unbalanced picture as well. Managers are less likely to seek feedback from peers in general, and when they do, they tend to seek—or even to subtly publicize—positive feedback more than negative feedback. While managers may be hesitant to seek negative feedback from peers because they may appear unsure of themselves, research shows the opposite is true.

Selected Research

- In his research on ability-relevant feedback, Brown (1990) found the search for feedback was most evident when individuals thought they would gain positive, rather than negative, information about themselves. However, even those led to believe that feedback might disclose incompetence did not completely refrain from further information seeking.

- Ashford and Tsui (1991) conducted a study that shows when managers sought negative feedback, this increased accuracy of understanding and enhanced superiors', direct reports', and peers' opinions of the manager's overall effectiveness. In contrast, seeking positive feedback decreased constituents' opinions of the manager's effectiveness.

- According to research by Larson (1986), if people frequently receive spontaneous positive feedback, seeking it actively isn't likely to yield much new information. Conversely, "actively seeking positive feedback may have no effect on the accuracy of a manager's understanding of constituents' evaluations." Individuals are more likely to give each other positive feedback spontaneously and withhold negative appraisals. Larson concludes that "people don't learn as much if they seek positive over negative feedback."

- According to Ashford (1986), feedback seeking can result in either a positive or a negative impression. "Managers seeking positive feedback may convey insecurity and a need for reassurance. Observers may question the seekers' self-confidence and reduce their opinions of the seekers' overall effectiveness."

- Results of a study (Palmer et al., 2001) examining the impression management orientation of 95 international middle- and upper-level business managers indicate that managers have primarily an acquisitive orientation. (An acquisitive orientation exists when an individual is concerned primarily with obtaining approval from the audience.)

So what difference do these findings make?

- Balance is best in all things. Seeking positive feedback (primarily on strengths) backfires as people generally lower their opinion of a person's effectiveness. Seeking constructive criticism and asking for suggestions to improve is a better strategy, coupled with feedback on strengths.

- It's human nature to want people to think well of you. The best way to do this is to be open and eager for improvement. This requires listening and responding to what you are told. If people see you respond to their comments, they will provide them in the future.

- The flow of positive feedback is significantly greater than negative feedback. Asking for and seeking more positive feedback doesn't actually increase new information.

- While people should be open and responsive to all feedback, seeking additional positive feedback is not helpful. Asking for "suggestions for the future" rather than "feedback on the past" often makes it easier for people to share ways to improve. People who seek and use feedback learn and progress more than those who do not.

Some Key Sources

Ashford, S.J. (1986). The role of feedback seeking in individual adaptation: A resource perspective. *Academy of Management Journal, 29,* 465–487.

Ashford, S.J., & Tsui, A.S. (1991). Self-regulation for managerial effectiveness: The role of active feedback seeking. *Academy of Management Journal, 34* (2), 251–280.

Brown, J.D. (1990, March). Evaluating one's abilities: Shortcuts and stumbling blocks on the road to self-knowledge. *Journal of Experimental Social Psychology, 26* (2), 149–167.

Larson, J.R. (1986). *Supervisors' performance feedback to subordinates. The impact of subordinate performance valence and outcome dependency.* Working paper, University of Illinois, Chicago.

Palmer, R.J., Welker, R.B., Campbell, T.L., & Magner, N.R. (2001). Examining the impression management orientation of managers. *Journal of Managerial Psychology, 16* (1), 35–49.

CAREER DEVELOPMENT

23.

What kinds of jobs matter most for long-term development?

SELECT ONE:

☐ A. Jobs requiring stark transitions and first-time experiences

☐ B. Functional switches (moving from one function to another).

☐ C. Multiple rotational assignments in early career.

☐ D. Product line or business unit switches.

☐ E. Being promoted to a boss's job.

23. What kinds of jobs matter most for long-term development?

The correct answer is A: Jobs requiring stark transitions and first-time experiences.

How sure are we at this time?

1	2	3	4	**5**
Hint	Suggestive	Trending	Substantial	**Solid**

Discussion

Significant development comes from the land of firsts—first jobs with unfamiliar responsibilities that people are not quite ready for; first time dealing with a particular group; first time in a job where failure is believed to be quite possible, even likely if learning does not take place. Development is a *demand pull*—the demands of the job pull the person to develop new skills and not rely on just successful habits of the past.

Successful leaders' careers are marked by a variety of specific, challenging, and stretch work assignments and disorienting experiences, like starting an operation from scratch, making a huge leap in scope of responsibility, or turning around a business in deep trouble.

Two characteristics of effective experiences come up consistently in the research. On-the-job learning is most likely to occur for both men and women when: first, individuals are placed in a variety of challenging situations with problems to solve and choices to make under conditions of risk; and second, individuals gain their experiences in a supportive environment with supervisors who provide positive role models and constructive support and mentors who provide counsel.

Selected Research

- Bennis and Thomas (2002) report on a study in which they interviewed 40 leaders whom they deemed either "geeks" (aged 21–34) or "geezers" (aged 70–82) to evaluate the effect of era on values and success. The two groups vary in terms of their ambitions, heroes, and family lives, but members of both sets share one common experience: All have "undergone at least one intense, transformational experience" which the authors call a "crucible." The authors offer interviews and statistical data as evidence for the value of the crucible experiences.

- According to research by Richardson (1992), one of the best ways to develop an executive's skills is to continually provide demanding jobs: "That every stage of development requires a new set of skills that, in turn, puts the executive in a better position for future promotions."

- In describing their research on executives, McCall et al. (1988) conclude that it is "critical to executive effectiveness for individuals to have experience with a wide variety of managerial roles; and that this diversity is not correlated with the number or frequency of promotions, rather with moves across problem domains."

- A fundamental conclusion of the McCall et al. (1988) study is that on-the-job learning is most likely to occur when managers are faced with challenging situations. The study results also revealed that what was learned from challenging on-the-job experiences was not technical in nature but consisted of leadership attributes, such as handling relationships, temperament, basic values, and personal awareness (in McCauley et al., 1994).

- A research model by Locke et al. (1990), called the High Performance (HPRF) Cycle, found that "success (in job satisfaction, which engenders commitment to the organization and its goals) is a combination of high challenge or difficult goals mixed with high expectations for success, feedback, adequate ability, and low situational constraints."

- Yukl's (1994) research, noted in his comprehensive book on leadership in organizations, reports that "managers are more likely to learn relevant leadership skills and values if they are exposed to a variety of developmental experiences on the job, with appropriate coaching and mentoring by superiors and peers" (p. 456).

- Research by Lyness and Thompson (2000) reveals how level and compensation are related to breadth of experience, and "developmental experiences are strongly related to career success."

So what difference do these findings make?

- On-the-job development is the most important of all development activities, especially putting people who are willing to learn and change into first-time, new, and tough situations. By going through this series of tough job assignments, people log an increasing number of lessons and templates that they can use later in similar situations.

- It is important to not rush to judgment when people take on tough assignments. Sometimes they will fail, and their ability to learn from the failure rather than be punished for it is key to long-term growth.

- Finding tough jobs for top candidates early in their careers is important for both their learning and probability that they will stay with the company.

Some Key Sources

Bennis, W.G., & Thomas, R.J. (2002). *Geeks and geezers: How eras, values and defining moments shape leaders.* Boston: Harvard Business School Press.

Locke, E.A., & Latham, G.P. (1990, July). Work motivation and satisfaction: Light at the end of the tunnel. *Psychological Science, 1* (4), 240–246.

Lyness, K.S., & Thompson, D.E. (2000). Climbing the corporate ladder: Do male and female executives follow the same route? *Journal of Applied Psychology, 85* (1), 86–101.

McCall, M.W., Lombardo, M., & Morrison, A. (1988). *The lessons of experience: How successful executives develop on the job.* Lexington, MA: Lexington Books.

McCauley, C.D., Ruderman, M.N., Ohlott, P.J., & Morrow, J.E. (1994). Assessing the developmental components of managerial jobs. *Journal of Applied Psychology, 79,* 544–560.

Richardson, H.S., Jr. (1992, November). *Some fairly obvious thoughts about selection of creative leaders.* Paper presented at the Executive Selection Conference, Center for Creative Leadership, Greensboro, NC.

Yukl, G. (1994). *Leadership in organizations* (3rd ed.). Englewood Cliffs, NJ: Prentice Hall.

SUCCESS PREDICTION

24.

How predictive (valid) are intelligence and technical/functional skills for selecting managers from a candidate slate of individual contributors?

SELECT ONE

☐ A. Together, they are the most important attributes to use in predicting who would make the best manager since past behavior is the best predictor of future behavior.

☐ B. They are important attributes to look at for potential managers along with many other competencies.

☐ C. They are most predictive if the manager's job is in a complex technical area.

☐ D. These two competencies correlate somewhat with performance in management roles but are usually readily available.

☐ E. Technical skills strongly relate to managing but intellectual skills less so.

24. **How predictive (valid) are intelligence and technical/functional skills for selecting managers from a candidate slate of individual contributors?**

The correct answer is C: They are most predictive if the manager's job is in a complex technical area.

How sure are we at this time?

1	2	3	**4**	5
Hint	Suggestive	Trending	**Substantial**	Solid

Discussion
A growing body of research indicates that learning agility is more important for predicting future performance as a manager or leader than intelligence and technical skills, which are more likely to explain why someone got hired or placed into a job or considered for promotion. Although many find it hard to accept, technical competencies don't make much of a difference in management jobs for two reasons:

1. Most people in technical roles are usually already smart (they were selected partly for this) and technically skilled (one of the factors used to make up the candidate slate—the best performers). It's part of the reason they performed well enough to be considered for promotion; and

2. The management job is not one where the job demands are primarily for the manager to engage in individual problem solving—the job involves more managing others and getting things done through others. The job involves managing processes and people and increasingly dealing with change. This is not to say smarts and technical skills never make a difference—in technical manager or highly

analytic roles, they may   it's just that, generally speaking, they become less important across time.

The evidence shows not that intelligence and technical skills don't matter for management jobs, rather, it shows that they have already been selected for, and unless the job is highly intellectual, that other factors make more difference. Technical skills may be seen as the ante, or necessary pre-condition; then the learning and softer skills become the wager or keys to success. Without the ante, or technical skills, the employee will not make the promotion slate. But, without learning agility, the promoted manager will not make the end of the year.

Selected Research

- In Sternberg's (1995) research, the best predictor of level attained was a measure of learning from experience; second best was IQ. Technical skills were far behind.

- In a study which related learning agility, IQ, and Big Five personality measures to job performance and measures of promotability, learning agility was by far the most related to performance and ratings of promotability. The other measures added very little to the regression equations (Connolly & Viswesvaran, 2002).

- Lombardo and Eichinger (2003) found that the best predictors of actual promotion were competencies measuring learning agility and drive for results (achievement motivation).

- Spencer and Spencer (1993) found that the need to achieve is the competency that most strongly sets apart superior and average executives and managers. Optimism is a key ingredient of achievement because it can determine one's reaction to unfavorable events or circumstances; those with high achievement are proactive and persistent, have an optimistic attitude toward setbacks, and operate from hope of success.

- According to research by Howard and Bray (1988), advancement was mostly related to early signs of the three basic types of ability—administrative, interpersonal, and cognitive—and to motivation, especially the drive to succeed. Far more than intelligence is involved, including having developmental jobs and developmental bosses.

- In 1973 David C. McClelland, in a paper titled "Testing for Competence Rather Than Intelligence," noted that academic overachievers are not always the most successful people in their professions and concluded that job selection and performance should be based on desired, observable behaviors instead of on traditional standardized tests (in Spencer & Spencer, 1993).

- Simonton (1987) observes, "Intelligence is a necessary but not sufficient cause of adulthood success in careers that demand creativity and leadership." While certainly related, excessive intelligence seems to hurt, with the most effective people being "somewhat smarter than the average for their group, but not too much smarter" (see Simonton, 1987; Most, 1990).

- Even when technical/functional skills and intellectual ability are significant, research shows that other skills are much more important—Time Management, Planning, Perseverance, Process Management, and Developing Direct Reports are the top five in one study (Clark & Clark, 1994).

- Formal education programs (Howard & Bray, 1988) emphasize the development of problem solving and decision making skills but give little attention to finding and exploiting opportunities or to dealing with potential problems. Effective managers, on the other hand, share characteristics that cannot be taught in a classroom: They need to manage, they need power, and they have the capacity for empathy. Furthermore, managers develop leadership capacities by firsthand observation of their environment and by an assessment of feedback from their actions. Managerial aspirants must be taught how to learn from their own firsthand experiences.

So what difference do these findings make?

- Selection variables—intelligence and technical skills—are mostly overweighted in selection and promotion decisions. They are overused and overconsidered. They are among the easiest to assess and, therefore, might make people more comfortable using them. It is too easy to rely on what is easy to measure more than what is right to measure. Learning agility is by far the more important characteristic to use in assessing how candidates will perform after promotion—especially into a first-time management job. Great managers are not always the smartest nor do they necessarily know the most about the technical side of the business, but they know how to learn.

- Intelligence and technical skills are necessary but insufficient predictors of future performance as a manager.

- The more productive discussion would be—among those candidates, all of whom are smart and technically skilled— who shows the best ability to learn new skills and behaviors? In screening, interviewers might also look for patterns of learning in previous jobs and life experiences. They might look for how candidates dealt with failure (hoping that they had some). They might give candidates an experience where learning may be assessed.

- Learn, as an organization, to assess learning agility. Learning has been defined as "the ability to generate and generalize ideas with impact," so learners are those who can generate new ideas or ways to solve problems and generalize their experience from one setting to another.

Some Key Sources

Clark, K.E., & Clark, M.B. (Eds.). (1994). *Choosing to lead* (pp. 58–59). Charlotte, NC: Iron Gate Press.

Connolly, J.A., & Viswesvaran, C. (2002, April). *Assessing the construct validity of a measure of learning agility.* A presentation at the Seventeenth Annual Conference of the Society for Industrial and Organizational Psychology, Toronto, Canada.

Howard, A., & Bray, D. (1988). *Managerial lives in transition: Advancing age and changing times.* New York: Guilford Press.

Lombardo, M., & Eichinger, R. (2003). *The LEADERSHIP ARCHITECT® norms and validity report.* Minneapolis: Lominger Limited, Inc.

McClelland, D.C. (1973). Testing for competence rather than intelligence. *American Psychologist, 46.*

Most, R. (1990). Hypotheses about the relationship between leadership and intelligence. In K.E. Clark & M.B. Clark (Eds.), *Measures of leadership* (pp. 459–464). West Orange, NJ: Leadership Library of America.

Simonton, D.K. (1987). Developmental antecedents of achieved eminence. *Annals of Child Development, 4,* 131–169.

Spencer, L., & Spencer, S. (1993). *Competence at work.* New York: John Wiley & Sons, Inc.

Sternberg, R.J., Wagner, R.K., Williams, W.M., & Horvath, J.A. (1995). Testing common sense. *American Psychologist, 50* (11), 912–927.

SELECTION

25.

What advantage do good-looking people have as candidates? (Notice our pictures at the front of this book. This is an important question for us!)

SELECT ONE:

☐ A. Physically good-looking people are hired at a greater rate than less attractive people.

☐ B. Physically good-looking people are offered higher starting salaries than less attractive people.

25

☐ C. Attractive women more than men have an advantage in both hiring rates and starting salaries.

☐ D. None. There is no real difference when you really look at the numbers.

☐ E. Both more attractive men and women get offered jobs at a higher rate and are offered higher starting pay.

25. What advantage do good-looking people have as candidates?

The correct answer is E: Both more attractive men and women get offered jobs at a higher rate and are offered higher starting pay.

How sure are we at this time?

1	2	3	**4**	5
Hint	Suggestive	Trending	**Substantial**	Solid

Discussion

Research shows that not only are good-looking applicants more likely to be hired, but they are likely to be hired at a higher starting salary. Attractiveness makes a difference with promotions, too. People ascribe more positive characteristics to attractive people. While beauty is in the eye of the beholder, there are consistent features that are seen as more attractive. Those with these features have more opportunities.

Selected Research

- According to Hatfield and Sprecher (1986), scientists find that most people react more favorably to good-looking people. Starting with grade school, studies show that good looks determine teachers' attitudes toward students and that good-looking children are perceived as being smarter than others. Hatfield points out that Title VII of the Civil Rights Act of 1964 forbids job discrimination on the basis of race, creed, color, sex, or national origin—but says nothing about physical attractiveness.

- In one study when interviewers were told applicants had been hired and they were to recommend a starting salary, they uniformly recommended higher starting salaries for the physically attractive candidates (Dipboye et al., 1977).

- Another researcher (Waters, 1980) discovered a "Cinderella syndrome." She found that HR managers and employment counselors gave a higher starting salary to a woman when she was made up attractively than when the same woman appeared not made up.

- A meta-analysis at the University of Michigan's Survey Research Center (Quinn, 1978) found that, for both men and women, physical attractiveness was tightly linked with income and occupational prestige.

- Researchers find we are "unbiased" in our biases. A study of work by artists, writers, students, and employees found that people are prejudiced in favor of the beautiful and against the ugly, regardless of the artists', writers', students', or employees' race, creed, or color (Maruyama & Miller, 1980).

- Quinn (1978) found that, for those not physically attractive, getting a job is tough in the first place. And, when they do get the job, studies show the less physically attractive have to work extra hard to get a good evaluation. Quinn found evidence that teachers and employers treat plain women and men's efforts with less respect than they deserve—especially when judgments have to be subjective.

So what difference do these findings make?

- Education of managers and supervisors can help promote acceptance of different levels of physical attractiveness, with the aim of alleviating the need to seek an attractiveness standard. Society accepts variation (eye and hair color, etc.) and should do the same with attractiveness. Remember, attractiveness may get someone the job, but it will not assure that they can do the job.

- The evaluations of less attractive employees may be skewed downward. You need to take caution when comparing two equally qualified employees, one more attractive and the other less so, for unintended bias. Examine less the physical features and more the social and emotional skills of a person.

Some Key Sources

Dipboye, R.L., Arvey, R.D., & Terpstra, D.E. (1977). Sex and physical attractiveness of raters and applicants as determinants of resume evaluations. *Journal of Applied Psychology*, *62*, 288–294.

Hatfield, E., & Sprecher, S. (1986). *Mirror, mirror...The importance of looks in everyday life*. Albany: State University of New York Press.

Maruyama, G., & Miller, N. (1980). Physical attractiveness, race, and essay evaluation. *Personality and Social Psychology*, *6* (3), 384–390.

Quinn, R.P. (1978). *Physical deviance and occupational mistreatment: The short, the fat, and the ugly.* Master's thesis, University of Michigan Survey Research Center, University of Michigan, Ann Arbor.

Waters, J. (1980, Winter). The Cinderella syndrome. *Farleigh Dickinson University Magazine*.

CAMPUS RECRUITING

26.

What are today's college graduates looking for in first-time employment?

SELECT ONE:

☐ A. Plain and simple as it has always been—best starting salary gets the most graduates; all else is a distant second.

☐ B. Geography and lifestyle perks are what drives the decisions Generation Xers are making today; they are quite different than the generation before them.

☐ C. They want to work for one of the 100 best places to work; money is way down the list.

☐ D. They look for a competitive pay package to narrow the field, then decide based on work culture and developmental opportunities, not always the best money offer.

☐ E. Total money package—including salary, incentives/bonuses and ownership are the biggest draws.

26. What are today's college graduates looking for in first-time employment?

The correct answer is D: They look for a competitive pay package to narrow the field, then decide based on work culture and developmental opportunities, not always the best money offer.

How sure are we at this time?

1	2	**3**	4	5
Hint	Suggestive	**Trending**	Substantial	Solid

Discussion

Despite conventional wisdom that says generations X and Y care less about money than about perks, the truth is that competitive organizations still offer competitive salaries, preferably sweetened with stock options or opportunities for economic gain through promotion or bonuses. After money and stock options, it's training and development opportunities—students look for employers who are generous with education benefits to keep their skills sharp. And a compelling work environment. Finally, students want to work where their friends work or where they might make friends.

Remember that students vary. The value proposition and what some students want may be different from that of other students. Value propositions change over someone's career and lifetime. What someone wanted in a job at 25 may differ at 35, 45, and 55. Evolving the employee deal is important to retain the right talent.

Selected Research

- In a survey by the National Association of Colleges and Employers (NACE), computer science graduates ranked "enjoying what they did" as the most important facet of a job, followed by the "opportunity to use their skills and abilities," and then, "opportunity for personal development." According to Thornberg (1997), money and ownership and signing bonuses—all are the price of admission. Beyond that, "research shows the two biggest attractions are training and development and a fun work environment."

- A survey by Poe (2000) noted these bargaining chips as being most important to current students and recent graduates: "Money (including signing bonuses), ownership (in the form of stock options), training and development opportunities, and a good work environment."

- A 2001 survey (NACE, 2001) reports that "money isn't everything to graduating college students who are preparing to enter the workforce. Although a good starting salary is important to them, they are most interested in jobs that offer room for advancement, a good benefits package, and the opportunity for continuing education or training."

- A national study (Bond et al., 1998) concluded that job and workplace characteristics far outweigh pay and benefits in predicting workplace productivity. They note that two things—work quality (job autonomy, challenges to learn on the job, and the meaning that people find in their work) and a supportive workplace (family friendly, supportive supervisors, relations with coworkers)—comprise positive job and workplace characteristics. The researchers also conclude that the same things that motivated workers 20 years ago still hold true today. The findings from 20 years ago showed pay was 12th and benefits 16th. "At the top of the list were accomplishing something worthwhile, autonomy, and chances to learn new things."

So what difference do these findings make?

- Attracting high-quality graduates is still a matter of offering a total package, which includes competitive dollars and, more importantly, a compelling place to work.

- Attracting the preferred graduates can be enhanced by relationship hiring where firms build relationships between current and future employees.

- A firm should create a clear and articulate value proposition that lays out what the new employee will get and what they in return must give to the firm. It is dangerous to hire a good performer who has expectations of what they will get and then not have those expectations met. These employees will leave and cost the firm time and money.

Some Key Sources

Bond, J., Galinsky, E., & Swanberg, J. (1998). *The 1997 National Study of the Changing Workforce.* Families and Work Institute: www.familiesandwork.org (Work-Life Research section).

National Association of Colleges and Employers (NACE). (2001). 2001 Graduating Student & Alumni Survey. (An annual study conducted by NACE.) *Journal of Career Planning & Employment.*

Poe, A.C. (2000, May). Face value. *HR Magazine.*

Thornberg, L. (1997, May). Employers and graduates size each other up. *HR Magazine.*

360 DEGREE FEEDBACK

27.

What length of time the rater has known the ratee yields the most accurate ratings?

SELECT ONE:

☐ A. It makes no difference. Ratings from anyone who has known you any length of time are OK.

☐ B. Less than two years known is most accurate; after that, they decrease in accuracy.

☐ C. One to five years known is most accurate.

☐ D. Five to ten years known is most accurate.

☐ E. Simply, the longer a rater has known the person, the more accurate the rating becomes.

27

27. What length of time the rater has known the ratee yields the most accurate ratings?

The correct answer is C: One to five years known is most accurate.

How sure are we at this time?

1	2	**3**	4	5
Hint	Suggestive	**Trending**	Substantial	Solid

Discussion

Knowing the person being rated for one to five years is the most accurate rater group. Studies show that ratings go up beyond five years and are less related to performance and more related to relationships. The same is true for people who have known the ratee for less than a year, but this information might still be useful because it would capture first-impression information. That might be quite helpful for someone with interpersonal issues.

Selected Research

- In his research, Mahler (1989) argued for the need to use evaluation methods that anchor conclusions about cognitive and behavioral competencies and traits to specific accomplishments over a period of several years.

- Similar research by Dachler (1989) concludes that raters needed to make "holistic assessments" by exploring patterns of behavior over time to analyze potential growth rather than single quantifiable dimensions at fixed points in time.

- According to Harris and Cleveland (1995), in order to manage our own careers effectively, we first have to "accept that our own self-view is not adequate, and then we have to supplement it with information from knowledgeable others. If we need information on our first impression, we need to look to people who have known us less than a year." (Harris and Murphy point out that studies show that feedback from people less than a year and beyond five years of knowing a person have higher ratings and are unrelated or less related to performance.)

- McEvoy and Beatty (1989) argue that asking raters to "rate behaviors they do not generally observe can be a frustrating experience for the rater and can provide data to the manager that are impossible to interpret." They add that, to the extent that items are included that are not necessarily ratable by all rater groups, response options such as "no opportunity to observe," "not applicable," or "don't know" can be used. In addition, items should either be ratable by all rater groups or targeted toward specific rater groups. The advantage of using the same items across rater groups is that it allows for comparison of the different rater views.

- Lombardo and Eichinger (2003) report that raters who have known the person being rated between one and five years yielded the highest accuracy. Those who had known the learner less than one year or more than five years gave ratings that were not significantly related with independent measures of performance. The raters who have known the person one to five years agree most with each other and least with the other groups (long- and short-timers). The one to two years known raters didn't even have significant agreement with the 10-plus years group. Overall, the most accurate raters had known the person one to three years. In the three to five years known period, the correlation dropped substantially but was still significant. "Before one year provides first impression data, but more than five years produces generalized or halo (depending on only a few key characteristics) ratings that lack differences and subtleties."

So what difference do these findings make?

• If you are interested in the most accurate data, select raters who have known the person being rated for one to five years. Keep track of this data when compiling 360 results.

• If you want to provide the person first impression data, select raters who have known the person being rated for less than one year.

• Be very careful of using raters who have known a person a long time (more than five years). The ratings tend to go up, get blandly positive with little differentiation, and be unrelated to performance.

Some Key Sources

Dachler, H.P. (1989). *Selection and the organizational context. Assessment and selection in organizations: Methods and practice for recruitment and appraisal.* Chichester, England: Wiley.

Lombardo, M., & Eichinger, R. (2003). *The LEADERSHIP ARCHITECT® norms and validity report.* Minneapolis: Lominger Limited, Inc.

Mahler, W.R. (1989). *The succession planning handbook for human resource executives.* Midland Park, NJ: Mahler Publishing Company.

McEvoy, G.M., & Beatty, R.W. (1989). Assessment centers and subordinate appraisals of managers: A seven-year examination of predictive validity. *Personnel Psychology, 42,* 37–52.

Murphy, K.R., & Cleveland, J.N. (1995). *Understanding performance appraisal.* Thousand Oaks, CA: Sage.

DEVELOPMENT

28.

What kinds of developmental changes occur during adulthood?

SELECT ONE:

☐ A. Very few; human personality is fairly set by age 18.

☐ B. None; human personality is largely genetic and the effects of environment are minimal after age 8.

☐ C. People go through similar developmental stages and phases throughout life, including late adulthood.

☐ D. People generally change in adulthood only as a result of experiences, crises, and trauma.

☐ E. Most people don't change much, but a few change fairly dramatically.

28

28. What kinds of developmental changes occur during adulthood?

The correct answer is C: People go through similar developmental stages and phases throughout life, including late adulthood.

How sure are we at this time?

1	2	3	**4**	5
Hint	Suggestive	Trending	**Substantial**	Solid

Discussion

Essentially, people get less interested in advancement and more interested in autonomy and achievement. Later on, most people become concerned with passing on wisdom and values to the next generation. There is some evidence that managers become cooler, tougher, more rational, and less interested in their own development over time.

Selected Research

- Howard and Bray (1990), reporting on a 20-year study, describe how successful managers' need for advancement declines with age, while the need for achievement, primacy of work, tolerance for uncertainty, and personal coolness (more rational, less nurturing) increases. What predicts success changes, not only with job and level changes, but also with human development and maturation.

- In their AT&T research, Howard and Bray found that careers in the Bell system had little resemblance to typical professional development tracks. Unlike many organizations, workers were promoted because of their knowledge of technology and job requirements. Most managers capitalized on this department- or subdepartment-specific informal and formal knowledge, focusing on the autonomy inherent in their jobs, and often "living out their careers in the same department or subdepartment." In the questionnaire that Howard and Bray administered, the "managers consistently scored high in terms of their pride in their jobs and their overall job satisfaction" (Howard & Bray, 1988, p. 132).

- Schultz and Schultz (1987) describe Erikson's Theory as including eight developmental stages covering a man's entire lifespan. They note that his theory is based on the view that the combination of the social environment and biological maturation causes a set of "crises" that need to be resolved (successfully or unsuccessfully) before a man can move on to the next stage. His three adult stages include: Intimacy versus Isolation—for young adults— where a man develops the ability to make long-term commitments to relationships; Generativity versus Stagnation—for middle adulthood—where a man develops an interest in guiding the development of the next generation; and Ego Integrity versus Despair—for older adulthood—where a man develops a sense of acceptance of the way he lived his life and the importance of the people and relationships he developed over the lifespan.

- In his book *Seasons of a Man's Life* (1986), Levinson reports on the results of a Yale study of forty men, ages 35 to 45, noting especially the mid-life transition that involves intense introspection. His research shows a "consistent pattern of adult life is an early struggle in adulthood to achieve a measure of success, followed by a mid life appraisal of ones' values and philosophy of life." Around 40, a man begins to reassess his life and begins "asking major questions like: Is this all I am going to do the rest of my life? Is this all I am going to achieve?"

- Jane Loevinger (1976) echoes Erikson's Theory that the progress from one stage to the next is "determined by an individual's psychological clock, not by chronological age or the social environment." In the independence stage, an individual attends college and lives away from home for the first time, becomes involved with a significant other, gets a job and begins paying their own bills. In the autonomous stage, an individual begins to question professional and social life choices but doesn't necessarily make changes involving these choices, plays corporate games, becomes focused on making a mark in life, becomes aware of the thoughts and goals of others, and gradually realizes that corporate games are becoming less important. The final stage is the integrated stage, where the individual takes greater interest in grandchildren, becomes interested in hobbies again, and in learning for the sake of learning instead of learning for the job, and "does community service and is quietly amused at any recognition received."

• In his book *Adaptation to Life* (1998), Vaillant noted that people with "poor psychological health," defined as an inability to cope with stress, were more likely to die young. In the study of a group of 185 people, 48 were identified as poor stress copers, 18 of whom died by age 53. In comparison, only two people with good "psychological health" (good stress copers) died by the same age. Vaillant also noted that psychologically healthy people are more adaptive and flexible and tend to have the following: stable family life, satisfying marriage, steady progression in their careers, and an absence of any disabling mental or physical illness.

So what difference do these findings make?
• What predicts success changes, not only with job and level changes, but also with human development and maturation. How employees define success also changes over time, thus changing what they want most from their jobs.

- Career ambition is an indicator of success but only early in one's career.

- Appealing to mature adults with promotion goals, career ambition goals, or money is less likely to work. Mature adults value autonomy and achievement much more. They also value the chance to pass on their information to the next generation of workers.

- People change rather dramatically in orderly and predictable ways. Trying to appeal to everyone as if they believed what they did when they started their careers is a losing strategy. Our focus should be on understanding key career timeline transitions.

- Building personalized career plans helps each employee know what is expected and what will be gained.

Some Key Sources

Howard, A., & Bray, D. (1988). *Managerial lives in transition: Advancing age and changing times.* New York: Guilford Press.

Howard, A., & Bray, D. (1990). Predictions of managerial success over long periods of time: Lessons for the management progress study. In K.E. Clark & M.B. Clark (Eds.), *Measures of leadership* (pp. 113–130). West Orange, NJ: Leadership Library of America.

Levinson, D.J. (1986). *The seasons of a man's life.* New York: Ballantine Books.

Loevinger, J. (1976). *Ego development.* San Francisco: Jossey-Bass.

Schultz, D.P., & Schultz, S.E. (1987). *A history of modern psychology.* Orlando, FL: Harcourt Brace.

Vaillant, G. (1995). *Adaptation to life.* Boston: Harvard Business School Press.

STRESS MANAGEMENT

29.

The majority of stomach ulcers are caused by:

SELECT ONE

☐ A. Prolonged stress that produces excess acid, which eats away at the stomach lining.

☐ B. Peak stress that overwhelms the body's defenses.

☐ C. Bacteria and anti-inflammatory drugs.

☐ D. Aggression, worry, and anger—Type A behavior.

☐ E. Heredity plus chronic stress.

29

29. The majority of stomach ulcers are caused by:

The correct answer is C: Bacteria and anti-inflammatory drugs.

How sure are we at this time?

1	2	3	4	**5**
Hint	Suggestive	Trending	Substantial	**Solid**

Discussion

For much of medical history, much was made of the connection between stomach ulcers and stress. The theory of excess stomach acid was the prevailing path. The remedy was a bland diet, acid reducing medication, and attending stress reduction therapy. Many Employee Assistance Programs followed that protocol, and employees were encouraged to reduce stress to avoid illness.

We now know better. The two most common causes of peptic ulcer disease are infection with *Helicobacter pylori* (*H. pylori*) bacteria and use of nonsteroidal anti-inflammatory drugs (NSAIDs). In the last 10 years, it has been shown conclusively that most (the vast majority) of stomach ulcers are caused by bacteria. Specifically, *Helicobacter pylori* (commonly referred to as *H. pylori*) bacteria. The treatment is two weeks of antibiotics. The fix has little to do with stress reduction. A bland diet wouldn't do any good.

How does stress play in the picture? Stress reduces the ability of your immune system to fight threats to your health. Specifically, stress of all forms increases the production of IL–6 (interleukin–6), a damaging chemical in blood. When under prolonged stress, the immune system can't fight normal attacks on various systems in your body, allowing things like

H. pylori to eat into the stomach lining. Normally, your immune system holds *H. pylori* in check.

So stress causes the immune system to be taxed, which in turn allows *H. pylori* to cause ulcers. If *H. pylori* isn't in your system, no amount of stress will cause ulcers. Stress might and does cause a lot of other problems, but not ulcers.

Selected Research

- A study of 119 men and women who were living under the stress of constant care giving as caregivers for spouses with dementia (CNN.com, 2003) reported higher levels of the chemical interleukin–6 in the blood of this group compared with the blood of others in the test. The study also found that the level remained higher in caregivers for up to three years following the spouse's death. The researchers (Kiecolt-Glaser & Glaser) explained the results by noting that people under stress tend to respond by doing things that increase their levels of IL–6, such as overeat, smoke, or not get enough sleep or exercise.

- A summary of research by two Australian researchers, Drs. Barry Marshall and Robin Warren, on the causes and treatment of ulcers (Slovut, 1997) reports that most ulcers are caused by a spiral-shaped bacteria, *Helicobacter pylori* rather than stress, as was previously suggested. The two researchers established that *H. pylori* infection causes ulcers in the stomach and the duodenum, noting that the "bug" seemed to cause about 50 percent of stomach ulcers and 90 percent of the more common duodenal ulcers.

- Marshall and Warren (1984) published the results of their study in the *Lancet*, noting that "the bacteria were present in almost all patients with active chronic gastritis, duodenal ulcer, or gastric ulcer and thus may be an important factor in the etiology of these diseases."

- In 1994, a U.S. National Institutes of Health Consensus Development Panel concluded that "infection appears to play an important contributory role in the pathogenesis of peptic ulcers," and recommended that antibiotics be used in their treatment. The report noted that peptic ulcers are fairly common, affecting up to 10 percent of the population (Thagard, 1999).

- A report in a Johns Hopkins White Paper (2002) notes that "as far back as 1886, researchers had documented a possible association between ulcers and spiral bacteria in the lining of the human stomach" but that mainstream medicine dismissed the finding because of the belief that "no bacteria could live in the acidic environment of the stomach." The paper further notes the efforts in 1991 of researchers at the Baylor College of Medicine in Houston, Texas, who used the first randomized study in the country to demonstrate the effectiveness of antibiotic therapy in the treatment of ulcers. Following that study, the National Institutes of Health recommended in 1994 that people with peptic ulcer and *H. pylori* infection receive antibiotics as a first-line therapy. They note that in 80 to 90 percent of people with peptic ulcers stemming from *H. pylori* infection (i.e., not related to other causes like nonsteroidal anti-inflammatory drugs), antibiotics combined with other treatments offer a permanent cure.

So what difference do these findings make?

- Stress reduction in general is a good idea. Excess stress can lead to all kinds of medical problems like heart disease, arthritis, diabetes, and even some kinds of cancer. And it can lead to poor performance because of bad judgment and decision making.

- Ulcers are caused by bacteria and treated with antibiotics. Reducing stress might decrease the chances of a recurrence. Elimination of *H. pylori* bacteria from your system will eliminate a recurrence.

- When you hear that an employee has an ulcer, it is not a correct conclusion that the employee is under excess stress or can't handle stress. When an employee is experiencing stress, changing diet is not the solution.

Some Key Sources

CNN.com (2003). *Study reveals how stress makes you sick.* Findings by the research group headed by Janice Kiecolt-Glaser and Ronald Glaser. Retrieved July 1, 2003, from CNN.com http://stress.about.com/cs/medicalconditions/a/aa071003a.htm

Johns Hopkins Digestive Disorders White Paper. (2002). *The H. pylori story: How two Australian researchers discovered the true cause of most peptic ulcers.* Retrieved July 17, 2003, from www.hopkinsafter50.com (Digestive Disorders Resource Center section).

Marshall, B.J., & Warren, J.R. (1984). Unidentified curved bacilli in the stomach of patients with gastritis and peptic ulceration. *Lancet, 1* (8390), 1311–1315.

Slovut, G. (1997, April 17). Antibiotics are the best way to fight ulcers. Minneapolis: *Star Tribune.*

Thagard, P. (1999). *How scientists explain disease.* Princeton, NJ: Princeton University Press.

WORKPLACE VIOLENCE

30.

*What does the phrase "going postal"
(post office workers showing violence)
demonstrate?*

SELECT ONE:

☐ A. The real problem is government service; the
screening process doesn't work; it allows
marginal people to be employed.

☐ B. The postal service has the largest percentage
of negatively discharged military-trained
employees.

☐ C. The postal service is not allowed to screen
based upon dishonorable discharge; most of
the violence has been committed by bad
characters with military training.

☐ D. The nature of the work and the work
environment itself is what relates to violence
in the workplace.

☐ E. Poor pay leads to workplace violence.

30

30. **What does the phrase "going postal" (post office workers showing violence) demonstrate?**

    The correct answer is D: The nature of the work and the work environment itself is what relates to violence in the workplace.

How sure are we at this time?

1	2	3	**4**	5
Hint	Suggestive	Trending	**Substantial**	Solid

Discussion

Studies have shown that it is the nature of the work environment that has led to workplace violence. Poor supervision, dull and repetitive work, poor communications, and ill treatment all have contributed.

Additionally, the work content and setting plays a role. About two million American workers are victims of workplace violence each year. Workplace violence can strike anywhere, and no one is immune. Some workers, however, are at increased risk. Workers who are at the greatest risk are those who: exchange money with the public; deliver passengers, goods, or services; work alone or in small groups during late night or early morning hours in high-crime areas; or those who work in community settings and homes where they have extensive contact with the public. These most at-risk groups include healthcare and social service workers such as visiting nurses, psychiatric evaluators, and probation officers; community workers such as gas and water utility employees, phone and cable TV installers, and letter carriers; retail workers; and taxi drivers.

Selected Research

• According to the Semiannual Report of the Office of Inspector General of the United States Postal Service (2000), violence in the workplace is still considered one of the biggest problems. The report revealed that "signs of workplace stress are present and that comprehensive steps are needed to improve the workplace climate, including aligning human resources with business requirements."

• Part of the above report documents a study on workplace violence requested by the Postmaster General. According to the commissioned workplace safety study, postal service employees believed they were at greater risk than the average worker in the United States to be a victim of workplace violence; however, they were no more likely to be victims of violence than employees in the national workforce.

• Violence in the workplace involving worker against coworkers is a problem of increasing magnitude. The risk of becoming a victim of a workplace homicide is higher for some industries and occupations and work settings (Diamond, 1997).

• From 1980 to 1989, homicides were the leading cause of fatal occupational injuries in retail trade (1.66 per 100,000); service (.61 per 100,000); finance, insurance, and real estate (.39 per 100,000). Additional National Institute for Occupational Safety and Health (NIOSH) data show that between 1980 and 1992, the greatest number of homicides occurred in retail trade (38 percent of total) and service industries as a whole (17 percent).

• For the similar period of 1983–1993, the workplace homicide rate for the postal service, 0.63 per 100,000 workers, was just under the workplace homicide rate for all occupations according to National Traumatic Occupational

Facilities (NTOF) surveillance system data. So "going postal" is not unique to the postal service.

- Coworkers appear disproportionately responsible for homicides that occur in the postal service. "From 1983 to 1989, 20 out of 35 work-related homicides were committed by coworkers or former coworkers, but 14 of these occurred in a single incident." According to a 1993 survey from the private agency, Northwestern National Life, of 89 workers who had been physically attacked at work at some point in their lives, 44 percent reported being attacked by a customer or client, 30 percent by coworkers or former employees, 24 percent by strangers, and 3 percent by someone else.

- Results of a 2002 Security Management and Salary Survey (*HR Focus*, 2003) found that companies that provide training to supervisors and employees in workplace-violence awareness are significantly cutting their incidence rate for employee-on-employee violence. Among the organizations that train supervisors to identify and address troubled workers, 20.2 percent reduced the number of violent incidents between employees. Only 17.9 percent of companies that don't conduct such training have been able to cut these incidents. "Providing workplace-violence training to all employees as opposed to just supervisors seems to make an even bigger difference: 21.9 percent of companies that do so reduced employee-on-employee violence, compared to 15.7 percent of companies that don't provide such training." Organizations with a written policy addressing workplace violence were 25 percent more likely to reduce violent incidents between workers in the past year than companies without such policies. Some but not all experts see drugs as a contributing factor in workplace violence. Of employers that conduct drug testing, 23.3 percent reported reductions in incidents of violence between employees compared to only 15.8 percent of companies that do no such testing. More than 20 percent of companies in the survey have no written policy; close to 40 percent provide no training on the subject; almost half (48 percent) say they drug-test all employees. The failure of almost 10 percent of companies currently to track incidents of workplace violence makes it more difficult to target solutions to the workers most at risk.

• Workplace violence has emerged as an important safety and health issue. Homicide, its most extreme form, is the third-leading cause of fatal occupational injury in the U.S. (OSHA). According to the Bureau of Labor Statistics (BLS) Census of Fatal Occupational Injuries, 639 workplace homicides occurred in 2001. They accounted for 15.3 percent of the total 5,900 fatal work injuries in the U.S. (excluding those deaths resulting from the September 11, 2001 terrorist attacks).

• Statistics show that the number of workplace-related violent incidents is increasing (Lipman, 1994). From 1980 to 1989, there have been 7,603 documented cases of workplace homicides all over the U.S., and surveys show that over 15 percent of American workers have fallen victim to some form of physical attack during their careers.

• An issue of *Trial Magazine* (Sakis & Kennedy, 2002) notes that each year between 1993 and 1999, an average of 1.7 million violent crimes were committed at work—not including about 900 work-related homicides annually. During the same period, workplace violence accounted for 18 percent of all violent crime in the United States. The Workplace Violence Research Institute of Palm Springs, California estimated that workplace violence costs $36 billion annually in lost productivity, work disruptions, employee turnover, litigation, and other losses.

So what difference do these findings make?

- Workplace violence is increasing everywhere and is not limited to the postal service. Policies, training, and communication have all been shown to reduce violence. Pay attention to the quality of the workplace environment, implement zero-tolerance policies, especially train supervisors to detect early signs, and have a prevention support program.

- Identify the early indicators of potential violence. Individuals who act "weird" often are. Monitor their behavior and follow up on even small dysfunctional actions.

Some Key Sources

Bureau of Labor Statistics. (2001). Census of Fatal Occupational Injuries, 2000. Washington, DC: U.S. Department of Labor.

Diamond, M.A. (1997, September). Administrative assault: A contemporary psychoanalytic view of violence and aggression in the workplace. *American Review of Public Administration*, *27* (3), 228(20).

Lipman, I.A. (1994, Summer). Violence at work. *Business Perspectives*, *7* (3), 14(6).

Office of Inspector General. (2000). *Semiannual Report to Congress: Including significant activities of the Inspection Service*, April 1, 2000–September 30, 2000.

Sakis, J.R., & Kennedy, D.B. (2002, December). Violence at work. *Trial Magazine*.

The most effective tool against workplace violence. (2003, February). *HR Focus*, *80* (2), 11, 13+.

PAY PRACTICES

31.

Paying managers one standard deviation higher than average market value results in:

SELECT ONE:

☐ A. An increase in market value of nearly 20% and profits by more than 25%.

☐ B. Little difference in organization performance because pay doesn't motivate.

☐ C. A 5% increase in overall firm performance.

☐ D. An increase of 10% in revenue and 5% in profits.

☐ E. Not possible to measure.

31. **Paying managers one standard deviation higher than average market value results in:**

   The correct answer is A: An increase in market value of nearly 20% and profits by more than 25%.

How sure are we at this time?

1	2	3	4	5
Hint	Suggestive	Trending	Substantial	Solid

Discussion
As astonishing as it may sound, overpaying managers results in increased outcomes. While it is probably true that differences in pay do not make people work harder or smarter, the best explanation is that paying higher than market attracts a higher level candidate, and good people tend to stay because it would be costly for other firms to hire them away. It probably also adds to personal pride in the sense of "I am worth high pay."

Selected Research
• Becker and Huselid (1996) found that for every one standard deviation increase in the compensation index, there was a 19 percent increase in firm value and a 27 percent increase in profits. The compensation index was a combination of six measures: amount of pay tied in to performance, amount of average pay compared to market, amount of share ownership, amount of annual pay increases over market, what percent of the workforce was eligible for bonuses, and amount of pension plan contribution on the part of the company.

So what difference do these findings make?

- Carefully track where your firm is on the six measures of the compensation index. Consider paying high as part of a long-term strategy to attract and retain top performers. But, be clear that where much is given, much is expected. Demand managers who are highly paid to be high performing. Set standards, monitor results, and give feedback so that high pay results in high performance. Also, let the managers know that they are being highly paid so that they are motivated to work to justify the high salary.

Some Key Sources

Huselid, M., & Becker, B. (1996). Methodological issues in cross-sectional and panel estimates of the HR-firm performance link. *Industrial Relations, 35,* 400–422.

DIVERSITY

32.

College entrance tests are . . .?

SELECT ONE:

☐ A. Now culture and gender bias free after two decades of effort.

☐ B. Now gender bias free and close to culture bias free.

☐ C. Now culture bias free and close to gender bias free.

☐ D. Now less relevant because they no longer predict academic achievement.

☐ E. Still show various but smaller degrees of both gender and culture bias.

32. College entrance tests are . . .?

The correct answer is E: Still show various but smaller degrees of both gender and culture bias.

How sure are we at this time?

1	2	**3**	4	5
Hint	Suggestive	**Trending**	Substantial	Solid

Discussion
While solid progress has been made to make college entrance exams free of racial, cultural, and gender bias, some still exist. Additionally, people in this debate are beginning to understand the limitations of this kind of testing on predicting academic and, more importantly, life success. Even if all entrance tests were culturally and gender bias free, they would still only partially predict academic success and predict even less of life success.

Selected Research
*   A decade of research on the disparity of SAT scores between men and women (Rosser, 1989) found that, when there is a large difference between male and female correct answers, the answer rates are biased in favor of males, "despite females' superior academic performance." Rosser found that females usually did better on questions asked about relationships, aesthetics, and the humanities, while males did better on questions about sports, the physical sciences, and business.

*   Since research shows that SAT scores predict only a small percentage of variance in college performance, Jencks and Phillips (1998) concluded that reliance on the scores "forces Blacks to pay for the fact that social scientists have

unusually good measures of a trait on which Blacks are unusually disadvantaged" (pp. 14–15). Even if the entrance exams were shown to predict differently for different protected groups, current practice and case law does not allow for different cutoff points or different weighting of tests.

- Research by Fernald (2002) and Geiser and Studley (2001) from the University of California shows that SAT scores are a weak predictor of freshman grades. High school grade point average and SAT II scores (achievement tests) are much better predictors. Preliminary data indicate they are also much better predictors of who goes on to graduate. Both high school grades and SAT II scores predict well across different racial/ethnic groups, family income levels, and for high schools of varying quality.

- While most researchers agree that some kind of testing must be done to create parity in admissions, research by Helms (1995) points out that the way a test is constructed determines what differences will be found among groups, and that preconceptions about group differences determine how one constructs the test.

- Blum and Levin (2000) point out that the uproar over admission of minority applicants into programs that rejected Whites with higher test scores "assumes that the test scores are an unassailable indicator of true merit."

So what difference do these findings make?
- While there is abundant support for the use of admissions testing to help predict those who would benefit most from the academic opportunity of a college or university experience, it is only a partial predictor and may still have some aspects of gender, racial, and cultural bias.

- Most universities are learning to rely on things other than pure testing for candidate admissions. Companies should do the same.

Some Key Sources

Blum, E., & Levin, M. (2000). Racial profiling: Wrong for police, wrong for universities. In F.J. Crosby & C. VanDeVeer (Eds.), *Sex, race and merit: Debating affirmative action in education and employment* (pp. 67–69). Ann Arbor: University of Michigan Press.

Fernald, J. (2002). *Preliminary findings on the relationship between SAT scores, high school GPA, socioeconomic status and UCSC freshman GPA.* Retrieved from http://www.ucop.edu/sas/research/researchandplanning/pdf/sat_study.pdf

Geiser, S., & Studley, R. (2001). *UC and the SAT: Predictive validity and differential impact of the SAT I and SAT II at the University of California.* Retrieved from http://www.senate.ucsc.edu/cafa/SATGPA.htm

Helms, J.E. (1995). Why is there no study of cultural equivalence in standardized cognitive ability testing? In N.R. Goldberger & J. Veroff (Eds.), *The culture and psychology reader* (pp. 674–719). New York: New York University Press.

Jencks, C., & Phillips, M. (Eds.). (1998). *The Black-White test score gap.* Washington, DC: Brookings Institution Press. http://www.policyideas.org/Issues/Education/Affirmative_Action.pdf

Rosser, P. (1989). *The SAT gender gap: Identifying the causes.* Washington, DC: Center for Women Policy Studies. http://www.centerwomenpolicy.org/pubfiles/1989SATgendergap.pdf

CAREER MANAGEMENT— INTERNATIONAL

How good are multinational companies in handling and managing their returning expatriates?

33

SELECT ONE:

☐ A. They tend to assign their best to international assignments and retain them after they return.

☐ B. Most multinationals only send high potentials to international assignments.

☐ C. Most multinationals struggle with the repatriation issue.

☐ D. High-tech companies do better at retaining their international managers.

☐ E. All multinationals lose the majority of returning expatriates to other companies.

33. How good are multinational companies in handling and managing their returning expatriates?

The correct answer is C: Most multinationals struggle with the repatriation issue.

How sure are we at this time?

1	2	**3**	4	5
Hint	Suggestive	**Trending**	Substantial	Solid

Discussion

It's the old good news, bad news story. Most multinational companies (MNCs) think that an increase in global competence is one of their biggest challenges and is one benefit of successful repatriation; that is, people who have served outside the home office country coming back with fresh perspectives...the good news. The bad news, and also a big concern to MNCs, is the low retention rate of global returnees. In the increasingly global world, managers and executives with international exposure and experience are worth a lot to MNCs. Unfortunately, many times it turns out that they are worth more to companies other than their own. While their own companies struggle with how to manage returnees, other companies recruit them. Retaining all they can after an international assignment should be a number one priority for MNCs.

Selected Research

- Research by O'Boyle (1989) found that between 20 and 25 percent of repatriated employees leave their firms within a year after returning to the U.S.

- Other repatriation studies (Black et al., 1992) found that 74 percent of repatriates did not expect to be working with the same company within one year after returning to their home country, 42 percent had seriously considered leaving their companies after repatriation, and 26 percent had been actively searching for other employment. Other results of their studies found that 77 percent of U.S. repatriates were demoted to a lower level position than what they had held during their global assignment.

- According to Wilson and Dalton (1998), a documented repatriation strategy is critical to the success of any global expatriation efforts.

- McCall and Hollenbeck (2002) stress the importance of strategic repatriation plans in global leadership development efforts. They reaffirm the importance of recognizing the expatriate's contribution to the organization and seeing their international experience as a "transformation" that needs to be incorporated in future globalization efforts.

- A study that examined the role of three sources of support in facilitating expatriate adjustment and performance (Kraimer et al., 2001) found that the feeling that they had organizational support had the most positive effect on expatriate adjustment after returning.

- Research to examine expatriates' decisions to quit their assignments (Shaffer & Harrison, 1998) found that a combination of the work-related factors of job satisfaction and organizational commitment had the most impact on their decision to quit their assignments. They also found that the nonwork satisfaction variables like family responsibility, spouse adjustment, and living conditions played a large role in their decision to quit their assignments.

- A 1994 Global Survey Relocation Report found that, while 97 percent of the U.S.-based MNCs in the survey offer to pay for return shipment of household goods, only 31 percent offer an expatriate career development assistance (Windham International & NFTC, 1994).

- According to Caligiuri and Lazarova (2000), successful expatriate programs include career planning, pre-assignment posting activities for the expatriate and family, establishing very specific terms and conditions of the assignment itself, educational and housing benefits, and, perhaps, repatriation planning before the assignment begins.

So what difference do these findings make?

- Companies keep trading past expatriates because they have such valuable experiences. No one doubts the added value of serving outside your home country. No one doubts globalization is one of the key challenges facing many companies. Everyone probably knows what to do to retain valuable international talent. But few do it well. What to do?

- Some practices suggested by Caligiuri (2000) for managing repatriation: Organizations should make an effort to manage expectations upon repatriation.

  - Offer career continuation planning and reentry management sessions well before end of an international assignment.

  - Offer a job upon return guarantee or repatriation agreement.

  - Use domestic mentors to keep expatriates abreast of company happenings.

  - Offer a reorientation program to brief returning expatriates.

- Offer repatriation seminars to employees and their families.

- Offer financial counseling and financial/tax assistance.

- Offer lifestyle counseling.

- Show that the organization values the international experience by promoting expatriates upon return, maintaining position status and bonus compensation for completing the assignment.

- Incorporating repatriation in planning (O'Boyle, 1989). While surveys address the need to use the skills acquired by the expatriate upon returning, little has been done to include the new knowledge and skills back into the business. Ask. Listen. Put past expatriates on taskforces. Have them selectively attend management meetings.

- Global assignments and repatriation (Black et al., 1992). To be strategic about international assignments, the purpose for selecting an individual in the first place, including plans after the assignment is completed, should be part of strategic succession planning.

Some Key Sources

Black, J.S., Gregersen, H.B., & Mendenhall, M.E. (1992). *Global assignments.* San Francisco: Jossey-Bass.

Caligiuri, P.M., & Lazarova, M. (2000). Strategic repatriation policies to enhance global leadership development. In M. Mendenhall, T. Kuehlmann, & G. Stahl (Eds.), *Developing global business leaders: Policies, processes, and innovations.* New York: Quorum Books.

Kraimer, M.L., Wayne, S.J., & Jaworski, R.A. (2001, Spring). Sources of support and expatriate performance: The mediating role of expatriate adjustment. *Personnel Psychology, 54* (1).

McCall, M.W., & Hollenbeck, G.P. (2002). *Developing global executives: The lessons of international experience.* Boston: Harvard Business School Press.

O'Boyle, T.F. (1989, December 11). Grappling with the expatriate issue: Little benefit to careers seen in foreign stints. *The Wall Street Journal*, pp. B1, B4.

Shaffer, M.A., & Harrison, D.A. (1998, Spring). Expatriates' psychological withdrawal from international assignments: Work, nonwork, and family influences. *Personnel Psychology, 51* (1).

Wilson, M.S., & Dalton, M.A. (1998). *International success: Selecting, developing, and supporting expatriate managers.* Greensboro, NC: Center for Creative Leadership.

Windham International and National Foreign Trade Council. (1994). *Global relocation trends: 1994 survey report.* New York: Windham International.

GENDER

34.

Which of the following is the most true about men evaluating women?

SELECT ONE:

☐ A. Men apply much higher standards when they rate women and rate them lower than men.

☐ B. Men and women rate each other on the same basis.

☐ C. Each gender holds the other to a higher standard.

☐ D. There are mixed results depending upon the rating situation, with men rating women slightly lower.

☐ E. Both men and women rate women significantly lower.

34. Which of the following is the most true about men evaluating women?

The correct answer is D: There are mixed results depending upon the rating situation, with men rating women slightly lower.

How sure are we at this time?

1	**2**	3	4	5
Hint	**Suggestive**	Trending	Substantial	Solid

Discussion

A lot of research has been done about the relationship between individual characteristics and rating tendencies. The research has focused on characteristics of the raters, the ratee, or both.

Research has generally shown that men use different standards when they rate women for the same job or task and therefore end up rating women lower. This trend may be abating. As more women enter the management ranks (46 percent of managers are women in the 2000 Census), this bias may dissipate.

Selected Research

- A study by Paludi and Bauer (1983) found that men reviewed research publications perceived to have been written by women less favorably than those thought to be written by men. (Women also rated male-authored papers more highly but not as highly as men rated male authors.)

- Eagly et al. (1992) cites men's higher status in society as an explanation [for harsh evaluations]. They may evaluate women more harshly (relative to men) in order to maintain their societal status.

- Two researchers, Christine Wennerds and Agnes Wold at Sweden's Goteborg University (May 22, 1997), examined the peer review system of the Swedish Medical Research Council, comparing male and female scientist productivity and found that reviewers consistently gave female applicants lower scores than equally productive men.

- A study by Sackett et al. (1991) found that women received lower ratings when they were a small proportion of the work group.

- Brown and Geis (1984) suggest that male raters use attribution theory to explain the success of women ratees. In this case, attribution theory suggests that raters search the environment for causes or reasons to explain observed events and that those reasons have to be found to explain the success of a woman manager. Very often, according to their research, male raters attribute women's success to factors other than skill.

- Cejka and Eagly (1999) argue that sex stereotyping in occupations is one of the primary reasons for today's division of labor between men and women. The researchers found that "success in occupations dominated by one sex requires the personal characteristics typical of that sex and that this stereotyping of occupations is reflected in performance evaluation." They conclude that, in male-typed occupations such as management, men rate men more highly than they rate women.

Counter Research
- Lombardo and Eichinger (2003) completed a study that found that "women and men rated their opposite gender the same on 84 percent of competencies noted in the study. Neither gender rated its own gender higher than it

rated the other overall, and male and female raters agreed much more with each other on people of either gender than with the person rated."

- Research by Chen and DiTomaso (1996) found that "while there is some evidence of rating bias between men and women, the effects are generally small."

- Research by Lombardo and Eichinger (2003) found that, in studies that "look at men and women in the same companies, in the same jobs, at the same level, with the same amount of managerial experience, effectiveness is about equal." Summarizing their research, they found: Gender was not related to promotion or performance overall or by level; men and women are not rated differently; people do not rate their gender higher (or lower) than the other; rating agreement between genders is high; women and men agree far more with each other than with the person rated, regardless of gender. They are primarily rating the person, not the person's gender; both women and men are rated higher by both genders on certain competencies; there are a few differences, with women scoring a little higher in some day-to-day management skills and interpersonal skills and men scoring higher in some problem-solving business skills; the differences are small and tell us nothing about an individual based on gender; the magnitude of the correlations with performance are the same for both genders.

So what difference do these findings make?

- Men give women lower ratings than for men in some settings and circumstances. Take this into account when looking at overall ratings.

- Women need to be aware of the rating biases of men and adjust their feedback results accordingly. They need to discount their results somewhat because there is more negative bias than is justified.

- Male raters need to be made aware of these results and trained to adjust their rating styles.

Some Key Sources

Brown, V., & Geis, F.L. (1984). Turning lead into gold: Evaluations of men and women leaders and the alchemy of social consensus. *Journal of Personality and Social Psychology, 46,* 811–824.

Cejka, M.A., & Eagly, A.H. (1999). Gender-stereotypic images of occupations correspond to the sex segregation of employment. *Personality and Social Psychology Bulletin, 25* (4), 413–423.

Chen, C.C., & DiTomaso, N. (1996). Performance appraisal and demographic diversity: Issues regarding appraisals, appraisers, and appraising. In E.E. Kossek & S.A. Lobel (Eds.), *Human resource strategies for managing diversity* (pp. 137–163). Oxford: Blackwell.

Eagly, A.H., Makhijani, M.G., & Klonsky, B.G. (1992). Gender and the evaluation of leaders: A meta-analysis. *Psychological Bulletin, 11,* 3–22.

Lombardo, M., & Eichinger, R. (2003). *The LEADERSHIP ARCHITECT® norms and validity report.* Minneapolis: Lominger Limited, Inc.

Paludi, M.A., & Bauer, W.D. (1983). Goldberg revisited: What's in an author's name. *Sex Roles: A Journal of Research, 9,* 387–390.

Sackett, P., DuBois, C., & Noe, A. (1991). Tokenism in performance evaluation: The effects of work group representation on male-female and White-Black differences in performance ratings. *Journal of Applied Psychology, 76* (2), 263–267.

Wennerds, C., & Wold, A. (1997, May 22). Nepotism and sexism in peer review. *Nature, 307* (6631), 341.

MEASUREMENT

35.

Are very small (below .20) correlations meaningless even if they are statistically significant?

SELECT ONE:

☐ A. Yes, they are essentially meaningless.

☐ B. They might have some small but unimportant value.

☐ C. They have great value because they are statistically significant; significance trumps size.

☐ D. It depends upon whether the result is measuring something very important or not.

☐ E. It all just depends.

35. Are very small (below .20) correlations meaningless even if they are statistically significant?

The correct answer is E: It all just depends.

How sure are we at this time?

1	2	3	4	**5**
Hint	Suggestive	Trending	Substantial	**Solid**

Discussion

How high a correlation has to be to be meaningful depends on the nature of the study. For example, most of us know that aspirin helps in the prevention of heart attacks, but you might not be very impressed with the correlation—it's .03 (Rosenthal, 1990). So why is it important and widely touted? Because of those suffering heart attacks, 65 percent of them were taking the placebo and only 35 percent were taking aspirin. The physicians abandoned the study because they thought it would be unethical to continue it when the value of aspirin was so obvious. Correlations work off variation and since 99 percent of the people in the study didn't have a heart attack, there was no relationship to measure. The "results" come from the remaining 1 percent. You should look carefully at small correlations—they can still significantly affect large numbers of people once you look at where the relationship came from.

On the other hand, if there is a study involving 1,000 men and 1,000 women, all of whom were measured on a dominance scale, and the correlation is .06 or .10, you should either ignore it or note it as a minor relationship, even if it is significant due to a large sample. Why? Because all the people contributed to the results (unlike the aspirin study above), and a small correlation tells us nothing important. There are undoubtedly other variables that explain male/female differences other than dominance.

Selected Research

- A report in the *Journal of Experimental Education* (Thompson, 1993) argues that use of the phrase "statistical significance" is often misleading. According to Thompson, the word "significant" itself causes professional practitioners and the lay public to think that the research results are important. He notes that even researchers and research journal editors could be swayed into thinking that a research result is important because it is "statistically significant," or the converse: that a research result is not important because it *is not* statistically significant. Statistical significance is often related to sample size. A large sample size will have statistically significant results of very small differences.

- Research by Sternberg (1996) makes an interesting point about correlations—that they do not prove causation, and that addressing causality needs to include other types of tests of reliability and validity (face, content, criterion, and construct validity). He explains the findings using height and weight. "Height and weight are correlated, but you do not get shorter when you lose weight." He adds that, just because one variable is related to another variable, doesn't mean the first variable "caused" the second variable. And, it's possible that the second variable could cause the first variable, or both the first and second variables could "be related to some third variable, which causes both of them."

So what difference do these findings make?

- Size of the correlation and statistical significance are only the starting points to determining whether the result is of practical use. Practical use depends upon a lot of factors. Look to the discussion of the findings to see if the author(s) discusses the practical utility of the findings.

- Relevance is often as important as significance. At times a small statistical difference might be very relevant for the particular study.

- In normal circumstances, follow the standard (Cohen, 1988) where .50 is a large correlation, .30 is moderate, and .10 is small. Normal is defined as a fairly small sample (say 30 to 200) with a good spread of ratings in both the predictor (e.g., competency ratings) and the criterion (e.g., performance ratings).

Some Key Sources

Cohen, J. (1988). *Statistical power analysis for the behavioral sciences* (2nd ed.). New Jersey: Lawrence Erlbaum.

Rosenthal, R. (1990). How are we doing in soft psychology? *American Psychologist, 45,* 775.

Sternberg, R.J. (1996). *Successful intelligence: How practical and creative intelligence determine success in life.* New York: Simon & Schuster.

Thompson, B. (1993). The role of statistical significance testing in contemporary analytic practice: Alternatives with comments from journal editors [Special issue]. *Journal of Experimental Education.* Washington, DC: Heldref Publications.

MANAGERIAL COMPETENCIES

36.

Can short managerial or leadership competency models predict individual success throughout an entire organization?

SELECT ONE:

☐ A. Most do if they are carefully constructed.

☐ B. There is no such thing as a small set of managerial or leadership competencies that predict individual success across entire organizations.

☐ C. They predict success only for core technical skills.

☐ D. They predict success only for managers and executives.

☐ E. They predict success only for individual contributors and professionals.

36. Can short managerial or leadership competency models predict individual success throughout an entire organization?

The correct answer is B: There is no such thing as a small set of managerial or leadership competencies that predict individual success across entire organizations.

How sure are we at this time?

1	2	3	**4**	5
Hint	Suggestive	Trending	**Substantial**	Solid

Discussion

Organizations often create and implement a managerial or leadership competency model which usually has 10 or fewer competencies (such as customer service, integrity, and communication). In these cases, the competencies are usually more a values statement that, while important for many jobs, does not define their total palette of required leadership competencies.

Many core competency models also contain competencies where most people always rate high, such as integrity, customer service, intelligence (as applied to solving problems), and functional/technical excellence. Measuring people on these generic and socially desirable dimensions won't tell an organization much, since people are and have been rated good at them since their individual contributor days. While important to continued performance, they are widely available (and sought after) in the marketplace and cannot make the difference in getting some sort of edge over one's competitors. These competency models are generic, not specific, and thus do not add to competitiveness.

What we know for sure is that the competencies that usually lead to success across a broad range of organizations differ by level. The mission critical competencies for individual contributors and professionals are different than those for supervisors and managers, which are again different for executives. So a single list of 10 or fewer competencies can't possibly predict much of success throughout an entire organization.

We also know for sure that the competencies that usually lead to success across a broad range of organizations also differ by function and by business strategy. The mission critical competencies for marketing will be different than manufacturing and in turn will be different for finance. The mission critical competencies for a business with a growth strategy will differ from one in a harvest strategy. So a single list of 10 or less competencies can't possibly predict much of success across an entire organization.

We would speculate that the competencies that usually lead to success across a broad range of organizations might differ by business unit. Possibly by country if the organization is international. Possibly by economic situation—a start-up will have a different list than a turnaround. Possibly by industry—high tech might be different than heavy manufacturing.

So for all of the sure and probable reasons above, we know for sure that a single list of 10 or less competencies will not say much, if anything, about success across all levels, functions, business units, and countries.

That said, a core competency list might be effective for managing culture and culture change. That is, you could specify that you will hold everyone in the entire enterprise accountable for integrity and ethics. That would not necessarily predict success in the sense of increasing revenue but might be effective in correcting an ethics problem.

To really define a single job or role or a job cluster takes about 20 to 30 competencies if you are really interested in accurate prediction. Ten or less just won't do the job.

Selected Research

- Studies by Spencer and Spencer (1993) suggest that the architecture of human competence can be defined as a series of layers: "The visible top or the first layer of the competence structure is concerned with the observable (instrumental) knowledge and skills that relate to the tasks and work; the second layer relates to non-job-specific skills that are applicable in various situations; the third layer in the competence structure consists of the values, standards, ethics, and morals of the person; and the fourth layer of the human competence structure consists of personal characteristics which are difficult to perceive and assess."

- Years of research by Lombardo and Eichinger (2002) reports that "many responsible institutions have competency lists or models, but they are hardly short lists. Hay-McBer has 21 general competencies that are tailored, along with some job-specific competencies; DDI has 70; Lominger, 67; PDI, 36; and SHL, 32. Which ones get applied vary by all the conditions described above."

- Research from the Center for Creative Leadership has shown that different job situations like start-ups, turnarounds, and scope jobs require a different set of competencies (McCall et al., 1988).

- A Lominger Norm Report (2003) has shown consistent differences by level and small samples of eight functions.

So what difference do these findings make?

- Don't assume a 10 or less list of core competencies is going to predict much about individual job performance across different kinds of jobs, levels, and functions. It sounds and feels nice to have a magic list, but it is just not sound practice.

- It takes many competencies to describe the complexities of performance.

- Those responsible for building managerial talent need to be thoughtful and rigorous in designing competency models that fit the unique situation of the organization and the individuals in it. Using a larger menu of choices, leaders can pick those competencies that work best for any particular individual or job. These tailored competency models then direct managerial attention and skills.

Some Key Sources

Lombardo, M., & Eichinger, R. (2004). *The leadership machine.* Minneapolis: Lominger Limited, Inc.

Lombardo, M., & Eichinger, R. (2003). *The LEADERSHIP ARCHITECT® norms and validity report.* Minneapolis: Lominger Limited, Inc.

McCall, M.W., Lombardo, M., & Morrison, A. (1988). *The lessons of experience: How successful executives develop on the job.* Lexington, MA: Lexington Books.

Spencer, L., & Spencer, S. (1993). *Competence at work.* New York: John Wiley & Sons, Inc.

CHANGE MANAGEMENT

37.

How successful have organizations been at achieving the expected or projected results through major change efforts, such as reengineering, TQM, value-based management, or Six Sigma?

SELECT ONE:

☐ A. 10% of the time or less.

☐ B. 20% to 33% of the time.

☐ C. 35% to 40% of the time.

☐ D. Half of the time (50%).

☐ E. More than 60% of the time.

37

37. **How successful have organizations been at achieving the expected or projected results through major change efforts, such as reengineering, TQM, value-based management, or Six Sigma?**

   The correct answer is B: 20% to 33% of the time.

How sure are we at this time?

1	2	3	4	**5**
Hint	Suggestive	Trending	Substantial	**Solid**

Discussion

Organizations have been spending millions of dollars to improve or change their processes to become more agile in responding to changes brought on by growing global competition. However, in spite of the enormous amount of money and effort expended, difficulties persist. About 75 percent of change efforts directed at processes like TQM, Six Sigma, or Process Reengineering fail to achieve the results that management hoped for.

Many change efforts fail because integrating new skills taught in seminars or workshops back into the workplace is not planned or supported. Executives and managers continue to complain that ineffective internal processes are hindering their organizations' ability to respond to the changing demands of the internal and external environment. An overwhelming sense of urgency often leads these organizations to begin efforts to change processes without a rigorous understanding of the efficacy of the methods being employed.

To make change really happen requires a number of support mechanisms. The change must be supported from the top down by communications, policies, and managerial attention. The change must be translated to employee behavior from the bottom up by engaging employees in what it means for their day-to-day behavior. The change must be sustained by changing processes, such as staffing, training, decision making, compensation, and resource allocation. Unless all these support mechanisms exist, desired changes fall short.

Selected Research

- A review of independent research by Arthur D. Little, Ernst & Young, Rath & Strong, McKinsey & Co., and A.T. Kearney concludes that only "about one-fifth—at best one-third— of TQM programs in the United States and Europe have achieved 'significant' or even 'tangible' improvements in quality, productivity, competitiveness, or financial returns." These same studies reveal that quality improvements using fully empowered, self-contained cross-functional teams show 200 percent to 600 percent improvement over their traditional functional pass-off counterparts (Harari, 1993).

- Pioneers of the business process reengineering concept, Hammer and Champy (1993) emphasize that "business process reengineering (BPR) is not an easy ride." Their studies show that 50 to 70 percent of all reengineering projects fail. The authors cite several reasons for this high rate of failure, including underemphasis on processes, lack of executive leadership, and premature implementation of the redesign.

- An Arthur D. Little study reports that two-thirds of the 500 quality initiatives launched by American firms "yielded no significant quality improvement." An A.T. Kearney review of TQM (Total Quality Management) initiatives at over 100 British companies showed much the same. And, Michael Hammer, guru of the "reengineering" craze, openly admits that 75 percent of such efforts fail (Rothschild, 1993).

- A study conducted by the National Center on the Educational Quality of the Workforce covering over 3,300 companies concluded that only 37 percent reported that they had adopted a formal Total Quality Management program (Pfeffer, 1998).

- In a survey presented in a White Paper for SHRM, 82 percent said their companies have implemented TQM / Continuous Improvement / Self-Managed Teams. When asked how well changes are working within their organizations, 46 percent were uncertain as to how well the changes are working, 44 percent report implemented changes are working at a good level, and a final 10 percent said the resulting changes were poor (Swist, 1997).

So what difference do these findings make?

- Major change is tough to do. There are ample best practices available to increase the chances of success. Most people know about them. Most do not follow them.

- A challenge of change is closing the "knowing/doing" gap, or turning what is known about change into practice. For example, we know that for successful organization change to occur, there must be:

  - Leadership support.

  - A clear need for the change.

  - A vision of the outcome for the change.

  - Mobilization of commitment to the change.

  - Translation of the change into managerial decisions.

  - Support of the change by HR, IT, and financial disciplines.

  - Early successes and continuous learning.

None of these ideas are new, but they are not done. It is imperative for managers to be rigorous and disciplined in doing what we know for change to occur.

Some Key Sources

Hammer, M., & Champy, J. (1993). *Reengineering the corporation.* New York: Harper Collins.

Harari, O. (1993, January). Ten reasons why TQM doesn't work. *Management Review.*

Pfeffer, J. (1998). *The human equation. Building profits by putting people first.* Boston: Harvard Business School Press.

Rothschild, M. (1993, October). Want to grow? Watch your language. *Forbes ASAP.*

Swist, J. (1997). Addressing the challenges of executing change. Published as a White Paper through the Society for Human Resource Management. Copyright© 1997–1999, *Applied Resource Management.*

FEEDBACK

38.

In general, how much feedback do people think they get to improve their job performance and manage their career growth?

SELECT ONE:

☐ A. More than enough.

☐ B. About the amount they say they want.

☐ C. About the amount that they need.

☐ D. Enough; about the right amount; sufficient.

☐ E. Less than they want and need to grow and develop.

38

38. In general, how much feedback do people think they get to improve their job performance and manage their career growth?

The correct answer is E: Less than they want and need to grow and develop.

How sure are we at this time?

1	2	3	**4**	5
Hint	Suggestive	Trending	**Substantial**	Solid

Discussion

Most employees want more feedback—any feedback, positive or even negative. The opportunity to grow and develop is in the top three things employees seek from their current company or in looking outside their current company. They uniformly cite receiving feedback as necessary to that growth. To attract and retain talented employees, the company has to train and prepare leaders to provide feedback. Unfortunately, providing feedback and development to employees is ranked as dead last in terms of managerial competencies.

So, what employees want and need is what managers least want to do.

Selected Research

- A Gallup Poll (reported in Buckingham & Coffman, 1999) examined the survey responses of more than 100,000 employees in a wide variety of industries to discover common themes for reasons employees decided to stay with or leave a company. The second most common reason for staying was "my supervisor cares about me and gives me regular feedback." (First was "I feel my job is important to the company.")

- A Horizons Human Resources newsletter (2001) reported on a retention survey that examined the results of 11,734 surveys that measured 99 work satisfaction questions for a statewide Department of Administration's Internet Coordination and Development Committee (ICDC). They found that 75 percent of employees stayed with their company because they were "satisfied with performance evaluation and feedback in their jobs."

- Results of McKinsey's War for Talent (2000) survey of 6,900 officers, executives, and mid-level managers at 56 cooperating companies demonstrate that the best efforts for building and retaining top talent include "giving people stretch jobs, informal feedback, coaching, and mentoring."

- In his research, Lawler (1994) found that employees wanted all types of and greater amounts of feedback, "not only compliments but also useful feedback about all aspects of their job performance—both supportive and constructive."

- In 1997, 71 percent of the respondents said that candid feedback on their performance was essential or very important to their development, but only 32 percent said that their companies provided such feedback. In 2000 an even greater proportion of the respondents—89 percent—said that candid feedback is important, but just 39 percent said they had received it (McKinsey's War for Talent 2000 in Axelrod et al., 2001).

- Van de Walle et al. (2000) reviewed research over the past 20-plus years on the amount of feedback individuals sought, the context for seeking feedback, and the types of people from whom they sought feedback. Some conclusions: The perceived value of the feedback was the most important determinant of feedback seeking. People sought feedback most from those whose opinion they respected most. Individuals with a learning goal orientation rather than a performance orientation—those seeking to develop by learning new skills—sought more positive or negative feedback. Those with a performance orientation rarely sought negative feedback. Individuals in an assigned goal condition were more likely than participants without an assigned goal to seek feedback about their performance. Individuals are more likely to seek feedback in a private context than in a public context. Individuals are more likely to seek feedback from a supervisor whose job relationships are characterized by mutual trust, respect for the subordinate's ideas, and consideration of their feelings.

- Research by Hillman et al. (1990) argues that providing ongoing performance feedback and coaching staff members as a formative or ongoing evaluation process is essential to good supervision.

- A key finding from Brooks et al.'s (2002) research on teaching strategies and performance-related feedback was the amount of feedback teachers provided students, specifically saying that "in essentially all cases, where one teaching strategy surpasses another in effectiveness, it also is characterized by having more performance-related feedback." They found that the "best instruction provides learners with much more feedback than does conventional instruction."

- Moerk (2000, pp. 6–7) found strong supporting evidence for what he called the "connectionist model" that uses more frequent and immediate performance-related feedback.

- Three research studies found significant learnings when they used a model consisting of exposure to examples followed immediately by feedback. Kellman (1994) noted dramatic improvements in learning to perceive and classify patterns in a study to measure training times for reading airplane cockpit dial displays. Chapman (1996), using the strategy, reported gains in detecting molecular geometries and Wise (2000) reported similar findings in measuring the results of teaching introductory organic chemistry.

- Although it may seem mildly counterintuitive, high potentials, and especially executives, get less feedback. They are more likely to be told how wonderfully they are doing; specific feedback or even formal performance appraisals can be rare (Kaplan et al., 1991).

So what difference do these findings make?

- People need, want, and many act on accurate, timely, important, actionable, and critical feedback, especially from people whose opinion they respect. We need to keep pushing bosses to deliver more of what they privately think and know but hesitate passing on.

- Leaders need to realize that giving feedback is: (1) a major part of their job, (2) done all the time whether the leader acknowledges it or not (the strongest feedback to a poor performer is no feedback which tells the poor performer that poor performance is OK); and (3) a skill set that can be learned.

- Effective feedback should be:

Immediate

Is offered as soon as behavior warrants it, not delayed to some future date (such as an end-of-year appraisal).

Consistent

Focuses on patterns of behavior, not any one individual behavior; offers one or two areas for improvement, not a long list.

Self-Monitored

Is defined and monitored directly by the recipient, not by someone else.

Honest

Is blunt, candid, and straight, and includes specific examples.

Behavioral

Focuses on future behaviors, not the person.

Followed Up

Encourages follow-up to ensure that changes occur.

Some Key Sources

Axelrod, E.L., Handfield-Jones, H., & Welsh, T.A. (2001). The war for talent: Part two. *The McKinsey Quarterly*, Number 2.

Brooks, D.W., Schraw, G.P., & Crippen, K.J. (2002). *Performance-related feedback: The hallmark of efficient instruction.* Unpublished manuscript, University of Nebraska, Lincoln, NE.

Buckingham, M., & Coffman, C. (1999). *First, break all the rules: What the world's greatest managers do differently.* New York: Simon & Schuster.

Chapman, O.L., Russell, A.A., & Wegner, P. (1996). The molecular science curriculum on the net. *Abstracts, 14th Biennial Conference on Chemical Education, 218.*

Hillman, L.W., Schwandt, D.R., & Bartz, D.E. (1990). Enhancing staff members' performance through feedback and coaching. *Journal of Management Development, 9* (3), 20–27.

Horizons Human Resources Newsletter, Issue #1. (2001, September 7).

Kaplan, R.E., Drath, W.H., & Kofodimos, J.R. (1991). *Beyond ambition.* San Francisco: Jossey-Bass.

Kellman, P.J., & Kaiser, M.K. (1994). Perceptual learning modules in flight training. *Proceedings of the 38th Annual Meeting of the Human Factors and Ergonomics Society,* 1183–1187.

Lawler, E.E. (1994). *Motivation in work organizations.* San Francisco: Jossey-Bass.

McKinsey & Company. (2000). *The war for talent 2000: Building a superior talent pool to drive company performance.* New York: McKinsey & Company.

Moerk, E.L. (2000). *The guided acquisition of first language skills.* Stamford, CT: Ablex Publishing Corp.

Van de Walle, D., Ganesan, S., Challagalla, G.N., & Brown, S.P. (2000). An integrated model of feedback-seeking behavior disposition, context, and cognition. *Journal of Applied Psychology, 85* (6), 996–1003.

Wise, J.A., Kubose, T., Chang, N., Russell, A., & Kellman, P.J. (2000, March). Perceptual learning modules in mathematics and science instruction. *Proceedings of TechED 2000,* 169–176.

SELECTION

39.

What seems to be the most accurate selection assessment method?

SELECT ONE:

☐ A. Across time the old reliable, grades in school (secondary plus college with more emphasis on their major) still do the best for selecting new hires who go on to be successful.

☐ B. Across time the old reliable, multiple interviews by people who know the jobs and the organization still do the best for selecting new hires who go on to be successful.

☐ C. Structured interviews, biodata, measures of cognitive ability, learning agility, and personality measures are the best selection methods.

☐ D. Personality and cognitive ability test batteries combined are the best selection method.

☐ E. Deep reference checks with people who really know the candidate turn out to have the most predictive value.

39

39. What seems to be the most accurate selection assessment method?

The correct answer is C: Structured interviews, biodata, measures of cognitive ability, learning agility, and personality measures are the best selection methods.

How sure are we at this time?

1	2	3	**4**	5
Hint	Suggestive	Trending	**Substantial**	Solid

Discussion

Because there is such a significant long-term economic value tied to it, the most important aspect of any selection assessment method is its ability to consistently predict long-term employee success.

Research shows that different assessment methods and combinations of methods vary significantly in the accuracy of predicting job performance. If you look at general buckets of methods, work samples, assessment centers, and biodata, structured interviews and measures of learning agility come out on top.

Others, such as GMA (also called general mental ability and general intelligence) tests and work sample measures, have high validity for predicting success as an individual contributor, less for managers.

Personality tests also have some validity as measures of leadership effectiveness but are considered intrusive by many job candidates who prefer strictly job-relevant measures.

Some, such as grades, outside interests, amount of education, informal interviews, and reference checks generally have very low validity.

Other methods, such as graphology (handwriting analysis), have no documented validity.

Over the years, structured interviews—those with a specific set of competencies and an interview template (specific questions and look for's) that get at those competencies—have probably done the best in predicting future success, assuming the competencies that were selected were right and the interviewers were trained. The second strongest measure is tests of general mental ability. Other useful methods are biodata, a fancy word for looking at background and past experience to predict future performance, and assessment centers. Informal or casual interviews, a method used by a majority of interviewers, do not predict much. Grades predict IQ and conscientiousness, which in turn predict some of future performance. Personality assessment is helpful in predicting future success as well, often in highly specific jobs and sometimes later in one's career.

To these we also make a case for measures of learning from experience. Research explicitly on measuring and developing learning from experience can be found in Wagner and Sternberg (1990), Sternberg et al. (1995), Spreitzer et al. (1997), Goleman (1998, 2000), and Lombardo and Eichinger (2000). These studies respectively look at measuring learning and its independence from intelligence (Sternberg), its use in identifying international executive potential, the measurement and development of emotional intelligence, and the measurement and application of learning in U.S. and Canadian organizations as a prime indicator of potential. Unrelated to intelligence see Sternberg et al. (1995) and Connolly and Viswesvaran (2002). Learning new behavior appears to make as much difference as IQ in success in a number of areas, including management. We do not include it as a prime predictor of success as yet because it has only been compared directly with other selection methods, usually IQ or personality measures, in a few studies. In the few cases where it has been compared, learning has come out on top.

Selected Research

- A report (Marshall, 2003) by the Merit Systems Protection Board states that their studies found that "structured interviews are twice as effective as unstructured interviews in predicting on-the-job performance."

- A study by Watson Wyatt Worldwide (1999) suggests that identifying and selecting highly qualified candidates is good business. They surveyed interviewing techniques of over 400 private-sector companies and found that "companies that hired workers well-equipped to perform their duties created more value for their shareholders than less-demanding companies."

- Schmidt and Hunter (1998) examined 85 years of research findings and concluded that "the average validity of the structured interview is 0.51 versus 0.38 for the unstructured interview."

- Dessler (1991) points out that the major disadvantage of unstructured interviews is that the same questions won't be asked of each of the candidates interviewed, and decisions will ultimately be based on different sets of criteria.

- Stone (1998, p. 626) found that "the most valid interviews use a consistent structure..." and, because the interaction between the candidate and the interviewer differs from one interview to the next, the results lack consistency and reliability.

- A University of Michigan study (Hunter & Hunter, 1984) analyzed interview processes and found that typical (unstructured) interviews increase your chances of choosing the best candidate by less than 2 percent. (They note that flipping a coin to decide is only 2 percent less reliable.)

- Schmidt and Rader (1999) used a meta-analysis of an extensive predictive validity database to review the validity of structured interviews, examining the process to see if the same concepts applied to structured telephone interviews. They found that, although the medium used to do the interview was different, the results were the same. "We hypothesize that this result obtains because different types of structured interviews all measure, to varying degrees, constructs with known generalizable validity (e.g., conscientiousness and general mental ability)."

- Research by Cortina et al. (2000) examined the incremental validity of predicting performance using three levels of structured interviews in best-, actual, and worst-case scenarios. They found that interview scores contribute to the prediction of job performance more than cognitive ability and conscientiousness (one of the personality traits they examined), with scores from highly structured interviews "contributing substantially to prediction."

- A meta-analysis by Wiesner and Cronshaw (1988) found that "structured interviews produced mean validity coefficients over *three times as high* as unstructured or informal interviews." Validity measures the degree to which an interviewer's ratings match actual on-the-job performance later. They looked at a total of 150 validities with a sample size of 51,459. Unstructured individual interviews had a mean validity of .20. In contrast, structured individual interviews had a mean validity of .63.

- Research by Dipboye (1994) claims that structured interviews are "valid predictors of future performance."

- Although larger organizations sometimes use psychological tests for candidates for middle-level positions, according to research by Van Clieaf (1991), the tests rarely "surpass the r = .53 level of validity in predicting job performance for lower- to middle-level positions."

- Meta-analytic findings of 85 years of research in personnel psychology showed that, in the 19 selection procedures reviewed, the top three combinations for predicting job performance as an individual contributor were: general mental ability (GMA) plus a work sample test; GMA plus an integrity test; and GMA plus a structured interview (Schmidt & Hunter, 1998).

- Schmidt and Hunter (1998) found "structured interviews" to be the same as general mental ability tests and only slightly under "work sample tests" as selection methods that were accurate in predicting overall job performance (.51 versus .54 for work sample tests). Flip of a coin was 0.00; job experience in years was .18; unstructured interviews was .38; integrity tests were .41; and general mental ability tests and structured interviews were .51.

- According to Sternberg et al. (1995), measuring practical intelligence (the ability to learn from experience) added 32 percent to the variance explained by IQ alone and "was the single best predictor of managerial performance." Research by Lombardo and Eichinger (2000) revealed similar results. For jobs requiring the learning of new behavior, learning from experience is highly related to performance. Connolly and Viswesvaran (2002) found that "a learning measure was much more highly related to performance than IQ or personality measures."

- According to research by Roth et al. (1996), grades have a "fully corrected validity in the mid .30s for predicting job performance." The nature of the jobs was not specified.

- In their study of five different ways to evaluate managerial candidates (Robertson & Makin, 1986), the researchers noted the reason for the infrequent use of proven personnel selection tools are the inherent disadvantages of the tools themselves—the inherent practical considerations in the use of each method, like ease of implementation, ease and cost of operation, and the amount of time to train interviewers.

- A survey by Robertson and Makin (1986) of 108 organizations showed that informal interviews and references (two of the least powerful predictors) were always used by 81 percent and 67 percent of the respondents, respectively. In contrast, three of the strongest predictors (assessment centers, cognitive tests, and biodata) were never used by over 70 percent of the firms surveyed.

- In their survey of interviewing techniques of industrial psychologists, Ryan and Sackett (1987) found that even the experts ignore proven selection techniques; only 18 percent always and 26 percent often validated the assessment process used. Additionally, only 40 percent said they conduct some kind of formal job analysis before interviewing candidates.

- A meta-analysis (Judge et .al, 2002) found a multiple correlation of .39 between Big Five personality measures and leadership effectiveness. The findings were stronger in student settings than in business, government, or military environments.

So what difference do these findings make?
- While all legitimate assessment methods add some predictive validity, structured and situational interviews are perhaps the top-rated best practices, especially when one of the measures is learning agility. Other methods help predict success more for entry jobs and individual

contributors (like grades, cognitive ability tests, and work samples) than for later jobs in management.

- Leaders should take the time to prepare a structured interview process for key jobs. The time spent up front in designing this process more than pays for itself later on.

Some Key Sources

Connolly, J.A., & Viswesvaran, C. (2002, April). *Assessing the construct validity of a measure of learning agility.* A presentation at the Seventeenth Annual Conference of the Society for Industrial and Organizational Psychology, Toronto, Canada.

Cortina, J.M., Goldstein, N.B., Payne, S.C., Davison, H.K., & Gilliland, S.W. (2000, Summer). The incremental validity of interview scores over and above cognitive ability and conscientiousness scores. *Personnel Psychology, 53* (2), 325–352.

Dessler, G. (1991). *Personnel/human resource management* (5th ed.). Englewood Cliffs, NJ: Prentice Hall.

Dipboye, R.L. (1994). Structured and unstructured selection interviews: Beyond the job-fit model. In G.R. Ferris & K.M. Rowland (Eds.), *Research in personnel and human resources management* (Vol. 4, pp. 79–123). Greenwich, CT: JAI Press.

Goleman, D. (1998). *Working with emotional intelligence.* New York: Bantam Books.

Goleman, D. (2000, March/April). Leadership that gets results. *Harvard Business Review*, 78–90.

Hunter, J.E., & Hunter, R.F. (1984). Validity and utility of alternative predictors of job performance. *Psychological Bulletin, 96* (1), 72–98.

Judge, T.A., Bono, J.E., Ilies, R., & Gerhardt, M.W. (2002). Personality and leadership: A qualitative and quantitative review. *Journal of Applied Psychology, 87*, 765–780.

Lombardo, M., & Eichinger, R. (2000). High potentials as high learners. *Human Resource Management, 39* (4), 321–330.

Lombardo, M., & Eichinger, R. (2003). *CHOICES ARCHITECT® promotion study results*. Minneapolis: Lominger Limited, Inc.

Marshall, S.T. (2003, February). *The Federal Selection Interview: Unrealized potential*. Merit Systems Protection Board. Retrieved February, 2003, from http://www.mspb.gov/studies/interviewing.pdf

Robertson, I.T., & Makin, P.J. (1986). Management selection in Britain: A survey and critique. *Journal of Occupational Psychology, 59*, 45–57.

Roth, P.L., BeVier, C.A., Switzer, F.S., & Schippmann, J.S. (1996). Meta-analyzing the relationship between grades and job performance. *Journal of Applied Psychology, 81*, 548–556.

Ryan, A.M., & Sackett, P.R. (1987). A survey of individual assessment practices by I/O psychologists. *Personnel Psychology, 40,* 455–488.

Schmidt, F.L., & Hunter, J.E. (1998, September). The validity and utility of selection methods in personnel psychology: Practical and theoretical implications of 85 years of research findings. *Psychological Bulletin, 24* (2), 262–274.

Schmidt, F.L., & Rader, M. (1999, Summer). Exploring the boundary conditions for interview validity: Meta-analytic validity findings for a new interview type. *Personnel Psychology, 52* (2), 445–464.

Spreitzer, G.M., McCall, M.W., & Mahoney, J.D. (1997). Early identification of international executive potential. *Journal of Applied Psychology, 82* (1), 6–29.

Sternberg, R.J., Wagner, R.K., Williams, W.M., & Horvath, J.A. (1995). Testing common sense. *American Psychologist, 50* (11), 912–927.

Stone, R.J. (1998). *Human resource management* (3rd ed.). Brisbane, Australia: Jacaranda Wiley.

Van Clieaf, M.S. (1991). In search of competence: Structured behavior interviews. *Business Horizons, 34* (2), 51–55.

Wagner, R.K., & Sternberg, R.J. (1990). Street smarts. In K.E. Clark & M.B. Clark (Eds.), *Measures of leadership* (pp. 493–504). West Orange, NJ: Leadership Library of America.

Watson Wyatt Worldwide. (1999). *Human Capital Index™— Linking human capital practices and shareholder value* (p. 5).

Wiesner, W.H., & Cronshaw, S.F. (1988). A meta-analytic investigation of the impact of interview format and degree of structure on the validity of the employment interview. *Journal of Occupational Psychology, 61* (4), 275–290.

40.

How much are these HR interventions worth, in terms of the return on investment, from best (most) to least?

SELECT ONE:

☐ A. Selection, training and development, and performance management.

☐ B. Performance management, selection, and training and development.

☐ C. Training and development, selection, and performance management.

☐ D. Performance management, training and development, and selection.

☐ E. Selection, performance management, and training and development.

40

40.   How much are these HR interventions worth, in terms of the return on investment, from best (most) to least?

The correct answer is D: Performance management, training and development, and selection.

How sure are we at this time?

1	2	**3**	4	5
Hint	Suggestive	**Trending**	Substantial	Solid

Discussion

Over the last 10 years, researchers have begun to try to determine the return on investment of various HR initiatives or interventions. Specifically, they have tried to compare using better selection methods, better training and development, and better performance management applications. These are extremely difficult things to compare and these studies are just now beginning to become part of the literature. All of these initiatives or interventions start with a rigorous study of the mission critical skills and competencies that make a statistically significant difference between high and low performers. Then those mission critical competencies are applied to selection (hiring people who already have the mission critical competencies), training and development (helping those current employees who do not have the mission critical competencies build them), or performance management (rewarding those who have them and deselecting those who don't).

Lyle Spencer has been a leader in this field of research. By reviewing the studies of the past along with his own research, he has determined that, at this time, the order from most to least is: Best = rigorous performance management, then training and development against the mission critical competencies, and then Least (but still positive) = selection against the mission critical competencies.

Those following this line of research have been surprised that selection was not higher or even first. Some have speculated that the reason for this is probably two-thirds of interviewers who are evaluating these outside candidates are not good at interviewing and judging others.

So the fastest way to improve the performance of any unit is to set rigorous performance standards and get rid of those who do not measure up—those who do not have the mission critical competencies. Next is to assess, give feedback to and train and develop current employees very specifically and very focused on the mission critical competencies. Last, but still useful, is using the mission critical competencies to guide selection decisions.

Performance management is three times more powerful than better selection interviewing and decision making, and training and developing current employees is two times more powerful than just hiring better employees in the first place.

This is an emerging field of research and is apt to change as more studies are reported.

Selected Research
- Becker and Huselid (1998) make a strong case for the emerging role of "human capital as a potential source of competitive sustainable advantage." Their argument centers around building a strategic advantage by using the HR applications that show the greatest promise in developing a high-performance workforce.

- Results of a four-year study by Morrow et al. (1997), designed to examine the bottom-line impact of different types of training programs—including managerial training and sales and technical training—varied significantly with the type of training. Managerial training had a mean ROI of 45 percent and sales/technical training had a mean ROI of 418 percent.

- In their research, Burke and Day (1986) found behavioral modeling training applications (often used to teach interpersonal skills to managers and supervisors) to be the most successful training method, especially when compared to others like peer training, self-study, and computer-assisted instruction (CAI).

- Spencer's (2001) long-term research on competencies argues that training and performance management is the highest EVA (economic value added) HR program. Spencer notes the gain from performance management (.67 of one standard deviation or effect size), training (.44), and selection (.22). Using one standard deviation above the mean to define superior performance, Spencer notes that a "superior worker is 148 percent more productive than the average worker." (He uses the example that a superior worker with a $100,000 salary has a productivity salary value of $148,000, and a poor performer—one standard deviation below the mean—has a salary value of only $52,000.)

So what difference do these findings make?

- All research-based and best practice HR initiatives and interventions probably have some return on investment. In particular, when one looks at the cost/benefit ratio and sees the benefits of HR interventions over time (year one, year two, and year three), the ROI of HR interventions is high. But at this time, it looks like the fastest way to improve the performance of a team, unit, or entire business is to separate those who aren't performing and replace them with people who have a higher chance of performing, while training those that remain in the mission critical skills.

This will require rigorous and tough-minded evaluation of performance and knowing what mission critical competencies make the difference.

- Putting performance standards in place requires that the strategy is clear and that the behaviors and outcomes of individuals and teams are clear and linked to the strategy. The process of setting individual and team standards is almost as important as the standards themselves. When employees participate in defining their expectations, they are more likely to live up to them.

- Training and development can be very profitable. Assessment of current employees on the mission critical competencies coupled with focused training and development has a healthy payback. There are four levels of the impact of training: (1) happiness with the program (smile sheets at the end of the training), (2) knowledge (increased understanding), (3) skill or behavioral change, and (4) economic impact. Most training evaluations are level 1 or 2, but we lean to level 3 and 4. When training can be measured in economic terms, it is easier to justify and more likely to be sustained.

- Learn how to measure ROI in your own organization. There is an emerging technology on how to measure the return on investment of various HR programs. Since we know that well-designed and statistically based initiatives pay for themselves, this could lead to better HR systems and practices that really impact the bottom line. For example, examine the performance of those who attended a training event and those who did not for the life cycle of the training (one to three years). Create a "difference in performance" index that captures the impact of the training. Using this number, you can begin to calculate an economic benefit of the training experience.

Some Key Sources

Becker, B., & Huselid, M. (1998). High performance work systems and firm performance: A synthesis of research and managerial implications. *Personnel and Human Resources Management, 16,* 53–101.

Burke, M.J., & Day, R.R. (1986). A cumulative study of the effectiveness of managerial training. *Journal of Applied Psychology, 71* (2), 232–245.

Morrow, C., Jarrett, M., & Rupinski, M. (1997). An investigation of the effect and economic utility of corporate-wide training. *Personnel Psychology, 50* (1), 91–120.

Spencer, L. (2001). The economic value of emotional intelligence competencies and EIC-based HR programs. In D. Goleman & C. Cherniss (Eds.), *The emotionally intelligent workplace: How to select for, measure, and improve emotional intelligence in individuals, groups, and organizations.* San Francisco: Jossey-Bass.

DIVERSITY

41.

When someone has benefited from an affirmative action program (given some advantage because of membership in a protected class) in their career, people . . .?

SELECT ONE:

☐ A. Hold it against them and evaluate them lower than might be justified.

☐ B. Tend to be happy that they were able to break out and succeed.

☐ C. Have no specific reaction.

☐ D. Try to continue to give them further advantages to assure success.

☐ E. Give them the benefit of the doubt and treat them more kindly.

41. **When someone has benefited from an affirmative action program (given some advantage because of membership in a protected class) in their career, people...?**

    The correct answer is A: Hold it against them and evaluate them lower than might be justified.

How sure are we at this time?

1	2	**3**	4	5
Hint	Suggestive	**Trending**	Substantial	Solid

Discussion

When members of the majority know that a member of a minority group (e.g., female or person of color) has been given a preference of some kind in the past, they are suspicious of the qualifications and skills of the person. They believe that the advantage was unfair and that they are not qualified on their own to make it. This negative reaction is especially true if the observer views the program as one of preferential treatment (like a quota system).

Selected Research

- Research by Heilman and Blader (2001) revealed that people tend to discount a person's abilities and merit if that person benefited from an affirmative action program.

- Maio and Esses (1998) found similar results. Even mentioning that a minority group may have benefited from an affirmative action or employment equity program led participants to derogate members of the minority group.

- This phenomenon occurred in the Judge Clarence Thomas hearings for a seat on the Supreme Court. Judge Thomas got into law school in a preference system. The press at the time, as one of the arguments against his candidacy, argued that that called his qualifications into question. In *Reflections of an Affirmative Action Baby* (1991), Stephen Carter, a Yale law professor, reviews research that points to the ironies of the career of Clarence Thomas, citing that Thomas' confirmation as a Supreme Court Justice was taken by many as an example of affirmative action being "used and then abused and abandoned." Discussing Clarence Thomas' confirmation as part of affirmative action, Deborah Stone (1996) writes "the real comeuppance for liberals is that they will have to stop relying on crude symbols of race and gender, and instead develop policy positions that speak to women and Blacks in all their diversity about issues of well-being, work, and family. This means going beyond the civil rights agenda of the '60s, and even the social equality agenda of the '70s and '80s...."

- Research by Bowen and Bok (1998) adds credence to the argument that providing preferences to all members of certain minority groups is not necessarily an indicator of disadvantage. In their study, the authors found that 86 percent of Black students at the selective colleges studied were from middle or high socioeconomic backgrounds. So if people think that all people who are advantaged by a protective group preference is in some way disadvantaged, this research argues against that.

- A *Wall Street Journal* article (Barrett & Stephen, 1991) surmises that the majority assumed that Clarence Thomas benefited from Holy Cross College and Yale Law School minority preference admission policies simply because the two schools had such policies. "The implicit assumption is that, if a quota system was in effect, *none of the admitted Blacks were qualified.*" While some of the Blacks may have been unqualified, it would be ridiculous to assert that none were, and, specifically, that Thomas was unqualified.

- In their research, Jencks and Phillips (1998) found that "admitting students on the basis of academic record would yield precious little diversity by race or class. Whites and Asians would constitute 96 to 97 percent of undergraduates at selective universities if a system of grades and standardized tests alone guided admissions."

- Using school ranking as a criteria for admissions is supported by research by Puma et al. (1997). In their national study, they found that "students receiving an A in high-poverty schools score about as well on the Comprehensive Test of Basic Skills as students receiving a C in low-poverty schools."

So what difference do these findings make?

- No good deed goes unpunished, as the saying goes. So trying to help give someone an extra chance at an opportunity to succeed can actually lead to another burden. Those from minority groups who are fully qualified may not be as credible because of affirmative action policies.

- In the organization, people advantaged by special diversity programming may have the extra burden of proving their qualifications above and beyond the normal.

- Leaders should give all employees equal opportunity to compete for key jobs.

Some Key Sources

Barrett, P.M., & Stephen, W. (1991, July 19). Judge Thomas, billed as conservative, may prove unpredictable. *The Wall Street Journal*, p. A1.

Bowen, W., & Bok, D. (1998). *The shape of the river: Long-term consequences of considering race in college and university admissions* (p. 341). Princeton, NJ: Princeton University Press.

Carter, S. (1991). *Reflections of an affirmative action baby.* New York: Perseus Book Group.

Heilman, M.E., & Blader, S.L. (2001). Assuming preferential selection when the admissions policy is unknown: The effects of gender rarity. *Journal of Applied Psychology, 86,* 188–193.

Jencks, C., & Phillips, M. (Eds.). (1998). *The Black-White test score gap* (pp. 7–8). Washington, DC: Brookings Institution Press. http://www.policyideas.org/Issues/Education/Affirmative_Action.pdf

Maio, G.R., & Esses, V.M. (1998). The social consequences of affirmative action: Deleterious effects on perceptions of groups. *Personality and Social Psychology Bulletin, 24,* 65–74.

Puma, M.J., Karweit, N., Price, C., Ricciuti, A., Thompson, W., & Vaden-Kiernan, M. (1997). *Prospects: Final report on student outcomes* (p. 12). Cambridge, MA: Abt Associates.

Stone, D.A. (1996). Race, gender and the Supreme Court. In W.F. Grover & J.G. Peschalk (Eds.), *Voices of dissent* (pp. 171–179). New York: Longman Publishing Group.

GOAL SETTING

42.

What is the impact of goal setting on individuals and teams?

SELECT ONE:

☐ A. Aggressive and stretch goals almost always lead to better results.

☐ B. Aggressive and stretch goals motivate individuals more than teams.

☐ C. Aggressive and stretch goals motivate teams more than individuals.

☐ D. Goals that people and teams can comfortably reach are more motivational than stretch goals.

☐ E. Goals that are the most effective are those that almost no one initially thinks they can meet but later find out they can.

42. What is the impact of goal setting on individuals and teams?

The correct answer is A: Aggressive and stretch goals almost always lead to better results.

How sure are we at this time?

1	2	3	**4**	5
Hint	Suggestive	Trending	**Substantial**	Solid

Discussion

Over the whole history of studying goal setting and subsequent performance, most have shown that moderately aggressive goals motivate best. Out-of-reach goals or goals that are too easy motivate less or not at all. The studies have also shown that goals work for individuals, teams, and entire enterprises. The lack of clear goals has also been associated to lack of performance across many venues.

Goals provide employees a focus. A focus means that attention (time, energy, and passion) is directed toward a common agenda. As such, the goal forces new behaviors and patterns.

Selected Research

- According to research by O'Leary-Kelly et al. (1994), groups that set goals perform one standard deviation higher than groups that do not.

- Taylor et al. (1992) found that a key success factor is the complexity of the task. He notes that "when tasks are complex, easier goals will result in greater performance. A difficult task may reduce the acceptance of the goal and, likewise, weaken the performance." He also concluded that setting easier goals for complex tasks resulted in earlier goal acceptance and commitment of resources.

- Research on the relationship between group goal difficulty and group performance (Weingart, 1992) reveals that, as group goals get more difficult, the effort exerted by members increases, with a resulting increase in performance.

- Research by Kaplan and Norton (1996) concludes that while 55 percent of *Fortune 1000* companies have implemented the Balanced Scorecard, individual and group goals and objectives need to drive the achievement of scorecard objectives and measures.

- Ulrich (1997) notes that the value proposition HR needs to create begins with "clearly defining the business strategy— stating the firm's goals so employees understand their roles and the organization knows how to measure success." Ulrich argues that "the activities of HR appear to be and often are disconnected from the real work of the organization" and that the new HR agenda is one in which "every HR activity in some concrete way helps the company better serve its customers or otherwise increase shareholder value."

- Locke and Latham (1990) found that, in a team's planning process, goals provide a valuable guide for the integration of individual efforts. "Research has clearly pointed out the fact that goals are highly motivational, encouraging persistence, as well as strategy development."

- According to Earley and Shalley's (1991) work, "when an individual is presented a goal, he or she may initially opt to accept, reject, or evaluate it further, and that when a goal is accepted, it becomes a personal goal that the individual is willing to work toward." They also note these results: "Organizational norms or a sense of duty to others may be extremely persuasive in acceptance of the goal; if the goals are determined in what is perceived to be a fair manner, they are more likely to be accepted; individuals who self-set goals will not be as accepting of goals which are assigned."

- Since goals are observable and measurable, each team member can clearly see when the team is making strides toward fulfilling their larger purpose (Katzenbach & Smith, 1993). Measurable refers to determining who sets the goals; what they are; when the goals must be completed; specifically how goals will be accomplished; and where the work will take place.

So what difference do these findings make?

- Goal setting is a known technology with abundant research and best practices. Support of goal setting processes should be a high priority for all. Effective goals should be specific so they can be monitored, behavioral so they can be accomplished, important so they link with strategy, doable so they are within the control of the individual trying to achieve it, and demanding but attainable so they push for new behaviors.

- Goal setting is an effective practice for individuals, teams, and entire enterprises. Leaders who set goals begin by examining the opportunities and threats in their environment, then selecting a vision that lays out the future, and goals that indicate progress towards the vision.

Some Key Sources

Earley, C.P., & Shalley, C.E. (1991). New perspectives on goals and performance. In G.R. Ferris & K.M. Rowland (Eds.), *Research in personnel and human resources management* (pp. 121–157). Greenwich, CT: JAI Press.

Kaplan, R.S., & Norton, D.P. (1996). *The Balanced Scorecard: Translating strategy into action.* Boston: Harvard Business School Press.

Katzenbach, J.R., & Smith, D.K. (1993). *The wisdom of teams: Creating the high-performance organization.* New York: Harper Collins.

Locke, E.A., & Latham, G.P. (1990). *A theory of goal setting and task performance.* Englewood Cliffs, NJ: Prentice Hall.

O'Leary-Kelly, A.M., Martocchio, J.J., & Frink, D.D. (1994). A review of the influence of group goals on group performance. *Academy of Management Journal, 37* (5), 1285–1301.

Taylor, L.A., III, Cosier, R.A., & Ganster, D.C. (1992). The positive effects of easy goals on decision quality and risk propensity in a MCPLP task. *Decision Sciences, 23,* 880–898.

Ulrich, D. (1997). Measuring human resources: An overview of practice and a prescription for results. *Human Resource Management, 36* (3), 303.

Weingart, L.R. (1992). Impact of group goals, task component complexity, effort, and planning on group performance. *Journal of Applied Psychology, 27* (5), 682–693.

INTERVIEWING

43.

What structure is the best for outside candidate interviews?

SELECT ONE:

☐ A. It's best to structure the questions asked but leave the rest alone.

☐ B. It's best to structure all aspects of the interview content and process.

☐ C. A casual, natural style interview is the most productive and liked most by interviewees.

☐ D. The interview process should be structured, but the content should be left loose and flexible to fit each candidate.

☐ E. No real work has been done on the structure of the interview outside of the questions.

43. What structure is the best for outside candidate interviews?

The correct answer is B: It's best to structure all aspects of the interview content and process.

How sure are we at this time?

1	2	3	**4**	5
Hint	Suggestive	Trending	**Substantial**	Solid

Discussion

There are as many interview structures as there are interviews, but research comes down strongly on the side of structured interviewing techniques. A structured interview technique means that the interviewer has done research to figure out what specific competencies are required for a job, then has a series of questions that will probe the extent to which the candidate has or has not demonstrated these competencies in previous assignments. When multiple interviewers use the same structured format with the same candidate, a more robust and precise image of the candidate's skills follows.

Selected Research

- Research has indicated that interviews can have higher average validities than researchers originally believed (McDaniel, Whetzel, Schmidt, & Maurer, 1994). Their study examined the validity of selection interviews as a function of format (individual versus board), structure, content, and criterion type. In general, these studies have found that interview scores are predictive of job performance, and that structured interview scores are more strongly related to job performance than are unstructured interview scores. Specifically, these studies have shown the overall relationship between interview scores and job performance to be between .37 and .47, with the validity for structured interviews lying between .44 and .63, and the validity for unstructured interviews lying between .20 and .35. McDaniel et al. found interviews conducted by individuals to have higher validities than did those conducted by panels (.43 versus .32).

- Research by Campion et al. (1997) identified 15 components of structure that may enhance either the content of the interview or the evaluation process in the interview. The research further evaluated each component in terms of its impact on numerous forms of reliability, validity, and user reactions, and found that interviews can be easily enhanced by using selected structural components. Some of the components that add to the accuracy of the interview are: base questions on a job analysis, ask the same questions of each candidate, use a longer interview or larger number of questions (longer interviews are more structured because they obtain a larger amount of information), rate each answer or use multiple scales, use the same interviewer(s) across all candidates, and provide extensive interviewer training.

- According to research by Raffonni (1999), case interviewing is the most useful of interviewing techniques. Used by strategy consulting firms for years, case interviewing depicts real-life scenarios that the candidate might encounter on the job. It helps the candidate to better understand the job and tests a variety of skills, such as problem solving abilities. Even with the best recruiting system available, you won't get the right person in the right job if your interviewing methods are lacking. That means getting past the typical canned conversation topics and drilling down for information about how candidates conducted themselves in specific situations—situations that are likely to arise in your organization.

- Research in the last 15 years has shown that cognitive ability, conscientiousness, and interviews all contribute to prediction of job performance for a variety of jobs (Ganzach et al., 2000). One way of making decisions on the basis of qualitative impressions is to identify a number of relevant dimensions, translate the impressions into quantitative ratings on each of the dimensions, and integrate the ratings using a mechanical combination scheme. The paper compares the output of this method to global (clinical) judgment. The basis for the comparison is a large database that includes both information collected in a structured interview and a relevant criterion. The results clearly suggest that mechanical combination outperforms clinical judgment but also that the combination of both schemes produces the highest accuracy. It also means that preparing ahead of time exactly what you are going to ask and how you are going to evaluate it is the best process.

- Results from a study by Cortina et al. (2000) suggested that interview scores contribute to the prediction of job performance to the extent that they are structured, with scores from highly structured interviews contributing substantially to the prediction of success.

- Campion and his colleagues (Campion, Pursell, & Brown, 1988) found consistent relationships between scores on structured interviews and scores on cognitive ability tests. Later research by Campion et al. (1994) found that structured interviews had incremental validity above and beyond a battery of cognitive ability tests when predicting supervisory ratings of job performance.

- A study by Schmidt and Rader (1999) uses meta-analysis of an extensive predictive validity database to explore the boundary conditions for the validity of the structured interview. Although the interview examined differed from traditional structured interviews in being empirically constructed, administered by telephone, and scored later based on a taped transcript, this nontraditional employment interview was found to have essentially the same level of criterion-related validity for supervisory ratings of job performance as other structured employment interviews. These findings suggest that a variety of different approaches to the construction, administration, and scoring of structured employment interviews may lead to comparable levels of validity. The researchers hypothesize that different types of structured interviews all measure to varying degrees constructs with known generalizable validity (e.g., conscientiousness and general mental ability). (The interview examined here was also found to be a valid predictor of production records, sales volume, absenteeism, and job tenure.)

- The hiring process has begun to increasingly rely on competency assessment as a decision making tool. According to research by Meade (1998), competency assessment lets organizations develop competencies by position and generate interview guidelines that are more likely than traditional models to help the staff hire the best person for the position and the organization. In addition to saving money, there is a serious contention that competency-based hiring is legally more defensible than more traditional methods.

- The legal strength of competency-based hiring is partially based in the scrapping of unnecessary restrictions that are not related to the competence to perform the job—this greatly benefits both women and ethnic minorities (Schofield 1993).

- A longitudinal field study was designed to examine the relationships between job information sources, self-esteem, and perceptions of person-job (P-J) and person-organization (P-O) fit, as well as the relationships between perceptions of fit and work outcomes (job satisfaction, organizational commitment, organizational identification, intentions to quit, stress symptoms, and turnover). The results indicate that the number of formal job information sources and self-esteem were positively related to perceptions of P-J fit, and formal job information sources were positively related to perceptions of P-O fit. Perceptions of P-J fit were positively related to job satisfaction, organizational commitment, and organizational identification, and were negatively related to stress symptoms and intentions to quit. Perceptions of P-O fit were negatively related to intentions to quit and turnover. In addition, perceptions of fit mediated the relationships between job information sources and self-esteem with job satisfaction, intentions to quit, and turnover. These results highlight the job applicant's perspective of fit, and demonstrate the importance of both P-J and P-O fit perceptions (Saks & Ashforth, 1997).

So what difference do these findings make?

- Unstructured, casual, seat-of-the-pants interviewing may feel good, but that's all. The more structure and job relevance the better. As they say, you would not buy a car you would not drive around and learn about, so why hire someone without full assessment. The time spent preparing for interviews and doing thorough interviews is well worth it.

- It is important to have different people interview the same candidate on similar dimensions to see if there is a consensus emerging.

- It is important to have a clear set of competencies that the job requires so that the interview focuses on the right issues.

Some Key Sources

Campion, M.A., Campion, J.E., & Hudson, J.P. (1994). Structured interviewing: A note on incremental validity and alternative question types. *Journal of Applied Psychology, 79*, 998–1002.

Campion, M.A., Palmer, D.K., & Campion, J.E. (1997, Autumn). A review of structure in the selection interview. *Personnel Psychology, 50* (3).

Campion, M.A., Pursell, E.D., & Brown, B.K. (1988). Structured interviewing: Raising the psychometric properties of the employment interview. *Personnel Psychology, 41*, 25–42.

Cortina, J.M., Goldstein, N.B., Payne, S.C., Davison, H.K., & Gilliland, S.W. (2000, Summer). The incremental validity of interview scores over and above cognitive ability and conscientiousness scores. *Personnel Psychology, 53* (2), 325.

Ganzach, Y., Kluger, A.N., & Klayman, N. (2000, Spring). Making decisions from an interview: Expert measurement and mechanical combination. *Personnel Psychology, 53* (1), 1.

McDaniel, M.A., Whetzel, D.L., Schmidt, F.L., & Maurer, S.D. (1994). The validity of employment interviews: A comprehensive review and meta-analysis. *Journal of Applied Psychology, 79*, 599–616.

Meade, J. (1998). Identifying criteria for success helps in making effective hiring decisions. *HR Magazine, 43* (5), 49–50.

Raffonni, M. (1999, July 1). Use case interviewing to improve your hiring. *Harvard Management Update.* Retrieved from http://www.hbsp.harvard.edu/hbsp/prod_detail.asp?U9907E

Saks, A.M., & Ashforth, B.E. (1997, Summer). A longitudinal investigation of the relationships between job information sources, applicant perceptions of fit, and work outcomes. *Personnel Psychology, 50* (2).

Schmidt, F.L., & Rader, M. (1999, Summer). Exploring the boundary conditions for interview validity: Meta-analytic validity findings for a new interview type. *Personnel Psychology, 52* (2).

Schofield, P. (1993). Improving the candidate job-match. *Personnel Management, 25* (2), 69.

DIVERSITY

44.

What effect have affirmative action plans and programs had on producing diversity in the workplace?

SELECT ONE:

☐ A. While many remedies have been tried, very little progress has been demonstrated.

☐ B. There is some economic benefit for those firms who are more successful with their affirmative action efforts.

☐ C. While affirmative action has been effective in increasing representation of protected classes, no economic benefit has been documented.

☐ D. More diverse firms are actually at a disadvantage because managing diversity is more difficult.

☐ E. Diversity only matters if the market for the firm is diverse.

44. What effect have affirmative action plans and programs had on producing diversity in the workplace?

The correct answer is B: There is some economic benefit for those firms who are more successful with their affirmative action efforts.

How sure are we at this time?

1	**2**	3	4	5
Hint	**Suggestive**	Trending	Substantial	Solid

Discussion

While you can always argue about whether the pace is satisfactory, there is substantial evidence that the result of a whole host of affirmative action programs is steady increases in the representation of women and covered minorities. Those organizations with stronger programming (government) have shown the most progress. Additionally, there is evidence that diversity increases the quality of thinking, ideas, decisions, and, in particular, innovation. The research on diversity leading to productivity and economic bottom line is still emerging.

Selected Research

• Several researchers report results that demonstrate an increasing number of women and people of color in the marketplace. Badgett (1999) reports that people of color constitute a greater percentage of the public (i.e., governmental) workforce than of the private workforce, and they advance further in the former than in the latter (Konrad & Pfeffer, 1991).

• With three million employees, the federal government is the single largest affirmative action employer. Studies by

Rodgers and Spriggs (1996) revealed that federal contractors have hired more women and more people of color than other employers of similar size in the same sectors of the economy. Federal contractors have also granted more promotions to people of color and women than firms without affirmative action programs (Parker, Baltes, & Christiansen, 1997).

- The benefits that diversity brings to work organizations has been the subject of several research studies. Holzer & Neumark (2000) found that firms that aggressively pursue affirmative action in hiring perform as well as others economically.

- According to research by Reskin (1998), diversity brings an economic advantage to organizations because "a diverse workforce introduces varied points of view" which, in turn, increases a firm's ability to respond to challenges and problems. Reskin also notes that diversity efforts benefit firms by helping them to market products and services to previously unserved populations.

- A laboratory study by Milliken and Martins (1996) showed that diversity allows for a variety of perspectives to be presented which, in turn, enhances the potential for creative problem solving.

- A study by the Federal Glass Ceiling Commission (Crosby & Herzberger, 1996) documents the dramatic results a Miami, Florida car dealership realized when it hired bilingual sales staff and held special events targeting a Hispanic clientele. Sales increased by 400 percent over a six-year period and the dealership retained 50 percent of the Hispanic market.

- When researchers Williams and O'Reilly (1998) reviewed literature on diversity in groups, they found that diverse workplaces needed to be managed carefully to gain all the possible benefits diversity programs have to offer. They cited prejudice, discrimination, and in-group bias as examples that can harm productivity, performance, and working relationships.

- Richard (2000) suggests that the benefits of diversity are closely aligned with the goals the organization is pursuing.

So what difference do these findings make?

- Aside from the moral aspects of affirmative action, well-thought-through and executed programs can enrich the culture of the organization. In particular, if a company is striving toward innovation and new ideas or ways of thinking, then diversity programs bring into the company alternative perspectives.

- Diversity programs also have some economic benefit because when the employees have the same demographics as targeted customers, revenue per customer is likely to go up. The longer-term economic impact of diversity on productivity and performance has not yet been fully demonstrated.

Some Key Sources

Badgett, M.V.L. (1999). The impact of affirmative action on public sector employment in California, 1970–1990. In P. Ong (Ed.), *Impacts of affirmative action: Policies and consequences in California* (pp. 83–102). Walnut Creek: AltaMira Press.

Crosby, F.J., & Herzberger, S.D. (1996). For affirmative action. In R.F. Tomasson, F.J. Crosby, & S.D. Herzberger (Eds.), *Affirmative action: The pros and cons of policy and practice* (pp. 5–109). Washington, DC: American University Press.

Holzer, H., & Neumark, D. (2000). What does affirmative action do? *Industrial and Labor Relations Review, 53,* 240–271.

Konrad, A.M., & Pfeffer, J. (1991). Understanding the hiring of women and minorities in educational institutions. *Sociology of Education, 664,* 141–157.

Milliken, F.J., & Martins, L.L. (1996). Searching for common threads: Understanding the multiple effects of diversity in organizational groups. *Academy of Management Review, 21*, 402–433.

Parker, C.P., Baltes, B.B., & Christiansen, N.D. (1997). Support for affirmative action, justice perception and work attitudes: A study of gender and racial-ethnic group differences. *Journal of Applied Psychology, 82*, 376–389.

Reskin, B.F. (1998). *The realities of affirmative action in employment.* Washington, DC: American Sociological Association.

Richard, O.C. (2000). Racial diversity, business strategy, and firm performance: A resource-based view. *Academy of Management Journal, 43*, 164–177.

Rodgers, W.M., III, & Spriggs, W.E. (1996). The effect of federal contractor status on racial differences in establishment-level employment shares: 1979–1992. *American Economic Review, 86*, 290–293.

Williams, K.Y., & O'Reilly, C.A., III. (1998). Demography and diversity in organizations: A review of 40 years of research. In B.M. Staw & L.L. Cummings (Eds.), *Research in organizational behavior* (Vol. 20, pp. 77–140). Greenwich, CT: JAI Press.

45.

Do people know which competencies are most important for their jobs and jobs they are asked to rate?

SELECT ONE:

☐ A. People are more than 75% correct in identifying the most important competencies.

☐ B. People are about 60% correct.

45

☐ C. People are about half right; 50% are correct.

☐ D. People are about 40% correct.

☐ E. People get about 33% correct.

45. **Do people know which competencies are most important for their jobs and jobs they are asked to rate?**

The correct answer is B: People are about 60% correct.

How sure are we at this time?

1	2	**3**	4	5
Hint	Suggestive	**Trending**	Substantial	Solid

Discussion

People are about 60 percent accurate, but the problem is that the more subtle, long-term competencies get missed. Many of these are highly related to promotion and/or long-term performance.

Selected Research

- Lombardo and Eichinger (2003) looked at the top 22 (and ties) competencies most often related to long-term performance and looked at what individual contributors, managers, and executives said about how important they were.

Importance	Top 1/3	%	Middle 1/3	%	Bottom 1/3	%
Individual Contributors	15	**68**	5	**23**	2	**9**
Managers	16	**62**	6	**23**	4	**15**
Executives	14	**64**	3	**17**	5	**23**
Overall		**64**		**20**		**16**

- They also looked at current performance.

Importance	Top 1/3	%	Middle 1/3	%	Bottom 1/3	%
Individual Contributors	15	68	6	27	1	5
Managers	16	62	5	19	5	19
Executives	11	50	8	36	3	14
Overall		60		27		13

- What are the blind spots of raters? What do they miss? These competencies are related to long-term performance but are given a low importance rating by self and other raters (40th out of 67 or below).

Group	What do they miss?
Individual Contributors	Sizing Up People Standing Alone
Managers	Command Skills Conflict Management Standing Alone Perspective Creativity Innovation Management Political Savvy
Executives	Dealing with Ambiguity Learning on the Fly Perspective Creativity Innovation Management Political Savvy

So what difference do these findings make?

- Asking people to judge what's important in their own jobs or in the jobs of others is about a half-right technique.

- Doing actual research on what the best performers do and contrasting that to what the poorer performers do is a better strategy.

- Traditional job analysis, where professionals study the competencies needed for a particular job, is also a sound technique.

Some Key Sources

Lombardo, M., & Eichinger, R. (2003). *The LEADERSHIP ARCHITECT® norms and validity report.* Minneapolis: Lominger Limited, Inc.

SUCCESS PREDICTION

46.

What is the relationship between being smart (having a high IQ) and the ability to manage others effectively?

SELECT ONE:

☐ A. There is a strong relationship; the smarter you are, the better manager you can be.

☐ B. There is a moderate relationship; the smarter you are, the more likely it is you can manage others well.

☐ C. There is a small relationship; it helps but not much.

☐ D. There is no relationship; the level of your IQ has nothing to do with how well you can manage others.

☐ E. There is a negative relationship; the smarter you are the more likely it is that you won't listen or delegate.

46. What is the relationship between being smart (having a high IQ) and the ability to manage others effectively?

The correct answer is C: There is a small relationship; it helps but not much.

How sure are we at this time?

1	2	3	**4**	5
Hint	Suggestive	Trending	**Substantial**	Solid

Discussion

If a company hires smart people (those with 3.5 or higher grade point averages from good schools), success is assured, right? Apparently not. There is always a talent shortage. Every organization seems to lack bench strength for key management and leadership roles. If success were essentially a matter of IQ and grades in school, we would have that talent and bench problem solved.

Many mistake being brilliant with being learning agile. There is little or no connection between the two. In the population organizations recruit from (college graduates, 120+ IQ), the two are unrelated. While being smart is a very good thing, being learning agile may be even more important for business success. In two studies, learning agility was much more related to management performance than intellectual horsepower (Sternberg et al., 1995; Connolly & Viswesvaran, 2002). But managers have a better chance to be accurate on their assessment of intelligence than on learning agility, since intelligence is easier to assess and more familiar. In addition, many look for it and tend to overvalue smarts in making potential hiring decisions. Long-term managerial success in the face of faster-paced challenges actually rests on three legs: basic intelligence, which most organizations assure through their hiring practices (top grades at good schools); variety of experience; and continuously learning to do something new or different (learning agility).

So we are not arguing that no attention be paid to smarts, only that by the time someone is being considered for a management job, reasonable intelligence is assured. Smarts is somewhat more strongly related to the level of achievement. In jobs toward the top of an organization, more intellectual horsepower is required to process all the information and make good decisions. But even with that, smarts doesn't help much in predicting who will be good at managing people, not just things and projects.

Selected Research
- In her research, Howard (1986) found that "intelligence certainly helps in managerial jobs that are highly complex or technical in nature."

- Sternberg et al. (1995) conclude "learning new behavior is a powerful predictor of level attained, better than IQ."

- People with higher scores on a learning measure also performed significantly better once promoted (Lombardo & Eichinger, 2003).

- Connolly and Viswesvaran (2002) report that a measure of learning from experience was the best predictor of performance and promotability, far better than IQ or personality measures.

- Historical studies looking back across 85 years have found that IQ accounts for 25 percent or more of job success. (Schmidt & Hunter, 1998). Other studies that include newer measures have argued that the average validity coefficient between cognitive-ability tests and measures of job performance is about .20, which means that only 4 percent of the variation among people in their job performance is accounted for by cognitive-ability test scores (Sternberg, 1996, p. 224).

- In a study of 181 competency models, Goleman (1998) found that "67 percent of the abilities deemed essential for effective performance for managers were emotional competencies." And, compared to IQ and technical expertise, emotional competence mattered twice as much.

- In a meta-analysis of the effectiveness of training across 70 studies, Burke and Day (1986) identified behavior modeling training (a type of training based on social cognitive theory which suggests that effective performance will be enhanced if the learner has first had an opportunity to observe others performing the behavior) and role playing as methods associated with positive results for skill-based training.

- Lyle Spencer, Jr., former director of Research and Technology at Hay-McBer, says that "what you learned in school distinguishes superior performers in only a handful of the five or six hundred jobs for which we've done competence studies. It's the emotional intelligence abilities that matter more for superior performance." In a presentation to the International Family Business Program Association, Spencer said that cognitive knowledge and skills are only the tip of the iceberg, and the other 90 percent of the iceberg is made up of four areas: cognition, motivation, perception, and regulatory functions (Spencer, 1997).

So what difference do these findings make?
- Most people overvalue smarts as a predictor of managerial success. While it's not unimportant, it isn't worth the weight that most give it. The same is true for technical or functional skills. Being stupid is not necessarily a good thing either and we don't advocate hiring stupid people, but having a threshold of smarts is sufficient.

- Learn to assess learning agility and add it to your list of criteria for selecting and promoting managers. Learning agility can be assessed by past experiences (how did the applicant handle difficult tasks, particularly those where he failed); by horizontal thinking (how would candidates handle some unique situation, how creatively do they approach problems); and by being reflective and self-aware so they do not make the same mistakes twice.

- Look to other variables that really relate to managing others like EQ and other softer competencies in hiring decisions.

Some Key Sources

Burke, M.J., & Day, R.R. (1986). A cumulative study of the effectiveness of managerial training. *Journal of Applied Psychology, 71* (2), 232–245.

Connolly, J.A., & Viswesvaran, C. (2002, April). *Assessing the construct validity of a measure of learning agility.* A presentation at the Seventeenth Annual Conference of the Society for Industrial and Organizational Psychology, Toronto, Canada.

Goleman, D. (1998). *Working with emotional intelligence.* New York: Bantam Books.

Howard, A. (1986). College experiences and managerial performance. *Journal of Applied Psychology Monograph, 71* (3), 530–552.

Lombardo, M., & Eichinger, R. (2003). *CHOICES ARCHITECT® promotion study results.* Minneapolis: Lominger Limited, Inc.

Schmidt, F.L., & Hunter, J.E. (1998, September). The validity and utility of selection methods in personnel psychology: Practical and theoretical implications of 85 years of research findings. *Psychological Bulletin, 24* (2), 262–274.

Spencer, L. (1997, July 10). Presentation to the International Family Business Program Association hosted by the UMass Family Business Center.

Sternberg, R.J. (1996). *Successful intelligence: How practical and creative intelligence determine success in life.* New York: Simon & Schuster.

Sternberg, R.J., Wagner, R.K., Williams, W.M., & Horvath, J.A. (1995). Testing common sense. *American Psychologist, 50* (11), 912–927.

MEASUREMENT

47.

A standard deviation is a common method of expressing the size of a difference between groups. How large does it need to be to make a difference?

SELECT ONE:

☐ A. Two standard deviations is the standard.

☐ B. One standard deviation is practically different.

☐ C. Between one-half and one standard deviation is practically different.

☐ D. One-half standard deviation is practically different.

☐ E. You can't make that decision based upon the standard deviation difference.

47. **A standard deviation is a common method of expressing the size of a difference between groups. How large does it need to be to make a difference?**

The correct answer is D: One-half standard deviation is practically different.

How sure are we at this time?

1	2	3	**4**	5
Hint	Suggestive	Trending	**Substantial**	Solid

Discussion

The standard deviation is one of several indices of variability (another is the t or F test) that statisticians use to characterize the dispersion among the measures in a given population. For example, if 10 sales clerks averaged 100 sales per month and the standard deviation were 10, then 68 percent of the sales representatives sold between 90 and 110 sales. If the standard deviation were 20, then 68 percent of the sales clerks sold between 80 and 120 sales. The higher the standard deviation, the greater the variability.

One-half standard deviation is the standard in viewing two groups as different. In a commonly accepted text (Cohen, 1988), .2 standard deviations is a small difference, .5 is medium, and .8 and higher is considered a large difference. The common way to express this is with the letter d, so if you see $d = .5$, this means the groups differ by one-half standard deviation. However, much lower values yield meaningful differences as well. Spencer (2001) reports the average gain due to improved selection practices as .2 (an increase of about 8 percent). In one study, a training program that produced an 8 percent gain in productivity netted a savings of $2.3 million across one year (Clark & Clark, 1994). The key is to look at real-world impact, which can be substantial even with smaller standard deviations. Higher values are used as well. When comparing an individual to a norm group on a 360 feedback instrument, one convention is to use the 75th percentile as the beginning of high scores and the 25th percentile as the beginning of low scores (this is 1 1/3 standard deviations). Other instruments use the 84th and 16th percentiles as high/low breakpoints (two standard deviations). This is ordinarily because the person's ratings are based on the ratings of only a few people and instrument makers have adopted a conservative approach. The standard in looking at the difference between superior and average performers is often one standard deviation (or effect size). It is a convention statisticians use to describe the significance of their findings.

In a normally distributed population:

- 68 percent of all scores are within one standard deviation above and below the average.

- 95 percent of all scores are within two standard deviations above and below the average.

- 99 percent of all scores are within three standard deviations above and below the average.

Two questions arise about any hypothesized relationship between two variables: (1) What is the probability that the relationship exists? (2) If it does, how strong is the relationship? There are two types of tools that are used to address these questions: the first is addressed by tests for statistical significance, and the second is addressed by measures of association. Tests for statistical significance are used to address the question: What is the probability that what we think is a relationship between two variables is really just a chance occurrence? If we selected many samples from the same population, would we still find the same relationship between these two variables in every sample? If we could do a census of the population, would we also find that this relationship exists in the population from which the sample was drawn? Or is our finding due only to random chance? Tests for statistical significance tell us what the probability is that the relationship we think we have found is due only to random chance. They tell us what the probability is that we would be making an error if we assume that we have found that a relationship exists. We can never be completely 100 percent certain that a relationship exists between two variables. There are too many sources of error to be controlled—for example, sampling error, researcher bias, problems with reliability and validity, simple mistakes, etc.

Using probability theory and the normal curve, we can estimate the probability of being wrong, if we assume that our finding a relationship is true. If the probability of being wrong is small, then we say that our observation of the relationship is a statistically significant finding. Statistical significance means that there is a good chance that we are right in finding that a relationship exists between two variables. But statistical significance is not the same as practical significance. We can have a statistically significant finding, but the implications of that finding may have no practical application. The researcher must always examine both the statistical and the practical significance of any research finding.

Selected Research

- According to Hunter et al. (1990), at the group level, one standard deviation can be a huge difference, involving "large amounts of money and quite notable differences." He notes that, depending on the complexity of a job, the value is 19 to 48 percent of output for nonsales jobs and 48 to 120 percent for sales jobs.

- Research by Spencer and Spencer (1993) notes the same thing: "The dollar amounts can be huge—in a survey of 44 firms, superior salespeople sold on average $6.7 million and average performers sold on average $3 million. Each superior salesperson returned $3.7 million in additional sales, a difference worth 89 times the average employee's salary!"

- Using statistical correlations as an example to explain the importance of statistical data analysis, Sternberg (1996) points out that "the most important thing to remember about correlations is that they do not prove causation. Height and weight are correlated, but you do not get shorter when you lose weight. Addressing causality must include other types of tests: Reliability, Validity—face, content, criterion, and construct validity."

- Devore and Peck's (2001, Fourth Edition) statistics reference book is often used as a textbook for college entry-level statistics courses. Fundamental concepts in the book include the connection between four statistical areas: (1) predicting population parameters from sample values; (2) the relationship between the size of the sample, the error tolerances, and the degree of confidence; (3) the concept that, with smaller error tolerances you either need to lower the degree of confidence or increase the sample size; and (4) there is a basic formula that is used that says, when predicting a given need, if you specify two of the values, you can calculate the third value.

So what difference do these findings make?

- When someone tests two groups or a person against a standard and says there is a one-half standard deviation difference between the two, there is a strong likelihood that the difference is real and, most likely, has practical significance.

- Although one-half standard deviation indicates a meaningful difference, a smaller difference may also indicate a real-world impact.

- When comparing mean scores, you should always ask for standard deviations to determine the ranges. For example, if one group scored 3.2 and had a *SD* of .2, and the other scored 3.2 and had a *SD* of 1.2, the second group has a much larger range in their responses. Although the means are the same (3.2), the two groups got there very differently.

Some Key Sources

Clark, K.E., & Clark, M.B. (Eds.). (1994). *Choosing to lead* (pp. 64–65). Charlotte, NC: Iron Gate Press.

Cohen, J. (1988). *Statistical power analysis for the social sciences* (2nd ed.). New Jersey: Lawrence Erlbaum.

Devore, J.L., & Peck, R. (2001). *Statistics: The exploration and analysis of data* (4th ed.). Belmont, CA: Duxbury Press.

Hunter, J.E., Schmidt, F.L., & Judiesch, M.K. (1990). Individual differences in output variability as a function of job complexity. *Journal of Applied Psychology, 75* (1), 28–42.

Spencer, L. (2001). The economic value of emotional intelligence competencies and EIC-based HR programs. In D. Goleman & C. Cherniss (Eds.), *The emotionally intelligent workplace: How to select for, measure, and improve emotional intelligence in individuals, groups, and organizations.* San Francisco: Jossey-Bass.

Spencer, L., & Spencer, S. (1993). *Competence at work* (pp. 14–15). New York: John Wiley & Sons, Inc.

Sternberg, R.J. (1996). *Successful intelligence: How practical and creative intelligence determine success in life.* New York: Simon & Schuster.

FEEDBACK

What is the effect on others of a person asking for and seeking negative feedback?

SELECT ONE:

☐ A. Others often think the person lacks self-confidence.

☐ B. Others expect the person to be defensive if they respond and therefore don't.

☐ C. Others think more positively of the person.

☐ D. Others respond by actually increasing positive feedback to counter the request.

☐ E. It has no measurable impact on others.

48

48. **What is the effect on others of a person asking for and seeking negative feedback?**

   The correct answer is C: Others think more positively of the person.

How sure are we at this time?

1	2	3	**4**	5
Hint	Suggestive	Trending	**Substantial**	Solid

Discussion

Seeking negative feedback enhances superiors', direct reports', and peers' opinions of the manager's overall effectiveness. This also increases self-knowledge, and we know that people who know themselves better generally are more successful.

Those who seek feedback are more likely to be learning agile and able to adapt to new situations. However, it is important not only to seek feedback, but to be willing to assimilate and act on it. Hearing feedback but not acting on it creates cynicism in others.

Selected Research

- Ashford and Tsui (1991) conducted a study that shows when managers sought negative feedback, this increased accuracy of understanding and enhanced superiors', direct reports', and peers' opinions of the manager's overall effectiveness. In contrast, seeking positive feedback decreased constituents' opinions of the manager's effectiveness.

- In their research on feedback, Ilgen et al. (1979) found that individuals who actively seek negative feedback have a more tempered view of their abilities, their performance, and their standing in an organization than those who don't. They also have a better basis for taking corrective action.

- A study designed to measure sensitivity to feedback (Edwards & Pledger, 1990) examined four factors—Sensitivity to Attention, Sensitivity to Socially Desirable Feedback, Sensitivity to Socially Undesirable Feedback, and Anticipation of Response—and found that "Sensitivity to Feedback was positively correlated with self-monitoring, self-esteem, and interaction involvement, and negatively correlated with communication apprehension."

- Kale (1989) examined the motivation for seeking negative feedback and reached two conclusions: Since managers depend on their superiors for resources (budget) and rewards (salary increases and promotions), they might be more motivated to seek feedback from them than from peers and direct reports; and, managers may also be hesitant to seek feedback from peers because of a concern that their peers might perceive them as lacking confidence and self-assurance.

- Research by Ashford (1986) examined three situations when individuals seek negative feedback and found that seeking negative feedback is seen to convey an image of the seekers as eager to perform well and interested in improving their behavior; employees with long company tenure were less likely to seek feedback than relative newcomers; and though managers are less likely to go to direct reports for feedback, they may seek negative feedback if they think doing so will convey an image of responsiveness, caring, and interest.

So what difference do these findings make?

- People know how hard it is for someone to publicly admit weaknesses, so they are more likely to give you the benefit of the doubt going forward when you ask for feedback.

- Individuals who actively seek feedback perform better in their jobs than those who don't because they have more insight into where their behavior is off track with respect to the goals they're pursuing.

- The people who look for feedback, especially negative feedback, are usually more self-aware and self-assured.

- Feedback givers should not be hesitant to deliver accurate, timely, and actionable negative feedback. In general, it will have a net positive impact. It is better if the person solicits the feedback before it is given. It is also better if the feedback is given in a private setting with attention paid to how it will be used.

- People with potential for progressing in their career should be made aware of the benefits of asking for and seeking negative feedback.

- When hiring, it is helpful to assess if people are open to feedback and improvement.

Some Key Sources

Ashford, S.J. (1986). The role of feedback seeking in individual adaptation: A resource perspective. *Academy of Management Journal, 29,* 465–487.

Ashford, S.J., & Tsui, A.S. (1991). Self-regulation for managerial effectiveness: The role of active feedback seeking. *Academy of Management Journal, 34* (2), 251–280.

Edwards, R., & Pledger, L. (1990, December). Development and construct validation of the sensitivity to feedback scale. *Communication Research Reports, 7* (2), 83–89.

Ilgen, D.R., Fisher, C.D., & Taylor, M.S. (1979). Consequences of individual feedback on behavior in organizations. *Journal of Applied Psychology, 64,* 359–371.

Kale, S.H. (1989). Dealer dependence and influence strategies in a manufacturing-dealer dyad. *Journal of Applied Psychology, 74,* 379–384.

GENDER

Are men and women different? The following statements: Women understand nonverbal communications better than men, women express emotion more comfortably than men, and women are more trusting and more nurturing than men on average, are examples of:

SELECT ONE:

☐ A. Stereotypical beliefs and myths that are not true.

☐ B. Prejudice and bias on the part of men.

☐ C. Actual facts.

☐ D. True statements but of little practical significance.

☐ E. The result of how culture looks at gender.

49

49. The following statements: Women understand nonverbal communications better than men, women express emotion more comfortably than men, and women are more trusting and more nurturing than men on average, are examples of:

The correct answer is C: Actual facts.

How sure are we at this time?

1	2	3	**4**	5
Hint	Suggestive	Trending	**Substantial**	Solid

Discussion

As hard as it is for some to accept, there are research-based differences between men and women on average. On average means there are sensitive men and clueless women but, on average, there are differences. Whether those differences are due to culture, upbringing, or even underlying neuroanatomy and neurophysiology are beyond the scope of this chapter. The fact is that there are real gender differences.

Selected Research

• Crucian and Berenbaum (1998) tested hemispheric differences between men and women and found that the right hemisphere in a man's brain is primarily specialized for spatial ability while the right hemisphere in a woman's brain is primarily specialized for emotional perception. They point out, however, that there was "no evidence for the hypothesized negative correlation between spatial ability and emotional perception."

• A study of 95 college students designed to measure perception of nonverbal cues (Hall et al., 1999) found that females scored higher in correctly perceiving facial expressions than did men.

- Kring and Gordon (1998) examined the expressive, experiential, and physiological emotional responses of men and women. Compared to men, "women were more expressive, but did not differ in reports of experienced emotion, and demonstrated different patterns of skin conductance (one measure of emotional activity) responding."

- Four meta-analyses by Feingold (1994) revealed that males were more assertive and had slightly higher self-esteem than females. The research also showed that females were higher in extraversion, anxiety, trust, and what they refer to as tender-mindedness (nurturance).

- According to research by Loring-Meier and Halpern (1999, September), there are significant gender differences in visuospatial tasks, with "large differences favoring males on tasks that require transformations in visuospatial working memory." They point out that males responded more quickly to all four tasks in the study and that speed in transforming the visual image could also speed up the decision making process.

- Lewin et al. (2001) found sex differences favoring women in their research on episodic memory. Their study examined sex differences in verbal, nonverbal, and visuospatial episodic memory tasks. Results showed that "although women performed at a higher level on a composite verbal and nonverbal episodic memory score, men performed at a higher level on a composite score of episodic memory tasks requiring visuospatial processing." They summarize the results to mean that men excel in visuospatial memory, and women excel in episodic memory when the material is verbally available.

- Sax (2001) argues that one of the problems with our current education system is that "5-, 6-, and 7-year-old children—especially boys—are not well suited to a school day that consists entirely of reading, writing, and arithmetic." He notes further, that since "boys' brains are physiologically one to two years less mature than girls' brains at this age, many boys are incapable of mastering a kindergarten curriculum that emphasizes reading, writing, and math." He cautions that if boys don't excel in either artistic or athletic areas, boys can label themselves as failures and lose interest in school.

So what difference do these findings make?

- There are practical differences between the genders which may have some impact on doing certain jobs over others. Men and women, on average and in general, have slightly different skill sets in specific areas. Knowing what the differences are and taking them into account in human capital applications is more intelligent than believing there are no differences.

- It might mean that when very specialized skills are needed to do a job—very fine motor skills or reading nonverbal communications—that the gender with less of that skill might be offered more training.

- It is important to not make gender the only or overriding criterion in assigning tasks. While there are average differences between genders, there are clearly distributions of skills for both men and women. On average, women are better at relationships than men, but the normal distribution would suggest that some women are worse and some men are better. Don't overgeneralize mean scores and apply them to all people.

- Relating these differences to the nature/nurture debate, the best guess now is that it is fifty-fifty.

Some Key Sources

Crucian, G.P., & Berenbaum, S.A. (1998, April). Sex differences in right hemisphere tasks. *Brain and Cognition, 36* (3), 377–389.

Feingold, A. (1994, November). Gender differences in personality: A meta-analysis. *Psychological Bulletin, 116* (3), 429–456.

Hall, C.W., Gaul, L., & Kent, M. (1999, December). College students' perception of facial expressions. *Perceptual and Motor Skills, 89* (3 Pt.1), 763–770.

Kring, A.M., & Gordon, A.H. (1998, March). Sex differences in emotion: Expression, experience, and physiology. *Journal of Personality and Social Psychology, 74* (3), 686–703.

Lewin, C., Wolgers, G., & Herlitz, A. (2001, April). Sex differences favoring women in verbal but not in visuospatial episodic memory. *Neuropsychology, 15* (2), 65–73.

Loring-Meier, S., & Halpern, D.F. (1999, September). Sex differences in visuospatial working memory: Components of cognitive processing. *Psychonomic Bulletin and Review, 6* (3), 464–471.

Sax, L. (2001). Reclaiming kindergarten: Making kindergarten less harmful for boys. *Psychology of Men and Masculinity, 2*, 3–12.

CAREER DEVELOPMENT

50.

What is known about the developmental power of line and staff jobs to develop future general managers?

SELECT ONE:

☐ A. Line jobs on average deliver much more development than staff jobs.

☐ B. Line jobs deliver somewhat more development than staff jobs.

☐ C. Even though the lessons learned are somewhat different, they are about equal.

☐ D. Staff jobs deliver somewhat more development than line jobs.

☐ E. Staff jobs deliver much more development than line jobs primarily because of the political and strategic nature of the environment.

50. **What is known about the developmental power of line and staff jobs to develop future general managers?**

   The correct answer is A: Line jobs on average deliver much more development than staff jobs.

How sure are we at this time?

1	2	3	**4**	5
Hint	Suggestive	Trending	**Substantial**	Solid

Discussion

Hands down, line jobs deliver more developmental lessons that lead to eventual success as a general manager. The lessons of line and staff assignments are, of course, different, and both are important, but typical line jobs deliver more lessons than typical staff jobs at the same level. It's still important for future general managers to have service in both staff and line jobs, but the majority of the service should be in a variety of line assignments.

Line jobs give managers the chance to have more clear-cut accountability and responsibility for results. They allow managers to develop leadership skills in directing the work of others. Staff jobs give managers the chance to process information, prepare conceptual roadmaps, and learn to influence from the side.

Selected Research

- Staff, from bottom to top, has had far fewer of the high-powered assignments that teach. The difference is on the order of 2 to 1 in favor of the line. The most common experiences reported by line executives are turnarounds, leaps in scope or scale, and start-ups. For staff executives, they are projects, incidents revealing the values of others, role models (usually direct bosses), and early non-management jobs. Limited experiences create limited learning as well. On 360 results collected as part of this study, line executives were rated significantly higher on 11 of the 16 effectiveness scales. On the remaining 5, there was no difference (Lombardo & Eichinger, 1990).

- For women and African Americans, the difference is more like 3 to 1, as they are more often in nonmanagerial and/or staff roles. (Morrison et al., 1992; see Lombardo & Eichinger, 2002 for a review of this literature).

- Staff jobs are seen as less significant than line jobs (Hurley & Sonnenfeld, 1998; McCall et al., 1988).

So what difference do these findings make?

- Future general managers should have a diverse mix of both line and staff jobs and headquarters and field, but the dominant portion of their formative years before becoming a general manager should be in line jobs like start-ups, turnarounds, heavy strategy assignments, and heavy people-management responsibilities.

- Leaving people in a line assignment until there are clear outcomes is also important. Moving a line manager before you can report if he has succeeded or not will not give him full development in the assignment. The cycle for task completion and outcomes varies by the task, but leaving line managers through at least one round of a project is important.

- For staff, find ways for staff to work on line issues. Use projects to teach staff about the technical business core. The goal here is to understand and contribute, not to actually do core jobs in most cases. Look for line-like jobs in staff units. Examples are payroll, compensation and benefits processing, or hardware and report generation

Staff jobs are also good breeding grounds for lateral influence, where the staff person has to learn to influence through relationships and expertise rather than authority and power. Line managers who misuse power might be well served to work in staff roles where they have to learn to influence laterally.

Some Key Sources

Eichinger, R., & Lombardo, M. (1990). *Twenty-two ways to develop leadership in staff managers* (Technical Report No. 144). Greensboro, NC: Center for Creative Leadership.

Hurley, A.E., & Sonnenfeld, J.A. (1998). The effect of organizational experience on management career attainment in an international labor market. *Journal of Vocational Behavior, 52*, 172–190.

Lombardo, M., & Eichinger, R. (2004). *The leadership machine* (pp. 360–368). Minneapolis: Lominger Limited, Inc.

McCall, M.W., Lombardo, M., & Morrison, A. (1988). *The lessons of experience: How successful executives develop on the job.* Lexington, MA: Lexington Books.

Morrison, A., White, R., & VanVelsor, E. (1987, rev. 1992). *Breaking the glass ceiling: Can women reach the top of America's largest corporations?* Reading, MA: Addison-Wesley.

SUCCESS PREDICTION

51.

Is IQ (Intelligence Quotient) or EQ (Emotional Quotient) a better predictor of managerial success?

SELECT ONE:

☐ A. IQ is a much better predictor of success than EQ. There is no substitute to being bright enough to do the thinking part of the job.

☐ B. IQ is a slightly better predictor of success than EQ.

☐ C. IQ and EQ are about equal. They are both important and predict roughly an equal portion of success as a manager.

☐ D. EQ is a slightly better predictor of success than IQ.

☐ E. EQ is a much better predictor of success than IQ. Much of a manager's job is the "soft stuff" and therefore EQ is a stronger predictor of success as a manager than being bright.

51. Is IQ (Intelligence Quotient) or EQ (Emotional Quotient) a better predictor of managerial success?

The correct answer is C: IQ and EQ are about equal. They are both important and predict roughly an equal portion of success as a manager.

How sure are we at this time?

1	2	**3**	4	5
Hint	Suggestive	**Trending**	Substantial	Solid

Discussion

The latest meta-analysis by Schmidt and Hunter puts the correlation of IQ and level of organizational achievement at about .50. The work by Goleman and others on EQ put the correlation with managerial success at .55. About equal. Of course, the two co-vary at some level; those with EQ probably have more IQ.

Selected Research

- By 1996, employers said the three most highly sought after skills in new hires were oral communications, interpersonal abilities, and teamwork abilities. In tests with managers at *Fortune 500* companies, Yale psychologist Robert Sternberg discovered that practical intelligence seems to account for at least as much on-the-job success as does IQ (Sternberg et al., 1995).

- In one study, tacit knowledge (learning from experience) which is part of EQ was much more predictive of level achieved than was IQ (Sternberg et al., 1995). It's especially important as managers move up in their careers to senior level positions that require more complex and sophisticated reasoning and interaction.

- Findings from research by Carnevale (1989) noted that employers list "the underlying ability to learn on the job" as more important than technical skills.

- Historical studies looking back across 85 years have found that IQ accounts for 25 percent or more of job success (Schmidt & Hunter, 1998). Other studies that include newer measures suggest a more accurate figure may be no higher than 10 percent and maybe as low as 4 percent (Sternberg, 1996). According to Sternberg, IQ-based measures typically account for less than 10 percent of the variation among those people who are more and those who are less successful according to societal standards.

- Lyle Spencer, Jr., former director of Research and Technology of Hay-McBer says that "what you learned in school distinguishes superior performers in only a handful of the five or six hundred jobs for which we've done competence studies. It's the emotional intelligence abilities that matter more for superior performance." In a presentation to the International Family Business Program Association, Spencer said that cognitive knowledge and skills are only the tip of the iceberg, and the other 90 percent of the iceberg is made up of four areas: cognition, motivation, perception, and regulatory functions (Spencer, 1997).

- In their research, Lombardo and Eichinger (2003) found that "people with higher scores on a learning measure also performed significantly better once promoted."

- Similarly, a measure of learning from experience was the best predictor of promotability, far better than IQ or personality measures (Connolly & Viswesvaran, 2002).

So what difference do these findings make?

• When looking at potential candidates for management, look to those who have the requisite amount of smarts plus the people skills needed to get things done through others. That's about half of the success formula. The rest is learning from experience and motivation to achieve.

• Evaluate EQ by looking at how candidates worked with and were regarded by others, how they dealt with difficult tasks particularly when they failed, and how they managed power and authority when they had it.

Some Key Sources

Carnevale, A.P. (1989). *Workplace basics: The skills employers want.* U.S. Department of Labor Employment and Training Administration.

Connolly, J.A., & Viswesvaran, C. (2002, April). *Assessing the construct validity of a measure of learning agility.* A presentation at the Seventeenth Annual Conference of the Society for Industrial and Organizational Psychology, Toronto, Canada.

Lombardo, M., & Eichinger, R. (2003). *The LEADERSHIP ARCHITECT® norms and validity report.* Minneapolis: Lominger Limited, Inc.

Schmidt, F.L., & Hunter, J.E. (1998, September). The validity and utility of selection methods in personnel psychology: Practical and theoretical implications of 85 years of research findings. *Psychological Bulletin, 24* (2), 262–274.

Spencer, L. (1997, July 10). Presentation to the International Family Business Program Association hosted by the UMass Family Business Center.

Sternberg, R.J. (1996). *Successful intelligence: How practical and creative intelligence determine success in life.* New York: Simon & Schuster.

Sternberg, R.J., Wagner, R.K., Williams, W.M., & Horvath, J.A. (1995). Testing common sense. *American Psychologist, 50* (11), 912–927.

DIVERSITY

52.

Studies on bias have shown that . . .?

SELECT ONE:

☐ A. People are aware of their biases.

☐ B. People are aware of other people's biases but not their own.

☐ C. Few people are overtly biased now in the workplace.

☐ D. After almost 40 years of affirmative action efforts, the workplace is now mostly free of bias.

☐ E. People are still unaware of how their biases affect their decision making.

52. Studies on bias have shown that . . .?

The correct answer is E: People are still unaware of how their biases affect their decision making.

How sure are we at this time?

1	2	3	**4**	5
Hint	Suggestive	Trending	**Substantial**	Solid

Discussion

Since the Civil Rights Act of 1964, there has been significant progress made on the attitudes and overt biases of the majority toward protected classes. In self-report surveys and studies, the majority reports increasing intentions of being less biased in their thinking and less biased in their actions and decision making. On the other hand, studies continue to show unintended biases still affect decision making, even when the person is convinced that no such bias exists.

This refers to all kinds of biases, including majority to minority biases, but also gender and many other groupings (race, religion, etc.). We often don't look in our own bias mirrors. Since we grow up with our biases, we don't realize they are there until someone points them out to us.

Selected Research

- A study by Frazer and Wiersma (2001) points out that, while Whites reported that they were equally likely to hire Black or White job applicants, they recalled Black applicants as being significantly less intelligent than White applicants, even though they had identical responses to interview questions.

- Dovidio and Gaertner (2002) found similar results. Research they conducted found that many subjects demonstrated prejudices and resulting discriminatory behaviors that were outside their conscious awareness.

- Research by Lueptow, Garovich-Szabo, and Lueptow (2001) revealed that sex stereotyping hasn't changed much in 25 years.

- Research by Rudman and Kilianski (2000) demonstrates that sexism in the workplace isn't limited to men. Women may show less overt gender prejudice than men, but their beliefs about the connection between status and gender appear to be the same as men.

- Morrison (1992) found that Caucasians reported that people of other ethnic backgrounds are less intelligent and less hardworking. Mount et al. (1997) found that African American managers gave African American direct reports higher ratings.

- Often referred to as "benevolent sexists," Rudman and Glick (1999) report that many still assume that women are unsuited to the challenge of high-status jobs.

- Sackett et al. (1991) reports that women received lower ratings when they were a small proportion of the work group. Morrison (1992) had similar findings—identical resumes were sent with different photographs. Executives selected the women for administrative tasks, the men for line assignments. When the experiment was repeated with minority women, the results were the same. They also picked the men for the line assignments.

- Graves and Powell (1995) report that female recruiters saw male applicants as more similar to them and more qualified than female applicants.

So what difference do these findings make?

- While espoused bias has been greatly subdued, actual bias has not yet disappeared. While most educated people now reject protected group discrimination and declare themselves to be free from bias, studies show that they are not yet at zero bias.

- While overt bias has all but disappeared from the workplace, vigilance is required to track actual decisions to make sure unintended prejudice is not still operating.

- We all need constant vigilance and training to uncover our hidden biases. While few admit biases openly, they continue to exist privately. Talking about our heritage and sources of possible biases may help uncover real biases we have and help overcome them.

- When seeing behavior evidence of a bias (e.g., a racial remark or prejudice against a group), a leader must quickly and clearly point out the bias to the individual involved. If this behavioral bias continues, more stringent action can be taken.

Some Key Sources

Dovidio, F.J., & Gaertner, S.L. (1996, Winter). Affirmative action, unintentional racial biases, and intergroup relations. *Journal of Social Issues, 52* (4), 51–75.

Frazer, R.A., & Wiersma, U.J. (2001). Prejudice versus discrimination in the employment interview: We may hire equally, but our memories harbor prejudice. *Human Relations, 54,* 173–191.

Graves, L.M., & Powell, G.N. (1995). The effect of sex similarity on recruiters' evaluations of actual applicants: A test of the similarity-attraction paradigm. *Personnel Psychology, 48,* 85–98.

Lueptow, L.B., Garovich-Szabo, L., & Lueptow, M.B. (2001). Social change and the persistence of sex typing: 1974–1997. *Social Forces, 80,* 1–36.

Morrison, A. (1992). *The new leaders.* San Francisco: Jossey-Bass.

Mount, M.K., Sytsma, M.R., Hazucha, J.F., & Holt, K.E. (1997). Rater-ratee races effects in developmental performance ratings of managers. *Personnel Psychology, 50,* 51–70.

Rudman, L.S., & Glick, P. (1999). Feminized management and backlash toward agenic women: The hidden cost to women of a kinder, gentler image of middle managers. *Journal of Personality and Social Psychology, 77,* 1004–1010.

Rudman, L.S., & Kilianski, S.E. (2000). Implicit and explicit attitudes toward female authority. *Personality and Social Psychology Bulletin, 26,* 1315–1328.

Sackett, P., DuBois, C., & Noe, A. (1991). Tokenism in performance evaluation: The effects of work group representation on male-female and White Black differences in performance ratings. *Journal of Applied Psychology, 76* (2), 263–267.

SUCCESSION PLANNING

53.

How early can potential be identified after a person is hired?

SELECT ONE:

☐ A. After one year on the job.

☐ B. Within two years on the job.

☐ C. After two bosses have watched them in two different jobs.

☐ D. After three or more jobs along a known career path.

☐ E. After a minimum of five years with the firm.

53. How early can potential be identified after a person is hired?

The correct answer is C: After two bosses have watched them in two different jobs.

How sure are we at this time?

1	2	3	4	5
Hint	Suggestive	Trending	Substantial	Solid

Discussion

Being a high potential involves a combination of having the "right stuff," the foundational characteristics of achievers (like intelligence, a bias for action, being results oriented, customer focused, etc.) to begin with, plus the ability and willingness to learn from life and job experiences.

Learning from experience is highly related to later success because later success requires a different set of competencies and skills than current success. Learners succeed when jobs change in demand requirements. People who stay the same are less successful over time because times and jobs change.

How much one learns can be assessed before hire for a first estimate. Most people have had quite diverse experiences and exposures in their life where they had the opportunity to adjust and think and behave differently. Watching how the person adjusts to a second job unlike the first is the earliest you could be comfortable with a long-term potential estimate. Obviously, if they go through a series of similar jobs in a functional silo, you may never know for sure.

With better measures of learning from experience, especially under first-time conditions for the person, potential could be assessed fairly early. It will ordinarily take a couple of jobs and first-time tasks for this to be seen.

Not everyone can assess learning from experience. It is a technology that many would have to be trained in order to use for assessment.

Selected Research

- Jaques (1986, 1989) designed a grid on which candidates are sorted into six strata of capacity and "argues for facilitated, executive judgments about the potential for a field of promotable candidates based on forced comparisons of candidates." Jaques claims you can largely do it at time of hire, adding that the amount of time to determine potential depends a lot on the work the high potential is doing.

- According to VanVelsor and Leslie (1991) relatively few leadership tests have been studied for predictive validity; that is, there is no firm evidence that performance on the test today will predict successful leadership over a period of years.

- Results of a CCL study (Ruderman et al., 1997) that reviewed the promotions of 13 Caucasian women and 16 Caucasian men found that decision makers, when asked about promoting men, mentioned having a high level of comfort with the candidate in 75 percent of the cases and in only 23 percent of the cases with women.

So what difference do these findings make?

- Some researchers argue that identifying high potentials early isn't a good idea. When young people get singled out, given special treatment through courses and visits with VIPs and the like, the confident, aggressive, independent syndrome can set in long before there are any real accomplishments to buttress it. It's better to hire for learning, to develop learning, and consider jobs the developmental test where people show they can learn how to handle the new and different. Development specialists suggest that you can figure out who your budding high potentials are by thinking of all early jobs as 20 percent developmental.

- The earlier learning potential is assessed, the longer you have to get people prepared for future management and executive responsibility.

- This would be especially important in increasing diversity.

- The assessment methods exist to assess learning from experience. It is of critical importance that firms learn how to use these techniques to assess the potential of their people.

Steps to Being a Learner

Step One: Choice

Learners seek alternatives. They see what might be, not what has been or has to be. They are able to quickly brainstorm multiple ways of approaching and defining problems rather than relying on old methods of solving them:

- Comparing: *Learners look around and see what others do. They encourage their own creativity when they identify alternatives by examining how other people have approached similar problems.*

- Experimenting: *Learners are willing to try new things and take risks. They create alternatives by testing new ways to do things—even if the old ones are still working—by setting up mini-experiments where they do something one way and see the impact, then try another.*

- Being willing to look stupid: *Learners accept that they probably won't get it right the first time. They are willing to* make mistakes and don't become captive to the mistakes. When learners make a mistake, they take it in stride, figure out why it happened, adapt, and try to not make the same mistake twice. They don't blame, they reflect.

- Volunteering for tough assignments and projects: Learners increase choices by taking on assignments that stretch their thinking and approaches.

- Asking "What if?" Learners moderate fear of failure and facilitate generation of new ideas by thinking through "what if" questions:

  - What if I don't succeed? What is the worst possible thing that can happen? Am I OK with that?

  - What if I don't try something new? How will I feel about myself in the future?

  - What if I try to do this another way? How would someone else approach this experience? What insights can I gather from seeing this project through someone else's eyes?

Learners create choices and seek alternatives.

Step Two: Consequence

Every choice has a consequence—some good, some not. Learners instinctively connect choice and consequence. They see the impact of their choices, both positive and negative. They constantly play the "if, then" game: If I make this decision, then such and such is likely to happen. In the "if, then" game, they can see future consequences of present decisions. They envision a future and fold it into the present.

Step Three: Correction

Learners adjust and adapt to the choices and consequences they experience. They constantly need to take corrective action to inform the next cycle of choices. Effective learners are feedback junkies—they always want to know how their work is seen by and affects others. They ask what worked and what did not so they can adapt and improve their work. Rather than being satisfied with the status quo, they always want to improve and make things better.

Some Key Sources

Jaques, E. (1986). The development of intellectual capability: A discussion of Stratified Systems Theory. *Journal of Applied Behavioral Science, 22,* 361–384.

Jaques, E. (1989). *Requisite organization.* Arlington, VA: Carson Hall Publishers.

Ruderman, M.N., Ohlott, P.J., & Kram, K.E. (1997, April). Managerial promotion: The dynamics for men and women. *HR Magazine.*

VanVelsor, E., & Leslie, J.B. (1991). *Feedback to managers. Volume II: A review and comparison of sixteen multi-rater feedback instruments.* Greensboro, NC: Center for Creative Leadership.

ROI

54.

How much gain in organization financial results might you expect by having a top-flight HR function?

SELECT ONE:

☐ A. It could have as much as a 10% impact on the bottom line.

☐ B. There is no practical way to measure the impact.

☐ C. It could have as much as a 25% impact on the bottom line.

☐ D. There is no relationship.

☐ E. Every 5% increase in the quality of the HR staff has a 1% impact on the bottom line.

54. How much gain in organization financial results might you expect by having a top-flight HR function?

The correct answer is A: It could have as much as a 10% impact on the bottom line.

How sure are we at this time?

1	**2**	3	4	5
Hint	**Suggestive**	Trending	Substantial	Solid

Discussion

There are two lines of research that address this proposition. The first is a study of the qualities of individual HR professionals. Since 1989, Ulrich and Brockbank have studied what the difference is between high- and low-rated HR professionals. Customers were asked to do the ratings. Ulrich and Brockbank then separated the highest rated from the lowest rated to see what the skill and competency differences might be. Their research has shown a consistent set of skills and competencies that make a difference. Although they have changed slightly over the three runs of the study, they are business knowledge, HR technology knowledge and delivery, personal credibility, and change management and strategic skills. In their most recent (2003) round of surveys, Ulrich and Brockbank compared the company performance of the organizations populated with the best collection of HR professionals to those with the less skilled. They found about a 10 percent difference in financial performance. The causation here is difficult, and more successful financial firms might have resources to provide for more qualified HR professionals, but Brockbank and Ulrich also argue that more qualified HR professionals make things happen in ways that affect the bottom line.

The second line of inquiry comes from a different level of analysis. Becker and Huselid have studied the bottom-line impact of HR systems across entire enterprises. They have found that HR systems which are aligned with enterprise strategy return more to the bottom line than those that are more random. Additionally, they found that those HR systems in which the individual elements were coordinated, integrated, and synergistic return more to the bottom line. Together, aligned and integrated HR systems are capable of delivering about 10 percent to the value of an enterprise.

Making the leap that high-quality HR professionals (Ulrich & Brockbank, 1995) are the ones who put together aligned and integrated HR systems (Becker & Huselid, 1998), then the best data we have at the moment is that HR can have as much as a 10 percent impact on organization results. In other words, good and sound HR pays.

Selected Research
- Brockbank and Ulrich (2003) have now studied over 27,000 HR professionals from hundreds of companies with about half from the USA and the others from around the world.

- Becker and Huselid (1998) have studied the relationship between the quality of the enterprise-wide HR system and financial value of firms.

- Brockbank and Ulrich (2003b) found that the ability of HR professionals to make a "strategic contribution" had the most impact on business performance and "personal credibility" had the most impact on personal performance.

So what difference do these findings make?
- It's a case of physician heal thyself. The HR function should give a high priority to improve its own quality. In turn, that higher quality can lead to more value added throughout the enterprise.

- Learn how to align the various pieces and parts of the total HR system to the strategic plan of the organization. For example, some firms hire for skills A,B,C, then train for M,N,O, and then pay for X,Y,Z, and wonder why their HR systems are not having an impact. It is important to have a similar logic for hiring, training, and paying so that consistency emerges.

- As HR creates and implements the various pieces of a total HR system, work to make sure it is integrated (e.g., a single competency library is used throughout all applications).

Some Key Sources

Becker, B.E., & Huselid, M.A. (1998). High performance work systems and firm performance: A synthesis of research and managerial implications. *Personnel and Human Resources Management, 16,* 53–101.

Brockbank, W., & Ulrich, D. (2003). *Competencies for the new HR.* Washington DC: Society for Human Resource Management.

Brockbank, W., & Ulrich, D. (2003b). *The new HR agenda: 2002 Human Resource Competency Study (HRCS).* Ann Arbor: The University of Michigan Business School.

Ulrich, D., Brockbank, W., Yeung, A., & Lake, D. (1995). Human resource competencies: An empirical assessment. *Human Resource Management Journal, 34* (4), 473–496.

RECURITING

55.

What has been the effect of online recruiting?

SELECT ONE:

☐ A. It has caused alienation of potential candidates and has not led to improvement of the process.

☐ B. e-Recruiting is more cost effective and leads to better employees.

☐ C. Younger people report they like it and older people do not.

☐ D. It has led to discrimination toward poorer people who do not have access to computers.

☐ E. It is more cost effective per employee hired, but the success rate per employee has dropped proportionately.

55

55. What has been the effect of online recruiting?

The correct answer is B: e-Recruiting is more cost effective and leads to better employees.

How sure are we at this time?

1	2	**3**	4	5
Hint	Suggestive	**Trending**	Substantial	Solid

Discussion

Ethics. Loyalty. Privacy. Availability. Online recruiting and other new hiring technology bring new issues to the HR table. The primary difference, of course, is time. All of the data entry into the HR database is done directly over the Web by the job applicant, which frees the HR department to spend more time actually analyzing and manipulating the data. Research to date has been generally positive toward online recruiting.

A key to online recruiting is that the criteria for the job are clearly laid out and that candidates can do some self-selection based on those criteria.

Selected Research

- According to research by Cappelli (2001), 18 million resumes are posted on Monster.com alone, the largest Internet job site. Monster.com boasts it has almost 500,000 jobs available. Cappelli argues "with more than 5,000 job boards where resumes and job opportunities are posted, the Internet has become, by far, the most effective way to broadly disseminate information about the availability of jobs and people."

- Nike in Las Vegas, who used computer-assisted interviewing to screen 6,000 applicants for 250 positions, found that using computer-assisted interviewing helped reduce turnover in the retail division by 21 percent in two years (Thornberg, 1998).

- Crispin (2000) reports on a 1998 survey by J. Walter Thompson in Los Angeles that found that 70 percent of the 550 HR professionals it polled used the Internet for recruiting, compared to 21 percent in a similar 1996 study. He added that, according to one researcher with extensive online recruiting expertise, at least 30,000 Web sites are trying to gain a piece of the online recruiting market. An estimated 75 percent of *Fortune 500* companies are posting jobs on their own sites, and "perhaps a million corporate Web sites from the smallest to the largest of companies are posting jobs."

- According to Dysart (2001), "while dozens of interactive tools are popping up on the Web, at least four—Web site search engines, interactive job application forms, e-mail autoresponders, and e-mail mailing lists—are appearing more frequently and gaining considerable popularity on HR Web sites." Dysart notes that the primary purpose of these tools is that they allow HR departments to link their company databases with the Web site and enable applicants to interact with a company more efficiently.

So what difference do these findings make?

- Benefits of interactive recruiting sites (Dysart). Applicants are more than willing to fill out interactive job application forms posted on the company's e-Recruiting site. The forms can be mined for predictive demographic data. The data can be mined to determine least and most popular jobs and company locations, as well as the salary level applicants expect. HR departments looking for more in-depth analyses of applicant data could post a survey to ask job seekers why they are applying, what they think they would like most about working for the company, and what they look for in a new employer. An online relationship allows a quick and easy dialogue. Applicants become part of the HR database. And the data can be manipulated to trigger an e-mail notification of a new job opening.

• Equity issues (Cappelli). "Issues of fairness, with respect to things like compensation, opportunities, etc. [used to be] all based on internal criteria. Now, increasingly, they are based on external criteria. The rate of pay we [the employer] decided was fair for you used to be based on how long you've been with the company, your job title and position within the hierarchy of the company. Now it's increasingly based on the rate for similar jobs elsewhere, and that's pretty much it. It makes the balance of power [between employer and employee] much more based on a market relationship rather than on a kind of inside political relationship."

• Setting criteria. A challenge of online recruiting is to have criteria for a job clearly defined. In one company, employees who work in a technical area are charged with defining the criteria for future employees. As they put together the criteria, they become more aware of what their job entails and are able to communicate this to potential applicants.

• Eroding loyalty (Cappelli). Online recruiting may erode loyalty. Before the Internet made information so easy to access, an employee competed mainly with others in the same firm for raises and promotions. No longer. Today, anyone doing a specific job anywhere is competition. "It's now so much easier to hire talent on the outside than it was," Cappelli says. "It's so much easier to get information about passive applicants that it alters the balance between inside development and outside hiring. It throws everybody into a more open labor market."

- Privacy Issues (Cappelli). There are privacy issues, particularly when it comes to the so-called "passive applicants." Many companies take job applications and screen applicants online. Some companies ask for personal information. JP Morgan's application, for example, is in the form of a game. The answers, says Cappelli, "reveal information about interests and attitudes of applicants." Cisco Systems offers facilities like libraries to identify and track users to recruit in the future. Some track potential applicants by asking questions to user groups and recording those who answer the questions correctly.

- Reduced hiring time (Thornberg). Technology can reduce the hiring cycle time, anticipate what skills will be in demand, and call up instant information about a potential hire. Interactive voice response technology (IVR) is beginning to be used to capture information about potential employees.

- Beware of the hype (Crispin). Most agree that posting openings on the largest and best-known job boards works well. However, experts caution that you should not be taken in by claims that a site has the "largest resume database available" or is the "most visited job site on the Internet."

Some Key Sources

Cappelli, P. (2001). *Topics and tactics. How online recruiting changes the hiring game.* Philadelphia, PA: The Wharton School, University of Pennsylvania.

Crispin, G., & Mehler, M. (2000). *CareerXroads 2000: Where talent and opportunity connect on the Internet.* Indianapolis: Jist Works.

Dysart, J. (2001, August 22). HR recruiters build interactivity into Web sites. *HR Magazine.*

Thornberg, L. (1998, February). Computer-assisted interviewing shortens hiring cycle. *HR Magazine.*

56.

What makes the least difference in team effectiveness?

SELECT ONE:

☐ A. Teams managing talent and skill acquisition themselves.

☐ B. The personality and style of the team leader.

☐ C. The net functional skills of the team to do the work.

☐ D. The absolute number of talented individuals on the team.

56

☐ E. Organizational support for the team.

56. What makes the least difference in team effectiveness?

The correct answer is B: The personality and style of the team leader.

How sure are we at this time?

1	2	**3**	4	5
Hint	Suggestive	**Trending**	Substantial	Solid

Discussion

There has been extensive research on what makes teams effective. The findings, while broad, point to some certain principles. Teams that have the talent and skills to basically manage themselves do better. A dominant team leader doesn't seem to lead to long-term and consistent performance. Organizational support makes a difference. How the team reacts to its customers and runs itself internally all make a difference. Net talent (how the talent of the individuals works together) is more important than having single-talented people. Having fun, enjoying one another, and liking each other don't seem to relate to high performance.

Selected Research

- In his book on myths and truths about teams, Hackman (2002) argues that "anyone who succeeds in getting performance-enhancing conditions in place, or helps strengthen them, is exercising team leadership." The author further believes that an individual's management style isn't as important as how well they design and support a team so that the team can end up managing itself. He bases the book on the conditions that need to exist for a team to be successful: It needs to be a "real team"; the team needs to have a compelling direction; the organization has to provide an enabling structure that allows it to work efficiently; and, finally, the team needs both a supportive context and competent coaching. Specific examples of successful teams include: Tektronix reports that one self-directed team now turns out as many products in three days as it once took an entire assembly line to produce in 14 days; FedEx, using work teams, cut service glitches (i.e., incorrect invoices and lost packages) by 13 percent; and Shenandoah Life processes 50 percent more applications and customer service requests—with 10 percent fewer people—using work teams.

- In *Designing Team-Based Organizations*, Mohrman et al. (1995) emphasize that teams are most effective when they're implemented in the "context of an organization that is designed to support them." The book is based on the results of four years of research conducted in two phases: The first phase involved comprehensive interviews with 25 teams in four companies; and the second phase included the study of 26 team-based business units in seven corporations. While the book addresses a wide variety of team design, management, and implementation issues, it focuses on three or four important findings. One finding they emphasize is that "leadership within the team is critical for success, and the organization needs to give the team its charter and scope of responsibility." Another finding is that many organizations establish teams but fail to establish the supporting structures and processes, almost dooming a team to failure. A third emphasis is managing performance. "This frequently overlooked aspect of team performance is critical in aligning individual and team goals and in making sure that behavioral changes in employees—and management—take place."

- Marshall et al. (2003) looked at 12 effective versus 12 average to low-performing teams. Teams were consistently rated differently by internal customers on items relating to effective team functioning. For example, more effective teams focused less on work atmosphere and more on achieving results and efficiency. They took a collective view of talent and were characterized by little competition among team members. Being better at these behaviors accounted for about $4 million in sales per team.

- Numerous studies have shown that self-managed work teams have higher performance and lower turnover and absenteeism. According to Spencer (2001), self-managed work teams pay more attention to skill acquisition than traditional teams. Additionally, Spencer found that a superior team is 30 percent more productive than an average team.

- Research by Cohen and Ledford (1994) points out that "the workplace is no longer the frontier of individual achievement for the 'top gun' graduate, but is painted more as a 'networked' environment peopled by graduates with the skills to work in a team setting." The researchers note that self-managed teams are considered both an advanced and aggressive form of employee involvement with benefits to the organization, the team, and individuals that comprise the team.

- Lawler (1996) outlines six organization design principles for overhauling an enterprise from bottom to top and "bringing it into alignment with the realities of today's marketplace." The fourth principle (that lateral processes are the key to organizational effectiveness) argues that "using the right combination of project teams, problem solving teams, work teams, overlay teams, and management teams, it is possible to develop organizations that are entirely team-based." Another principle demonstrates that managerial and employee involvement is the most effective source of control. "Typical management activities—goal setting, giving credit for a job

well done, and developing and nurturing competencies—
must be done with the entire team. Managers must also
provide teams with a sense of mission, direction, and
purpose."

- Results of a study by Lawler et al. (1998) review high-
involvement work practices—that are increasingly being
adopted by *Fortune 1000* companies—to demonstrate the
value of teams in creating more effective organizations.
They point to several interrelated work-system features,
such as "involvement/empowerment, trust, goal alignment, development, teamwork, performance-enabling
work structures, and performance-based rewards" as being
especially important in creating these high-performance
work systems.

So what difference do these findings make?

- There is a well-known and researched set of principles and
best practices to bring out the best in teams. It is readily
available with many talented practitioners and experts
available to train and implement.

A synthesis of this work follows in the table on the following
page.

CRITERIA OF EFFECTIVE TEAMS	DETAILS	
PURPOSE: To what extent does our team have a clear purpose?	**Strategy:**	Do we know what we are doing to win in the competitive marketplace?
	Mind-set:	Do we have a unity about what we want to be known for by our best customers?
	Priority:	Do we have the top priorities for the organization and for the team?
DECISION: How well do we make decisions?	**Decision Protocol**	
	Clarity:	Are we clear about the decisions we have to make?
	Accountable:	Are we able to assign accountability for who will make decisions?
	Timeliness:	Are we clear about how much time to spend on decisions?
	Process:	Do we have processes for making decisions (allocating resources, speed of decision, degree of risk, involvement)?
	Return & Report:	Do we stick with decisions? Have clear follow up to make sure it sticks?
RELATIONSHIP: How well do we work together?	**Conflict:**	Do we deal with conflict openly and clearly?
	Affect:	Do we communicate appreciation and support?
	Style:	Do we know and act on our style that works?
	Difference:	Do we appreciate differences and leverage them?
LEARNING: How well do we learn from successes and failures?	Do we process the things that worked and did not work in the last 90 days? Do we not make the same mistakes again? Do we not blame, but learn?	

- The higher performing work team's technology should be part of the arsenal of any organization.

Some Key Sources

Cohen, S.G., & Ledford, G.F., Jr. (1994). The effectiveness of self-managing teams: A quasiexperiment. *Human Relations, 47* (1), 13–43.

Hackman, J.R. (2002). *Leading teams: Setting the stage for great performances.* Boston: Harvard Business School Press.

Lawler, E.E. (1996). *From the ground up.* San Francisco: Jossey-Bass.

Lawler, E.E. (1998). *Strategies for high performance organizations.* San Francisco: Jossey-Bass.

Marshall, S., Lombardo, M., & Leming, J. (2003, June). *High vs. low performing teams.* Lominger Annual Users Conference, San Diego, CA.

Mohrman, S.A., Cohen, S.G., & Mohrman, A.M. (1995). *Designing team-based organizations.* San Francisco: Jossey-Bass.

Spencer, L. (2001). The economic value of emotional intelligence competencies and EIC-based HR programs. In D. Goleman & C. Cherniss (Eds.), *The emotionally intelligent workplace: How to select for, measure, and improve emotional intelligence in individuals, groups, and organizations.* San Francisco: Jossey-Bass.

TALENT MANAGEMENT

57.

What's the most effective long-term talent acquisition path to follow?

SELECT ONE:

☐ A. It's always best to develop your own talent from within.

☐ B. To the extent possible, it's better to build your own talent and go outside for specialized and temporary needs.

☐ C. It's faster and cheaper to get most of your talent from the outside because you can never develop enough internal people to go around.

☐ D. It's always cheaper and faster to buy talent from the outside.

☐ E. Developing internal people just leads to increased turnover; it's a losing game.

57. What's the most effective long-term talent acquisition path to follow?

The correct answer is B: To the extent possible, it's better to build your own talent and go outside for specialized and temporary needs.

How sure are we at this time?

1	2	3	**4**	5
Hint	Suggestive	Trending	**Substantial**	Solid

Discussion

For many human resource departments, reacting to rapid changes in the economy and keeping up with technology have become full-time jobs. Then there are such added issues as the global shortage of qualified workers. It isn't difficult to see why more and more companies are outsourcing to meet talent needs.

Some of the outsourcing is for administrative, routine, standardized tasks that do not differentiate your firm from your competitors. It makes sense to outsource talent when you are seeking talent at the industry average. Go for the best price.

But, when seeking talent that gives you a competitive advantage, most studies say essentially the same thing: Get all the talent you can to begin with and then develop it aggressively while you have it. Since the amount of talent is restricted in the labor marketplace, just hiring talent generally won't do it. You have to develop people after they arrive. As it turns out, the developed people are a company's most important asset.

Going outside for key talent should occur when there is a need to change a culture or way of doing things; staying inside for talent will continue the status quo. In general, we have found about 80/20: 80 percent internal promotion to key jobs and 20 percent outside the existing business to bring in new ideas.

Another thing to remember is that people hoard talent, make irrational arguments about who to promote, won't make tough calls on stagnant performers, and do all the things they do to protect themselves. It's called human nature. And, although your competitors can buy some talent, no one can buy away the thousands to millions of hours invested in growth.

Selected Research

- A McKinsey survey of computer science and electrical engineering graduates, summarized in The War for Technical Talent (Bodden et al., 2000), predicted that falling numbers of middle-aged people, the movement of employees out of large corporations, and frequent job-hopping will force employers to offer top dollar to the best performers. The researchers report that companies are finding that people who can fill key technical jobs are in critically short supply. According to the U.S. Bureau of Labor Statistics, one-tenth of the more demanding technical openings (such as those related to information technology and electrical engineering) already can't be filled within a reasonable time.

- Reporting on a similar study, the McKinsey War for Talent study, Chambers et al. (1998) found that three-fourths of corporate officers surveyed said their companies had insufficient talent or that talent was in short supply across the board.

- According to studies at AT&T (Howard & Bray, 1988), twice as many AT&T low-assessed people got to third-level management than did the high-assessed if the low-assessed's developmental opportunities were significantly better.

- By studying the lives of 35 accomplished adults, Bloom's (1985) research on talent development revealed that the role of quality instruction and master teaching is central to talent development. According to Bloom, talent development consisted of several variables: a nurturing and supportive family, the right teacher at the right time, the opportunity to become fully immersed in their area of talent, and the opportunity to enter competitions and exhibitions.

- Lombardo and Eichinger (2002) say that "looking for top talent only is a losing strategy." They argue that there is "only 5 percent to go around, and firms with big purses and new e-commerce start-ups snap up most of it"; adding that, since grades in school, IQ scores, and college quality aren't overwhelmingly predictive of success, hiring some 3.0 GPA students who are high in nonacademic learning is a better approach.

- Ulrich and Lake (1990), in a University of Michigan study, found that the most profitable mix across businesses was to hire 80 percent inside/20 percent outside: 80 percent for continuity and keeping promises to employees, 20 percent for freshness and unblocking paths.

- An article in *Workforce Magazine* (1997) by Jac Fitz-enz notes that "companies lose huge amounts of dollars when their good employees leave." He estimates organizations lose $1 million on average when they lose 10 professional and managerial employees. "Assuming your organization has a 10 percent after-tax profit, that's a reduction of $100,000 from the bottom line." Fitz-enz estimates that the total potential costs of turnover can be measured in terms of three aspects: customer retention costs, marketing and sales spending to attract a new customer, and employee-based costs.

So what difference do these findings make?

• It is cheaper and surer to develop most, but not all, of your talent from within. Having a strong training and development system along with a best practices succession planning process pays off in the long-term. Good people stay longer with companies that provide opportunities to grow and develop.

• Sometimes going outside for great talent is deceptive because the grass often looks greener on the other side of the valley. New hires often come with challenges not always visible in the interviewing process. And, orienting and socializing new mid-level managers can be difficult. Finally, internal employees who wanted the job that was given to an outsider may be unsupportive and sabotage the newly hired employee. Our rule of thumb for going outside for mid or senior hires is 30 to 40 percent more qualified than internal candidates, to such an extent that internal candidates say "Aha, I would like to work for this person!" Then, the chances of success are better.

Some Key Sources

Bloom, B.S. (Ed.). (1985). *Developing talent in young people.* New York: Ballantine Books.

Bodden, S., Glucksman, M., & Lasky, P. (2000). The war for technical talent. *The McKinsey Quarterly,* Number 3.

Chambers, E.G., Foulon, M., Handfield-Jones, H., Hankin, S.M., & Michaels, E.G. (1998). The war for talent. *The McKinsey Quarterly,* Number 3, 44–57.

Fitz-enz, J. (1997, August). It's costly to lose good employees. *Workforce, 76* (8), 50–52.

Howard, A., & Bray, D. (1988). *Managerial lives in transition: Advancing age and changing times.* New York: Guilford Press.

Lombardo, M., & Eichinger, R. (2004). *The leadership machine.* Minneapolis: Lominger Limited, Inc.

Ulrich, D., & Lake, D. (1990). *Organizational capability.* New York: Wiley.

INTERVIEWING

58.

How accurate are untrained managers at figuring out what characteristics to interview for—things that will actually predict performance and potential?

SELECT ONE:

☐ A. More right than wrong; over 50%.

☐ B. More wrong than right; less than 50%.

☐ C. About half right.

☐ D. Very accurate for performance and not accurate for potential.

☐ E. Very accurate for the first job, much less accurate for jobs after that.

58

58. **How accurate are untrained managers at figuring out what characteristics to interview for—things that will actually predict performance and potential?**

The correct answer is B: More wrong than right; less than 50%.

How sure are we at this time?

1	2	3	**4**	5
Hint	Suggestive	Trending	**Substantial**	Solid

Discussion

In one study, managers were asked to select 12 factors to be used in the hiring process that they thought would accurately predict performance and potential. They picked 3 that had a positive correlation and 5 with a negative correlation! Gut feel doesn't work in trying to figure out what drives performance—only science does. The best predictors of performance and potential are structured interviews measuring competencies, biodata, assessment centers, and specialized instruments. Informal judgment has little or no support as an accurate predictor. It is too easy for first impressions or other gimmicks used by those being interviewed to trick hiring managers into making false judgments.

Selected Research

- A study by Lawrence et al. (1982), in which managers were asked to predict 12 factors in the hiring process that would accurately predict tenure and performance, found that only 3 of the items the managers picked showed a positive correlation. Four of the factors were shown to have no predictive value at all, and 5 had a negative correlation to tenure and job performance.

- In his research, Clark (2001) found that 17 competencies accounted for 55 percent of the difference between average and high performing sales managers, a difference worth over a million dollars per manager. When current sales managers were asked to identify the key competencies needed for the positions, they chose only 6 of the 17 critical competencies.

- In a study by Adler (2002), 95 percent of hiring managers said they had made bad hiring decisions. He argues that a company would feel it needs to immediately address a flawed process that yields a 5 to 10 percent error rate but balk at spending the money or time on a process that research shows has a 40 to 50 percent error rate. He further noted in evaluating the hiring success of over 1,000 interviews that there was no correlation between interviewing skills and job competency.

- Research by Sachs (1994) found that "getting a good gut feeling" about an applicant is one of the strongest factors used in making hiring decisions and "the least accurate."

- In one study (Camp et al., 2001), even when told candidates may be lying, interviewers did not improve their ability to "detect deception." Additionally, although research shows that interviewers have the ability to detect the differences in personality between candidates, they were found to be unable to match the optimal personality type to the organization's cultural needs. Camp also found that the typical employment interview process provides an inaccurate "prediction of the candidate's ability to do the job."

- In her research, which included examining videotapes of hundreds of interviews, Rosenberg (2000) found that the majority of interviewers were unprepared for the interview, resulting in an inconsistency between candidates in questions asked and a further inability to evaluate the answers because they were busy formulating questions for the candidate. She argues that the purpose of the interview is not to exchange facts; rather, it is to determine if the candidate meets the basic qualifications to do the job.

* Bell (1999) reports that, while most *Fortune 500* companies and government agencies have implemented behavior-based structured interviewing programs for candidates for middle management and below, "in the hiring of their key people—upper management—little has changed. Seat-of-the-pants interviewing still rules, despite the very real danger that the company will find itself in court for discriminatory hiring practices."

* Skinner (2000) reported that "most managers fail to plan interviewing strategies, leaving them without accurate information for making an informed decision about the candidate."

* Another researcher (Bauer, 2000) found poor preparation to be the most common hiring mistake, noting that "most people simply 'wing it' and don't interview enough people each year to be especially good at it."

So what difference do these findings make?

* Asking line managers what to look for in the selection process is not a best practice. You have to actually study what the best performers are doing and contrast that to the worst performers to find the mission critical differentiating characteristics. Leaving it up to each manager to decide would not lead to success.

* It is useful to have managers involved in the hiring process since they will have to work with those who are hired. But, before having them do interviews, they need to be oriented and trained. They should be oriented to the competencies

they are looking for and how to structure an interview to assess those competencies. They should also be trained on how to pose questions and look for signals that the candidate is the best hire.

- It is often helpful to have candidates interviewed by multiple assessors. The insights from one may be different. One firm hiring senior managers set up a scenario where someone clearly in lower power (e.g., seasoned and trusted secretary) did an interview to see how the candidate responded when in a position of authority and power.

Some Key Sources

Adler, L. (2002). *Hire with your head: Using power hiring to build great teams* (2nd ed.). New York: John Wiley & Sons, Inc.

Bauer, B. (2000). The art of hiring smart. *Rough Notes, 143* (5), 16–18.

Bell, A.H. (1999, September). Gut feelings be damned. *Across the Board.* New York.

Camp, R.R., Vielhaber, M.E., & Simonetti, J.L. (2001). *Strategic interviewing: How to hire good people.* San Francisco: Jossey-Bass.

Clark, L. (2001, June). *Show me the money.* Presentation at the Lominger Leadership Architect Conference, Sedona, CA.

Lawrence, D.G., Salsburg, B.L., Dawson, J.G., & Fasman, Z.D. (1982, March). Design and use of weighted application blanks. *Personnel Administrator.*

Rosenberg, D. (2000). *A manager's guide to hiring the best person for every job.* New York: John Wiley & Sons, Inc.

Sachs, R.T. (1994). *How to become a skillful interviewer.* New York: AMACOM.

Skinner, M. (2000). Effective interviews. *Executive Excellence, 17* (11), 13.

SUCCESSION PLANNING

59.

What percent of identified high potentials succeed after they are promoted?

SELECT ONE:

☐ A. The great majority (90%) are still in place five years later and are successful.

☐ B. About 75% continue to be highly successful.

☐ C. About 50% continue to be successful.

☐ D. About 25% continue to be successful.

☐ E. While over 75% stay in their jobs, only 25% could be called successful.

59

59. What percent of identified high potentials succeed after they are promoted?

The correct answer is C: About 50% continue to be successful.

How sure are we at this time?

1	2	3	**4**	5
Hint	Suggestive	Trending	**Substantial**	Solid

Discussion

Historically, 50 percent or so of job placements with high potentials don't work. The reasons for this vary. Sometimes, what made a good employee in one job does not necessarily lead to being a good employee in a more demanding job. The popularized "Peter Principle" suggests that employees will be promoted to their level of incompetence because what they are promoted for does not necessarily mean that is what they will need to do in the new job. In addition, conditions may also change in the new job, and the skills required going into the job may change and not be easy for a new manager to learn.

Selected Research

- DeVries (1992), in a review, estimated that during the previous 10 years the failure rate among senior executives in corporate America had been at least 50 percent. Shipper and Wilson (1991), using data from 101 departments in a large southwestern hospital, reported that the base rate for incompetent management in that organization was 60 percent. Millikin-Davies (1992), using data from a large aerospace organization, estimated a 50 percent failure base rate. She gathered critical incidents of managerial incompetence which she rank-ordered in terms of frequency. The most common complaints from direct reports concerned (a) managers' unwillingness to exercise authority (e.g., "is reluctant to confront problems and conflict"; "is not as self-confident as others"), which characterized 20 percent of the sample of 84 managers; and (b) managers tyrannizing their subordinates (e.g., "manages his/her employees too closely; breathes down their necks"; "treats employees as if they were stupid"), which characterized 16 percent of the sample.

- Studies show that leaders are chronically short on the talent they need to succeed. The outcome of this is shown in a study in which only 15 percent of executive selections came from the succession plan (Bishop, 2000).

- Top executive failure rates are estimated as high as 75 percent and rarely lower than one-third (Sessa & Campbell, 1997).

- A survey of 150 *Fortune 500* companies conducted by Development Dimensions International (DDI), a global leadership assessment firm, noted that the average company expects 33 percent turnover at the executive ranks within the next five years, and fully one-third said they're not confident that they will be able to find suitable replacements (Byham, 2001).

- DDI asked 110 managers and executives to estimate first-year costs of filling an executive vacancy. The average one-year estimated replacement cost is $750,000—which includes finding the new person, training and development costs, and opportunity costs of getting the new hire up to speed" (Byham, 2001).

- McCall and Lombardo (1988) point out that many executives and managers do not always perform at the level of effective experiential learners. In fact, derailment among promising executives is common. "Perhaps 30 to 50 percent of high potential managers and executives derail" (p. 54). The primary cause of derailment among the group of 400 executives that were involved in the study was ineffectively managing the experiential learning cycle.

• Lombardo & Eichinger (2003) studied whether the people who were promoted were really high potentials (were high in learning agility) or not and found no relationship between assessed potential and who was subsequently promoted. After being promoted, those higher in learning agility performed better and did better the tougher the job was. This means that the call on potential was not correct in the first place and that had it been, a higher percentage would have been successful.

So what difference do these findings make?

• If the call on potential is correct to begin with, the success rate would be higher. Organizations need to add a measure of learning agility to their succession planning assessments.

• When starting a new job, managers need to go through an orientation that enables them to learn about the job and its expectations. This orientation has often been called a new manager assimilation where the new manager and employees share expectations and roles so they can build a learning contract. New manager assimilation helps high potentials get started in their new jobs.

• Sometimes high potentials come into new jobs and throw out previous work without sensitivity to the heritage of the business. By so doing, they overchange the organization and may lose credibility. In other cases, they underchange and wait too long to make difficult decisions.

• New managers need coaches who confide in them and give them feedback on the do's and don'ts of their role. New managers sometimes lack such support and thus make unattended mistakes that hurt their success.

Some Key Sources

Bishop, C.H. (2000). *Making change happen one person at a time*. New York: AMACOM.

Byham, W.C. (2001, May 3). Grooming next-millennium leaders. *HR Magazine*.

DeVries, D.L. (1992). Executive selection: Advances but no progress. *Issues & Observations, 12*, 1–5.

Lombardo, M., & Eichinger, R. (2003). *Learning agility as an aspect in promotion*. Minneapolis: Lominger Limited, Inc.

McCall, M.W., Lombardo, M., & Morrison, A. (1988). *The lessons of experience: How successful executives develop on the job*. Lexington, MA: Lexington Books.

Millikin-Davies, M. (1992). *An exploration of flawed first-line supervision*. Unpublished doctoral dissertation, University of Tulsa, Tulsa, OK.

Sessa, V.I., & Campbell, R. (1997). *Selection at the top*. Greensboro, NC: Center for Creative Leadership.

Shipper, F., & Wilson, C.L. (1991, July). *The impact of managerial behaviors on group performance, stress, and commitment*. Paper presented at the Impact of Leadership Conference, Center for Creative Leadership, Colorado Springs, CO.

60.

What is the economic impact on the bottom line of the use of competencies?

SELECT ONE:

☐ A. There is no research-based answer, just anecdotal case studies.

☐ B. The impact, if there is one, would not be traceable; there are too many variables.

☐ C. In the formal studies to date, there has been no demonstration of impact.

☐ D. In the limited research that has been done, some minor amounts of impact have been shown.

☐ E. In multiple research studies, the use of competencies has been justified by a significant return on investment.

60

60. **What is the economic impact on the bottom line of the use of competencies?**

The correct answer is E: In multiple research studies, the use of competencies has been justified by a significant return on investment.

How sure are we at this time?

1	2	3	**4**	5
Hint	Suggestive	Trending	**Substantial**	Solid

Discussion

The economic impact of managerial and employee competencies is one area where most researchers agree. Work on emotional intelligence, leadership development, training and development, selection tools, and succession planning systems all point to the benefit of selecting, developing, and planning for specific competencies.

Of course, to lead to significant return on investment, the competencies need to be derived in a rigorous and systematic way, not just a "wish list" created by a management or HR team. With valid and reliable competencies, decisions can be made to attract, motivate, compensate, and retain the most talented employees.

Selected Research

- Spencer (2001) concludes there is a significant economic value to both emotional intelligence competencies and EIC-based HR programs.

- Lombardo and Eichinger (2002) argue that "in many cases we know what competencies to develop in order to achieve these financial impacts. In one company, high performing managers are better at certain competencies, such as drive for results, perseverance, and basic management skills, such as priority setting and managing and measuring." Their research shows that being better at these competencies is worth $467,000 in commissions and $544,000 in reduced turnover—over a million dollars per manager. Being better at certain competencies explains 54 percent of the difference between superior and average managers for the company's overall measure of growth and profitability.

• According to Russell (2001), at executive levels the numbers can be even more impressive. Russell found that selecting for the right competencies was worth $3 million in profit per executive.

• Results of the McKinsey study (in Axelrod et al., 2001) found that "companies scoring in the top quintile of talent-management practices outperform their industry's mean return to shareholders by a remarkable 22 percentage points." The study also noted that "the best 20 percent or so of managers raise operational productivity, profit, and sales revenue much more than average performers do...." In one manufacturing company, the best plant managers increased profits by 130 percent; in an industrial services firm, the best operations managers achieved increases of 80 percent. (The worst managers in both companies brought no improvement.) The researchers found that paying an additional 40 percent to hire an "A" player could yield an overall return of 100 percent or more in a single year.

• Watson Wyatt's survey of 1,000 senior executives for its 1999 Leadership in the Global Economy study (in Axelrod et al., 2001) cited leadership development as the single most important human resource issue facing their companies. The study also found a statistically significant relationship between leadership development and financial success in four areas: shareholder return, growth in market share, growth in net income, and return on sales.

So what difference do these findings make?

- HR competes with every other function for capital investment funds. HR professionals are more likely to be able to convince customers to adopt programs if they can state the benefits offered by proposed efforts in economic terms. Investment proposals with "business cases" showing compelling ROI projections are more likely to be funded. "Soft" programs and staff lacking economic justification are more likely to be cut. Competencies is one HR investment that should be relatively easy to justify. It requires that HR professionals note the difference in economic results from higher and lower competent employees, then convince management that with a clearly articulated competence model that is used for people decisions, performance will increase.

- Economic results data enhance HR professionals' credibility. HR programs are increasingly emphasized in ISO 9000, JACHO, Deming and Baldridge audits and awards. Most of these assessments are qualitative. Economic value-added data provide much more powerful measures of HR quality. Hard data showing HR interventions that made a meaningful business contribution find their way into management reports and personnel folders and enhance HR staff careers.

- Competency models fail when managers delegate the project to a staff group or consultants, when more time is spent creating the competency model than using it for people decisions, or when competency models focus too much on what skills differentiated high and lower performers in the past versus the future. With careful planning, each of these concerns may be overcome.

Some Key Sources

Axelrod, E.L., Handfield-Jones, H., & Welsh, T.A. (2001). The war for talent: Part two. *The McKinsey Quarterly,* Number 2.

Lombardo, M., & Eichinger, R. (2004). *The leadership machine.* Minneapolis: Lominger Limited, Inc.

Russell, C.J. (2001, August). A longitudinal study of top-level executive performance. *Journal of Applied Psychology, 86* (4), 560–573.

Spencer, L. (2001). The economic value of emotional intelligence competencies and EIC-based HR programs. In D. Goleman & C. Cherniss (Eds.), *The emotionally intelligent workplace: How to select for, measure, and improve emotional intelligence in individuals, groups, and organizations.* San Francisco: Jossey-Bass.

CAREER DEVELOPMENT

61.

What kinds of jobs are likely to matter least for development?

SELECT ONE:

☐ A. Promotion into boss's job.

☐ B. Chair of a key task force.

☐ C. Changing lines of business.

☐ D. Job rotations (3 to 6 month functional assignments).

☐ E. Changing functions.

61. What kinds of jobs are likely to matter least for development?

The correct answer is D: Job rotations (3 to 6 month functional assignments).

How sure are we at this time?

1	2	3	**4**	5
Hint	Suggestive	Trending	**Substantial**	Solid

Discussion

The research on development makes it clear that low variety and low stress lead to low development. Development requires us to be kicked out of our comfort zone, to confront things we're not ready for. Of the jobs listed above, most do not demand much in the way of newness—in ordinary cases, the chance of failure is near zero. In A, you know all the players and most of the problems; in B, you need to learn new content and new people but are likely to be surrounded by experts who won't let anything bad happen; in C, you're doing more or less the same job albeit in another line of business; in D, it's unlikely you would be doing a real job at all—most of these rotations are glorified exposure experiences; and in E, you do meet new people and deal with different issues in a real job. So some of these jobs are somewhat developmental, but compared with the demands of first-time situations—a start-up, first corporate assignment, a fix-it, or a strategic assignment—coupled with unfamiliar people and responsibilities, they pale badly. Typical job rotation programs are the least developmental of the five options.

Selected Research

- In CCL's long-term studies (McCall et al., 1988; Morrison et al., 1987, rev. 1992) the jobs they identified as having the most learning value were "major shifts in challenges—multifunctional projects on pressing organizational issues." On the opposite end of the spectrum were job rotations, which, although they expose a person to various aspects of the business, were rarely cited as having developmental value.

- Many studies conducted around the world have reinforced these initial findings (McCauley et al., 1994; McCauley & Brutus, 1998; Mumford, 2000; Lyness & Thompson, 2000).

- Bray, Campbell, and Grant (1974) argue that "much if not most managerial-leadership development takes place on-the-job rather than in seminars or classrooms and that early leadership experiences are among the key influences on career development."

- Research by Guy (1994) ties gender to a lack of developmental opportunities in organizations. He notes "the glass ceiling concept is extended to include similar problems wherein women and minorities have experienced 'glass walls,' 'sticky floors,' and 'trap doors'—positions and assignments that lack the credibility and skill-building components that aid in development." He notes a danger inherent in the concept: "When nonpromotion and missed developmental opportunities involve individuals who have made valuable contributions to the organization and are expected to continue to do so in the future, the results can greatly, and adversely, affect motivation and productivity."

So what difference do these findings make?

- While the popularity of rotational training programs have waned a bit, they still exist. There are more powerful options. If the goal is to expose people to functional knowledge, targeted training is more effective than job rotations. If the goal is on-the-job knowledge, then training as a student on the job is more effective. If the goal is really to understand the contributions that different functions make, then projects are far and away the most powerful source of how those skills are applied to real-life situations.

* Asking high potential people to do their existing job while serving on a focused task force gives them exposure to new people and tasks, stretches them in their current assignment, and accomplishes the goal of the task force. It is also a better development experience than simple functional rotation where they might not be stretched as much.

Some Key Sources

Bray, D.W., Campbell, R.J., & Grant, D.L. (1974). *Formative years in business: A long-term AT&T study of managerial lives.* New York: Wiley.

Guy, M.E. (1994, Spring). Organizational architecture, gender and women's careers. *Review of Public Personnel Administration, 14* (2), 77–90.

Lyness, K.S., & Thompson, D.E. (2000). Climbing the corporate ladder: Do male and female executives follow the same route? *Journal of Applied Psychology, 85* (1), 86–101.

McCall, M.W., Lombardo, M., & Morrison, A. (1988). *The lessons of experience: How successful executives develop on the job.* Lexington, MA: Lexington Books.

McCauley, C.D., & Brutus, S. (1998). *Management development through job experiences: An annotated bibliography.* Greensboro, NC: Center for Creative Leadership.

McCauley, C.D., Ruderman, M.N., Ohlott, P.J., & Morrow, J.E. (1994). Assessing the developmental components of managerial jobs. *Journal of Applied Psychology, 79,* 544–560.

Morrison, A., White, R., & VanVelsor, E. (1987, rev. 1992). *Breaking the glass ceiling: Can women reach the top of America's largest corporations?* Reading, MA: Addison-Wesley.

Mumford, M.D., Marks, M.A., Connelly, M.S., Zaccaro, S.J., & Reiter-Palmon, R. (2000). Development of leadership skills: Experience and timing. *The Leadership Quarterly, 11* (1), 87–114.

DERAILMENT

62.

What most often gets managers and executives terminated?

SELECT ONE:

☐ A. Poor performance.

☐ B. Poor future prospects.

☐ C. Poor self-knowledge and relationships.

☐ D. Poor technical job skills.

☐ E. Poor track record overall.

62. What most often gets managers and executives terminated?

The correct answer is C: Poor self-knowledge and relationships.

How sure are we at this time?

1	2	3	**4**	5
Hint	Suggestive	Trending	**Substantial**	Solid

Discussion

In studies of success and derailment, failure to learn to do something differently in order to make key transitions has figured prominently in the results. Additionally, lack of self-awareness and a tendency to overrate oneself leading to poor relationships have been found to be crippling. Lack of learning may also come from a tendency to blame when things go wrong rather than to look for alternatives. Successful people learned more new behavior and were more self-aware. They kept their skills fresh. The other reasons above are more likely to weed out people early in a career or people who may have skills suited to some other organization or line of work.

Selected Research

- According to long-term research by Lombardo and Eichinger (2002), getting fired is more the flip side of promotion than performance. They report that people may excel at most of the competencies that are important to performance, yet still get fired. The authors noted that, when they looked at terminations, they found many competencies where being better at them did not get people promoted, but being worse at them got them fired. "What happens is that people run out of people to work with, wreck relationships, and destroy trust, and this inevitably erodes their ability to perform. While few sheer relationship skills ordinarily relate to performance, they play heavily in who gets ahead, who gets left behind, and who gets shown the door."

- An additional finding in studies by Lombardo and Eichinger (2003) is that, in a 360 evaluation, the higher the self-rating compared with the ratings of others, the more likely a person is to be fired. They tended to rate their interpersonal skills the highest, compared to how others rated them.

- On 360 degree competency assessments, average performers typically overestimate their strengths, whereas star performers rarely do; if anything, the stars tended to underestimate their abilities, an indicator of high internal standards (Goleman, 1998).

- Accurate self-assessment was the competency found in virtually every "star performer" in a study of several hundred knowledge workers—computer scientists, auditors, and the like—at companies such as AT&T and 3M. Since high potentials are the most self-aware, reviewing consistency between self and others' ratings would be helpful in identification of high potentials (Kelley, 1998).

- Among several hundred managers from 12 different organizations, accurate self-assessment was the hallmark of superior performance (Boyatzis, 1982). Individuals with the accurate self-assessment competency are aware of their abilities and limitations, seek out feedback and learn from their mistakes, and know where they need to improve and when to work with others who have complementary strengths (Boyatzis). Again, since there is usually a large gap between how individuals see themselves and how others see them, the view of what's needed in terms of development is going to be different.

- Lombardo and Eichinger (1989) report that "the most visible group of derailers are those high in independence and low in affiliation needs who tend to be bright, technically proficient problem solvers with poor team-building skills."

- Research by Lombardo and McCauley (1988) found that factors for derailment are clustered into six flaws: problems with interpersonal relationships; difficulty molding a staff; difficulty making strategic transitions; lack of follow-through; overdependence on a mentor or boss; and strategic differences with management. They concluded that interpersonal flaws "are more likely to affect a person's ability to handle jobs requiring persuasion or the development of new relationships."

- According to Shipper and Dillard (2000) who conducted an analysis of the performance of more than 1,000 middle managers at a national high-tech firm, "managers who overestimate their own abilities are often ineffective and fail to learn from management development programs." They further said that, no matter what the industry, managers most likely to derail are usually those who have too high an opinion of their own skills and abilities compared to managers who underestimate their abilities. They note that "those rating themselves high often demonstrate traits such as lack of self-awareness and arrogance, usually associated with ineffective management."

- Lombardo and Eichinger (2002) report that, when people get terminated, it's usually for one of three reasons: They have poor work relationships; they can't get the work out; or they are nonstrategic.

- McCall and Lombardo (1983) in a study of what derails previously successful people stated that "the most frequent cause for derailment was insensitivity to others." Other reasons included being arrogant, betrayal of trust, and overmanaging.

So what difference do these findings make?

- Early in one's career, a high potential should be exposed to the derailment research.

- High potentials should be assigned coaches or mentors who systematically give them feedback not tied to hierarchical position. This enables the high potential to hear about possible problems before they become a part of a formal evaluation.

- After a reasonable time in a new job (2 to 4 months), the new manager should have a review to learn what is working and what is not. This review would ideally include some anonymous 360 feedback from boss, peers, and employees. This data may help the new manager understand strengths and weaknesses for going forward.

Some Key Sources

Boyatzis, R. (1982). *The competent manager: A model for effective performance.* New York: John Wiley and Sons, Inc.

Goleman, D. (1998, November/December). What makes a leader? *Harvard Business Review.*

Kelley, R. (1998). *How to be a star at work.* New York: Times Books.

Lombardo, M., & Eichinger, R. (1989). *Preventing derailment: Why rising stars fail and how to avoid it.* Greensboro, NC: Center for Creative Leadership.

Lombardo, M., & Eichinger, R. (2004). *The leadership machine.* Minneapolis: Lominger Limited, Inc.

Lombardo, M., & Eichinger, R. (2003). *The LEADERSHIP ARCHITECT® norms and validity report.* Minneapolis: Lominger Limited, Inc.

Lombardo, M., & McCauley, C. (1988). *The dynamics of management derailment.* Greensboro, NC: Center for Creative Leadership.

McCall, M.W., & Lombardo, M. (1983). *Off the track: Why and how successful executives get derailed* (Technical Report No. 21). Greensboro, NC: Center of Creative Leadership.

Shipper, F., & Dillard, J. (2000). A study of impending derailment and recovery of middle managers across career stages. *Human Resource Management, 39* (4), 331–347.

RECRUITING AND HIRING

How often do external job applicants misrepresent their background, education, and job experience on resumes?

SELECT ONE:

☐ A. Less than 5% of the time.

☐ B. About 10% of the time.

☐ C. One out of four or 25% of the time.

☐ D. About one out of three or 33% of the time.

☐ E. More than half or 50% of the time.

63. **How often do external job applicants misrepresent their background, education, and job experience on resumes?**

   The correct answer is D: About one out of three or 33% of the time.

How sure are we at this time?

1	2	**3**	4	5
Hint	Suggestive	**Trending**	Substantial	Solid

Discussion

According to a nationally recognized reference checking firm, one in twelve applicants will report a bogus degree and, among sales candidates, about one in eight is guilty of claiming a degree not earned. And, things might be getting worse: The amount of misrepresentation reported by reliable surveys shows that the problem has been rising steadily over the past 20 years. Depending on who's doing the checking (*WSJ, Review of Business, Managing Office Technology*) the misrepresentation is anywhere from 20 to 64 percent.

All in, it looks to be about one of three candidates misreport or exaggerate something about their background.

Selected Research

- A survey of 7,000 executive resumes by Christian & Timbers (2001), a global executive recruitment firm, revealed that 23 percent of executives misrepresented their accomplishments. More specifically, they misrepresented the number of years they spent in a job 71 percent of the time, exaggerated accomplishments 64 percent of the time, indicated a partial degree as a full degree 48 percent of the time, and exaggerated jobs 44 percent of the time.

- According to Andler (1998), misrepresentation has doubled in the past 20 years or so. He reports "in 1997 misrepresentation was reported to be about 36 percent, which is the same result shown in a 1991 survey; in 1981 it was about 23 percent; and in 1979 it was only 17 percent."

- In *The Complete Reference Checking Handbook* (1998), Andler reports the following examples of misrepresentation: *The Wall Street Journal* said "34 percent of all application forms contain outright lies about experience, education, and the ability to perform essential functions on the job." *Review of Business* said that "one in four resumes contain false information pertaining to educational credentials, skill levels, or past experience." College and university registrars report that at least 60 percent of the verifications they receive contain falsified information (Testimony to House Select Committee, 1985). *Managing Office Technology* said 20 to 25 percent of all resumes and applications contain at least one major fabrication. *Small Business Reports* said "employees at all levels falsify their backgrounds. Twelve percent of job applicants inflate or falsify his/her education qualifications" (Andler, 1998).

- A 1998 reference checking survey of 854 HR professionals by the Society for Human Resource Management (SHRM) reports that "about one in five organizations refuses to give references at all, mainly because of liability concerns, and that 35 states have enacted laws that shield employers from civil liability when giving good-faith references" (Elizabeth Owens, state legislative affairs coordinator at the Society for Human Resource Management in Alexandria, VA; Hirschman, 2000).

So what difference do these findings make?

- Verify essential information. Don't take it at face value. Several coaching assignments have involved falsified educational background. Several CEOs of *Fortune 500* companies have claimed degrees they did not possess. It is not hard to verify the factual information (e.g., degrees, jobs held). It is also helpful to be networked with professionals in other firms who can give insight into the potential job candidate.

• The legal difference (Hirschman). Getting and giving references has always been a fine line, but now, with the possible legal ramifications (negligent hiring and providing negligent or incomplete references to other companies), companies have to check out employees more thoroughly. Some companies are hesitant to give out much information other than basic facts (e.g., the candidate worked here from date A to date B). Getting beneath the facts comes from relationships with colleagues in the candidate's previous firm, checking about specific projects the candidate claimed to have done, and seeing any inconsistencies in the resume. If a candidate misrepresents information on a resume, it is a good indicator of future integrity concerns.

• The cost difference (Andler, Hirschman, SHRM). Making a bad choice costs the company in actual costs (lost sales, production, training and overhead), in peripheral costs (morale, culture, team building, succession impact), and in PR costs (company position in the marketplace because of negative PR). Many put the cost of a hiring error (assuming no litigation) at two to three times salary. It is worth the time to be sure before hiring someone.

• Start with education (SHRM). As a result of their research, SHRM recommends starting reference checking with education. "With few exceptions, you can verify school attendance and degrees attained over the phone. It usually takes from four to eight minutes." They recommend calling your own school to see how easy it is to get this information and caution, "If you find a discrepancy, you may not want to go any further." They report that

15 percent of job candidates they check out do not get hired because of the information they uncover.

- It is kind to the candidate to tell them that you uncovered discrepancies in their information when they are not hired. Allowing lies to continue hurts the overall hiring process.

Some Key Sources

Andler, E.C. (1998). *The complete reference checking handbook.* New York: AMACOM.

Christian & Timbers. (2001, September 27). *Survey shows executive resumes misrepresent accomplishments 23% of the time.* Retrieved from Christian & Timbers Web site October 29, 2003. http://www.ctnet.com/pr/releaseDetails.asp?prid=92

Hirschman, C. (2000, June). The whole truth: How to get the real story when checking applicants' references. *HR Magazine,* 87–92.

MEASUREMENT

64.

Who is generally the best source of accurate feedback about performance, potential, strengths, weaknesses, and areas for development?

SELECT ONE:

☐ A. The person (self); he/she is in the best position to know.

☐ B. Boss.

☐ C. Direct reports.

☐ D. In-group peers; they work the most with the person.

☐ E. Customers.

64. **Who is generally the best source of accurate feedback about performance, potential, strengths, weaknesses, and areas for development?**

    The correct answer is B: Boss.

How sure are we at this time?

1	2	3	**4**	5
Hint	Suggestive	Trending	**Substantial**	Solid

Discussion

Different groups have different patterns of competency ratings. It is normal for them not to see a person the same—they see the same behaviors and interpret them differently, sometimes see different behaviors, or simply look to different behaviors as important. Boss may be most concerned about work objectives (and treatment of direct reports if the person rated is a manager), while peers may be most interested in negotiation skills, and subordinates in delegation and listening. Also, some sources are more accurate for some competencies than others. Delegation may be most accurately assessed by direct reports, strategy by bosses, and negotiating by peers. Overall, the one source which is the most accurate is the boss and the least accurate is the person (self), especially when it comes to helping a person get ready for increased responsibility.

Self is generally the worst judge of performance and potential. Self-ratings on competencies are often unrelated to job success (actual performance). Whether a person rates himself or herself high or low is unrelated to performance dimensions. On the other hand, the ratings of all the other sources generally show significant relationships with actual performance. Self-ratings are most accurate on strengths, less accurate on weaknesses, and least accurate on interpersonal skills and the impressions we leave on people (EQ). Most of the skills missing in managers and executives were those very same skills about which self-raters are least accurate (Lombardo & Eichinger, 2003).

In the reported studies, boss ratings were most accurate and have been related to assessment center ratings and long-term performance and promotion. It is often useful to map out how different stakeholders perceive the individual. Some employees are particularly good at "managing up" and might get a more positive response from their boss than peers and subordinates; others might be just the opposite. The 360 is a valued and valid way to provide employees feedback and to give managers a complete picture of employee performance.

Selected Research

- Lombardo and Eichinger (2003) found that boss was by far the best rater in a predictive study of long-term performance and promotion. Competency ratings from bosses on 59 of the 67 competencies used in the research predicted long-term performance, for example. Peers and direct reports added some value; customers and self did not.

- Lombardo and Eichinger (2003b) also found that people with higher scores on learning agility performed better once promoted. This finding was accounted for by boss ratings. The authors report a correlation of .45 between boss ratings and independent measures of performance. The correlation of other raters (mostly peers) with performance was -.02.

- Atkins and Wood (2002) reported that bosses were the best predictors of assessment center ratings. They were also better able to see through those who overestimate themselves in self-ratings.

- Kaplan and Kaiser (2003) found that boss ratings of versatility had the highest validity (relationship to effectiveness ratings).

- Antonioni and Park (2001) found that liking the person being rated affected leniency (giving higher ratings) for direct reports and peers more than for superiors.

- Conway and Huffcutt (1997), in their meta-analytic study, found that various feedback sources provide unique information. They found that "the average correlation between two supervisors is only .50, between two peers .37, and between two subordinates .30; between supervisors and peers .34; between supervisors and subordinates and supervisors and self .22; and between peers and self .19." The researchers conclude that this low agreement *between* sources needs to be analyzed the same way low agreement *within* sources is analyzed, noting that "if two supervisors can't agree, why would we expect a supervisor and a subordinate to agree?"

- In their research, Mount et al. (1998) collected ratings from bosses, peers, and subordinates, as well as self-ratings, and concluded that each of these sources provided "partially unique information." They itemize the value of each group's input, noting that supervisors are typically familiar with the job and provide the kind of feedback that can aid in development; peers and colleagues are likely to observe a high proportion of the employee performance, but "they may not be motivated to provide accurate assessments"; and direct reports provide a valuable perspective on managerial performance, but this may be limited to interactions that involve the supervisor. The same scenario may be true for information from customers and suppliers. They conclude by noting: "In a large-scale study of different rating sources, the researchers found that each rater's rating (self-ratings, two bosses, two peers, two subordinates) were different enough from each other to constitute a separate method. The implication for 360 degree feedback reports is that the information should be displayed separately for each individual rater. This would allow the ratee to examine patterns of each rater's ratings across the skills."

- Atwater et al. (1998) found that when "self- and other ratings are in agreement and high, effectiveness is high. Effectiveness decreases as self- and other ratings agree and become lower. In addition, effectiveness tends to be lower when self-ratings are greater than other ratings." Effectiveness was higher when self-ratings were lower than other ratings as well.

- Tornow (1993) suggests that there are benefits to having inter-rater variance in ratings. He argues that, for practical applications, "differences in ratings are not error variance, but meaningful differences in perspective that may enhance personal learning." He suggests that rating differences are valuable for development but need to be investigated if the 360 feedback is being used for administrative purposes (i.e., raises).

- Meta-analytic studies by Harris & Schaubroeck (1988) reveal that self-ratings have higher means than peer and supervisor ratings.

- Lanyon and Goodstein (1997) note that, because "self-report responses are a product of psychological, sociological, linguistic, experiential, and contextual variables, which may have little to do with the construct of interest," other evaluation methods are needed to get a true picture.

- Research by Walker and Smither (1999) suggests that upward feedback does improve performance. They note, however, that the effectiveness of upward feedback seems to depend on who is being appraised. In their study of 252 bank managers over a five-year period, they found that "poorly or moderately performing managers increased their performance over the five-year period following upward feedback." Another study (Johnson & Ferstl, 1999), found that "performance improvement depends on the manager's self-ratings: Managers whose subordinate ratings were lower than their self-ratings improved performance following upward feedback, whereas managers whose subordinate ratings were higher than their self-ratings decreased their performance."

So what difference do these findings make?

- Beauty is in the eye of the beholder and different rater groups have different perspectives and might be accurate on different issues. Also, some employees are predisposed to managing up, down, or sideways better than others.

- While other groups have valuable insights, the best judge of performance, potential, and promotion is the boss. In 360 feedback sessions, particular attention should be given to boss evaluations on competencies as they are most likely to be accurate. A 360 lacking a boss's input will not be very helpful; make sure the boss has filled out the form.

- It is important to train all raters. It is especially critical to train bosses.

- Self-assessment alone doesn't work.

Some Key Sources

Antonioni, D., & Park, H. (2001). The relationship between rater affect and three sources of 360 feedback ratings. *Journal of Management, 27* (4), 479–495.

Atkins, P.W., & Wood, R.E. (2002). Self versus other ratings as predictors of assessment center ratings. *Personnel Psychology, 55,* 871–904.

Atwater, L.E., Ostroff, C., Yammarino, F.J., & Fleenor, J.W. (1998). Self-other rating agreement: Does it really matter? *Personnel Psychology, 51,* 576–597.

Conway, J.M., & Huffcutt, A.I. (1997). Psychometric properties of multisource performance ratings: A meta-analysis of subordinate, supervisor, peer, and self ratings. *Human Performance, 10,* 331–360.

Harris, M.M., & Schaubroeck, J. (1988). A meta analysis of self-boss, self-peer, and peer-boss ratings. *Personnel Psychology, 41,* 43–62.

Johnson, J.W., & Ferstl, K.L. (1999). The effects of interrater and self-other agreement on performance improvement following upward feedback. *Personnel Psychology, 52* (2), 271–303.

Kaplan, R.E., & Kaiser, R.B. (2003). Rethinking a classic distinction in leadership: Implications for the assessment and development of executives. *Consulting Psychology Journal: Research and Practice, 55,* 15–25.

Lanyon, R.I., & Goodstein, L.D. (1997). *Personality assessment* (3rd ed.). New York: Wiley.

Lombardo, M., & Eichinger, R. (2003). *The LEADERSHIP ARCHITECT® norms and validity report.* Minneapolis: Lominger Limited, Inc.

Lombardo, M., & Eichinger, R. (2003b). *Learning agility as an aspect in promotion.* Minneapolis: Lominger Limited, Inc.

Mount, M.K., Judge, T.A., Scullen, T.E., Sytsma, M.R., & Hezlett, S.A. (1998). Trait, rater and level effects in 360 degree performance ratings. *Personnel Psychology, 51,* 557–576.

Tornow, W.W. (1993). Editor's note: Introduction to special issue on 360 degree feedback. *Human Resource Management, 32,* 211–219.

Walker, A.G., & Smither, J.W. (1999). A five-year study of upward feedback: What managers do with their results matters. *Personnel Psychology, 52* (2), 393–423.

DIVERSITY

65.

What is the current level of discrimination, prejudice, and stereotyping in the workplace?

SELECT ONE:

☐ A. As bad as ever, nothing has changed.

☐ B. Still around and having some influence on decisions.

☐ C. About gone.

☐ D. Minorities and women are actually at a slight advantage because organizations are stamping out discrimination, etc.

☐ E. Minorities and women are actually at a great advantage because organizations are stamping out discrimination, etc.

65

65. What is the current level of discrimination, prejudice, and stereotyping in the workplace?

The correct answer is B: Still around and having some influence on decisions.

How sure are we at this time?

1	2	3	**4**	5
Hint	Suggestive	Trending	**Substantial**	Solid

Discussion

Stereotyping and prejudice are real. Education can help. Overt prejudice is rare these days, as it should be. Minorities and women are advancing, albeit slowly. Yet it does exist. From the individual's perspective, stereotyping by gender or race means they miss out on career development opportunities. From the organization's perspective, they miss out because many of the passed over might have been valued contributors later. There are also prejudices for religion, weight, schools attended, family connections, political beliefs, region where raised, attractiveness, sexual preferences, country of national origin, etc. Learning to face and overcome each of these stereotypes is important in forming cohesive groups and a strong organizational culture.

In fact, it is important that companies encourage differences so that decisions take into account multiple points of view. For example, having sensitivity to Muslim, Jewish, and Christian worship and holidays is important for companies to fully leverage employee strengths.

Selected Research

- Research by Hakel (1992) concludes that "until that [executive] suite itself becomes more diverse (in such areas as demography, career histories, and functional areas of expertise), the leadership at lower ranks in the organization is likely to move at only a glacial pace towards diversity." Concerted effort to expand diversity at the executive level will probably only happen when executives themselves have some kind of powerful personal experiences with diversity.

- Eagly et al. (1995) reports no overall difference in male/female skill levels but notes that men do better in stereotypically masculine jobs and vice versa.

- According to Morrison et al. (1992), "prejudice and stereotyping cut both ways, against one's own group as well as for that group." In one study, identical resumes were sent with different photographs. Executives selected the women for administrative tasks, the men for line assignments. When the experiment was repeated with minority women, the results were identical! They also picked the men for the line assignments. In another study, female recruiters saw male applicants as more similar to them and more qualified than female applicants (Graves & Powell, 1995). The researchers argue that "this belief that senior executives have that women are less committed to their careers and less likely to show initiative or take risks than their male counterparts creates problems for women in terms of breadth of job experiences, with executives often less willing to take risks in giving them executive roles with significant responsibility and challenges."

- Catalyst research (1990) showed that senior executives still strongly believe that women are less committed to their careers and less likely to show initiative or take risks than their male counterparts.

So what difference do these findings make?

- Stereotyping and prejudice are real. Education can help. Prejudice and stereotyping are more complex than the old saying "Birds of a feather flock together." As we've seen, expectations can lead same group members to be biased against their own ethnic or racial group as well. Some biases are conscious, but many of them appear to be unconscious as well. When the unconscious is made conscious it is more likely to begin to change. This means that leaders should both reveal and talk about their personal prejudices, how they have overcome them, and encourage dialogue around how similar work can be done in the organization.

- Success has been reported in diversity courses where conscious and unconscious prejudices are exposed and explored. At their root is what we discussed earlier, differing expectations. Such courses backfire, however, when they become exercises in blame and bashing. To work, no one should be bashed. Everyone should face whatever conscious and unconscious prejudices they may have, including prejudices against their own nominal group.

- Often, prejudice comes from a lack of understanding. Asking people who are different to work together is one of the best ways to break down prejudices. After working on a business project with people who are different, it is helpful to process the experience with a question like, "What did you learn from working with people who are different from you?" Generally, people will respond with observations and insights that are positive and help overcome stereotypes.

Some Key Sources

Catalyst. (1990). *Women in corporate management: Results of a Catalyst survey* (Research Report No. 25). New York: Catalyst.

Eagly, A., Karau, S.J., & Makhijani, M.G. (1995). Gender and the effectiveness of leaders: A meta-analysis. *Psychological Bulletin, 117* (1), 125–145.

Graves, L.M., & Powell, G.N. (1995). The effect of sex similarity on recruiters' evaluations of actual applicants: A test of the similarity-attraction paradigm. *Personnel Psychology, 48,* 85–98.

Hakel, M.D. (1992, November). *Meta view, too.* Paper presented at the Executive Selection Conference, Center for Creative Leadership, Greensboro, NC.

Morrison, A., White, R., & VanVelsor, E. (1987, rev. 1992). *Breaking the glass ceiling: Can women reach the top of America's largest corporations?* Reading, MA: Addison-Wesley.

PERFORMANCE APPRAISAL

66.

How accurate are the ratings on formal performance appraisal evaluations?

SELECT ONE:

☐ A. People get higher ratings than they really deserve; ratings are generally inflated.

☐ B. Higher performers get inflated ratings but lower performers get accurate ratings.

☐ C. Higher performers get accurate ratings but the ratings of lower performers are inflated.

☐ D. Everyone gets accurate ratings in general.

☐ E. People get lower ratings than they really deserve.

66

66. How accurate are the ratings on formal performance appraisal evaluations?

The correct answer is A: People get higher ratings than they really deserve; ratings are generally inflated.

How sure are we at this time?

1	2	3	4	**5**
Hint	Suggestive	Trending	Substantial	**Solid**

Discussion

Most informal studies show that 85 to 95 percent are rated at or above average in formal performance appraisal processes. So as a practical rule, you can't depend on formal appraisals alone. They are probably as much as .75 higher on a five-point scale than the raters would admit to under truth serum, and there will be less negative (less helpful) information than the raters actually think.

Because bosses aren't good at giving critical feedback, they inflate their ratings and hold back negative opinions. And, because formal performance appraisal is many times tied to pay, that further complicates its accuracy. In the heyday of TQM, Edward Deming pronounced that performance appraisal was a failed system and should be dropped, primarily because it rarely differentiates levels of performance.

Selected Research

- According to research by London and Smither (1995), raters say they would change (mostly increase) the scores they gave if they thought the feedback results were to be used for administrative purposes (pay, promotion, etc.). Not surprisingly, inflated performance appraisals often provide discharged employees with an incentive to sue. ("When an employee with an inflated appraisal heads into court, an employer's claim that performance was woefully inadequate will be inconsistent with the prior appraisal.")

- In a study of 58,000 performance appraisals, scores went up significantly in public appraisal processes (Jawahar & Williams, 1997).

- Tornow et al.'s (1998) research revealed that, where trust is not high or feedback is new [to the organization], the display of individual rater responses, even when disguised by codes, might be detrimental to the goal of getting honest results. They give them a false sense of security and deprive them of the opportunity to improve. "Many management gurus advocate that coaching about performance for the purpose of improving performance is best separated in place and time from any performance appraisal discussions tied to salary decisions (where the manager has to play judge)."

- Murphy and Cleveland (1991) noted that the evaluation of a manager's performance depends, in part, on the relationships that the person has established with his or her subordinates.

- Bernardin and Klatt (1985) found that managers who were involved in multi-rater appraisal systems received significantly higher mean effectiveness ratings than those who received no subordinate feedback.

So what difference do these findings make?

- Organizations need to be cautious in taking performance evaluation ratings as is. In the same sense as discounted cash flow, performance ratings need to be discounted. Some organizations get more rating inflation than others. Probably the order of performance ratings, from highest (but inflated) rating to lowest (still inflated) is a better way to deal with the metrics of performance evaluation. In this way, people can focus on what they do best and where they most need to improve short-term performance.

Some Key Sources

Bernardin, H.J., & Klatt, L.A. (1985). Managerial appraisal systems: Has practice caught up to the state of the art? *Personnel Administrator, 30,* 79–86.

Jawahar, I.M., & Williams, C.R. (1997). Where all the children are above average: The performance appraisal purpose effect. *Personnel Psychology, 50* (4), 905–925.

London, M., & Smither, J.W. (1995). Can multisource feedback change self-evaluations, skill development, and performance? Theory-based applications and directions for research. *Personnel Psychology, 48,* 803–839.

Murphy, K.R., & Cleveland, J.N. (1991). *Performance appraisal.* Boston: Allyn & Bacon.

Tornow, W.W., London, M., & the Center for Creative Leadership Associates. (1998). *Maximizing the value of 360 degree feedback.* San Francisco: Jossey-Bass.

CAREER DEVELOPMENT— INTERNATIONAL

67.

To be a successful expatriate manager, what does research show is the best way of learning about a culture other than your own?

SELECT ONE:

☐ A. Living there leads to four times the lessons than traveling to, studying remotely and managing a business in that culture.

☐ B. You can learn just as much by managing a business remotely in a culture not your own than actually living there, as long as you travel there frequently (more than 10 times) and work with in-culture people.

☐ C. Being there is twice as powerful a teacher than managing remotely and traveling to.

☐ D. If you already know one culture other than your own, there is no difference.

☐ E. Learning about a culture remotely is actually superior because being part of it might bias you. It's easier to understand the forest if you are not in it.

67. **To be a successful expatriate manager, what does research show is the best way of learning about a culture other than your own?**

   The correct answer is A: Living there leads to four times the lessons than traveling to, studying remotely and managing a business in that culture.

How sure are we at this time?

1	2	**3**	4	5
Hint	Suggestive	**Trending**	Substantial	Solid

Discussion

There is no substitute for being there. Research by McCall and Hollenbeck showed that the difference in reported lessons was about 4 to 1. They also found that global companies are in the best position to develop global executives because they can more easily put people into a variety of countries and cultures.

While it is nearly impossible for everyone in a company to live in another country, some companies have made it a high priority that high potentials have at least one significant assignment in a country not their own. If these global assignments occur early in a career, they shape thinking later on. One company has mandated that to be an officer, the executive needs to have worked for a significant time (generally two to three years) in a non-home country.

Selected Research

- Basing his book *High Flyers* (1998) on the premise that "what people learn is driven by the kinds of things they have to contend with in that particular experience," McCall found that specific experiences have significantly more development potential. Describing the first of the four developmental categories he identified (job assignments), he notes that expatriate job assignments include all the core elements of powerful developmental experiences— unfamiliar responsibilities, high stakes, and external pressures inherent with working in a foreign culture.

- McCall and Hollenbeck (2002) in *Developing Global Executives*, argue that the cultural context has a significant impact on the way business is done. Their findings show that, while "many business lessons could be learned without expatriation, most cultural adaptability lessons cannot." Findings from their multiyear study, in which they interviewed 101 expatriates from 16 international firms in 34 cities, reveal that 54 percent of the "lessons learned" came from expatriate experiences versus 22 percent from those with international (not living there) responsibilities, and 24 percent from domestic experiences. Results were similar for business lessons learned—with 44 percent expatriate learnings, 29 percent international, and 27 percent domestic. Lessons of culture were predominantly expatriate (76 percent) versus international (19 percent). Being there was four times more powerful.

- In his book, Goldsmith (2003) defines five emerging characteristics of global leaders: the ability to think globally; an appreciation for diverse cultures; a willingness to develop technologically; the ability and desire to build partnerships and alliances; and the business, personal, and social skills to share leadership. Most notably, he argues, is the need for leaders to "see themselves as citizens of the world with an expanded field of vision and values." An appreciation for cultures other than your own drives one-fourth of success as a global leader.

So what difference do these findings make?

- If your current and future business depends upon having high performing global executives, expatriate assignments seem to be your best (and possibly your only) bet.

- Some companies, like Unilever, Siemon, Nestle, and Phillips have created a career track that they call "glopats." These employees decide early in their careers to be global expatriates. They spend two to five years in a country, then move to another country. They never "take an expat assignment, then return home" but live their careers in different settings around the world. These individuals often have unique rewards (e.g., schooling for children) and career tracks. Having glopats is a good idea for large global companies. It is a source of executive talent. It sets clear expectations early in a career. It allows the organization to embed truly global thinking.

Some Key Sources

Goldsmith, M., Bennis, W.G., & O'Neil, J. (2003). *Global leadership: The next generation.* London: Financial Times Prentice Hall.

McCall, M.W. (1998). *High flyers: Developing the next generation of leaders.* Boston: Harvard Business School Press.

McCall, M.W., & Hollenbeck, G.P. (2002). *Developing global executives: The lessons of international experience.* Boston: Harvard Business School Press.

DIVERSITY

68.

When people in protected classes are asked whether their group or themselves are more discriminated against, they . . .?

SELECT ONE:

☐ A. Reply that they are discriminated against more personally than other members of their group. They always personalize their own experience more directly.

☐ B. Respond that people in their group are more discriminated against than they are personally.

☐ C. Respond that there is no difference; both they and members of their group are equally discriminated against.

☐ D. Respond that each group is different; some say it one way and others the reverse.

68

☐ E. Say that their group is more discriminated against than other protected groups.

68. When people in protected classes are asked whether their group or themselves are more discriminated against, they . . .?

The correct answer is B: Respond that people in their group are more discriminated against than they are personally.

How sure are we at this time?

1	2	**3**	4	5
Hint	Suggestive	**Trending**	Substantial	Solid

Discussion

A long line of studies all show that, in general, members of a protected class see themselves as less discriminated against than other members of the same group. The phenomenon has been labeled by some as P/GDD (personal/group discrimination discrepancy) or denial in general.

This phenomenon is the same as "I love my congressman, but hate congress." It shows that stereotypes are often overcome by personal connection and relationships.

Selected Research

- Literature in social psychology has shown that historically disadvantaged groups recognize discrimination against their group but tend not to see themselves as personally disadvantaged (Crosby, 1984).

- Taylor, Wright, Moghaddam, and Lalonde (1990) found that members of disadvantaged groups recognized some personal disadvantage, although they had "imperfect awareness of their own disadvantage."

- A laboratory study by Operario and Fiske (2001) showed that Black students are more likely than White students to voice that they are subjects of discrimination, but at the same time, felt they were less disadvantaged than other members of their group.

- This proclivity to believe they are "less discriminated against than others in their reference group" supports the research that reveals that people think differently about events in their own life than they do about events in the lives of others (Norenzayan & Nisbett, 2000).

- Robinson and Ryff (1999) found this same tendency—people imagine that justice exists in their own worlds more than the world at large. They believe this to be part of an overall tendency for people to see themselves—and their situations—in a more positive, if less realistic, light.

So what difference do these findings make?

- Most people want to think that their situation is more positive than it might really be. There is also a reluctance to report negative experiences for fear of reprisals. There is also a hesitance to start a legal action for fear of reprisals and a lack of resources.

- Personal reality may have to be gently coaxed out of reluctant people to realize what's happening to them and to be an active part of the solution.

- Also, members of a protected class think others are in worse shape than they might actually be, so some reality coaching might be called for.

- When collecting data about diversity or possible discrimination, ask questions about the group rather than individual experiences.

Some Key Sources

Crosby, F.J. (1984). The denial of personal discrimination. *American Behavioral Scientist, 27,* 371–386.

Norenzayan, A., & Nisbett, R.E. (2000). Culture and causal cognition. *Current Directions, 9,* 132–135.

Operario, D., & Fiske, S.T. (2001). Ethnic identity moderates perceptions of prejudice: Judgments of personal versus group discrimination and subtle versus blatant bias. *Personality and Social Psychology Bulletin, 27,* 550–561.

Robinson, M.D., & Ryff, C.D. (1999). The role of self-deception in perceptions of past, present, and future happiness. *Personality and Social Psychology Bulletin, 25,* 595–606.

Taylor, D.M., Wright, S.C., Moghaddam, F.M., & Lalonde, R.N. (1990). The personal/group discrimination discrepancy: Perceiving my group, but not myself to be a target of discrimination. *Personality and Social Psychology Bulletin, 16,* 254–262.

DEVELOPMENT

69.

What is the order of influence on how a person ends up as an adult?

SELECT ONE:

☐ A. Biological makeup, peers, parents.

☐ B. Peers, parents, biological makeup.

☐ C. Parents, peers, biological makeup.

☐ D. Parents, biological makeup, peers.

☐ E. Biological makeup, parents, peers.

69

69. **What is the order of influence on how a person ends up as an adult?**

The correct answer is A: Biological makeup, peers, parents.

How sure are we at this time?

1	**2**	3	4	5
Hint	**Suggestive**	Trending	Substantial	Solid

Discussion

Since we know from the Twins studies that nature makes up at least 50 percent and maybe more, the order of answer A (biological makeup, peers, parents) is correct but at a low-level rating since this is the first treatment of the topic showing that peers have more influence than parents.

Behavioral geneticists studying adoptees and twins say that the effects of heredity can be gauged by measuring the degree to which people who share genes are more similar than people who do not share genes. Study results show that heredity accounts for roughly 50 percent of the variation in the samples of people tested, environmental influences for the other 50 percent.

Note: The fifty-fifty result (50 percent heredity, 50 percent environment) that behavior geneticists obtained doesn't mean that half of the correlation between parents and children is due to genes and the other half is due to environmental influences. The fifty-fifty result means only that 50 percent of the differences among the children, in some particular characteristic such as cordiality, can be traced to differences in their genes.

What about shared home experiences? To what extent do they contribute to the similarities and differences in siblings growing up in the same environment? Surprisingly, numerous studies of twins, and both biological and adopted siblings, have shown that shared home experiences have a minimal effect in shaping the personalities of children. The similarity in siblings reared together appears to derive mostly from their shared genetic inheritance and not from the home environment.

Selected Research

- Swiss researchers Ernst and Angst's (1983) conclusion, based on their study of 7,582 young adults and a survey of the literature on birth-order and family-size effects, was that family socialization doesn't appear to play an important role in the forming of adult personality characteristics.

- A study by socialization researchers Eleanor Maccoby and John Martin (1983) found that either the parents' child-rearing style has no effect on the children's personalities or that the only effective aspects of parenting must vary greatly from one child to another within the same family.

- Similar results in studies by Bouchard et al. (1990) reveal that, by the time they are adults, adoptive siblings who were reared in the same home bear no resemblance to each other in personality. Biological siblings reared in the same home will be somewhat more alike; even identical twins reared in the same home will not be identical in personality. They will not be noticeably more alike than identical twins reared in separate homes.

- Referring to a low but statistically significant correlation, one Swedish study (Harris, 1998) showed a behavior correlation of .19, which means that if you saw how a child behaved with her/his parents, you would be unlikely to predict correctly how she/he would behave with her/his peers. Harris also points out that the twins and adoptees studies are fairly conclusive. Heredity matters more than parents or peers.

- Bouchard and Maccoby (1990) note that here, too, the studies are pretty conclusive. Birth order doesn't matter; the number of siblings or only child doesn't matter; parental preference doesn't even matter.

So what difference do these findings make?

- With nature taking up 50 percent, peers and parents (home environment) have to split the remaining 50 percent. At this point in time, it appears that who you associate with during your formative years outweighs the influence of your parents and siblings. So mother was right: You need to pick your friends carefully, and hanging out with a bad crowd does make a difference.

- The fifty-fifty split does not mean "it is all genetics." It means that we have predispositions that lean us in one direction or another. It also means that these predispositions might be tailored or shifted by environmental experiences or training. One manager explained this by saying that at birth he was given a deck of 52 playing cards, his predispositions, but he had a choice about which cards to play and when.

- But what does this mean for HR? Personality isn't made of spun glass. If someone has a deep-seated obnoxiousness, lack of perseverance, prejudice, or is cold to the point of turning off coworkers, changing this behavior dramatically is unlikely. You need something to work with in development. Better strategies would be to have the person compensate in some other way, change jobs, or try to neutralize the tendency. Giving the person continual and honest feedback about the behavior helps with the change. The key question is what is the impact of these behaviors? A cold person, for example, can learn to mimic the behaviors of approachable people. While the person won't ever appear warm, the person can appear to be at least interested and responsive to others. This set of behaviors minimizes the impact of seeming disinterested.

- Leadership development, focused on experiential learning, can help adapt the 50 percent that is not genetically predisposed. Leaders are not born or bred; they are both. They are born with predispositions but shaped through experiences. The debate of whether good leaders are born or bred is silly.

Some Key Sources

Bouchard, T.J., Jr., Lykken, D.T., McGue, M., Segal, N.L., & Tellegen, A. (1990, October 12). Sources of human psychological differences: The Minnesota study of twins reared apart. *Science Magazine, 250,* 223–228.

Ernst, C., & Angst, J. (1983). *Birth order: Its influence on personality.* Berlin, Germany: Springer-Verlag.

Harris, J.R. (1998). *The nurture assumption: Why children turn out the way they do.* New York: The Free Press.

Maccoby, E.E., & Martin, J.A. (1983). Socialization in the context of the family: Parent-child interaction. In P.H. Mussen (Series Ed.) & E.M. Hetherington (Vol. Ed.), *Handbook of child psychology: Vol. 4, Socialization, personality, and social development* (4th ed., pp. 1–101). New York: Wiley.

MEASUREMENT

70.

When constructing scales to evaluate performance or skills, it is generally best to use:

SELECT ONE:

☐ A. Three distinctions: high = exceeded; middle = met; and low = missed. So from a research standpoint, a three-point scale is the best and is all you really need.

☐ B. Four or six distinctions: It's best if there is no middle value because it forces people to make a decision. That prevents too many people from copping out and defaulting to a middle average rating.

☐ C. Five distinctions or scale points.

☐ D. Seven distinctions or scale points.

☐ E. It really depends upon the application; there really isn't any general rule on scale points.

70

70. **When constructing scales to evaluate performance or skills, it is generally best to use:**

    The correct answer is C: Five distinctions or scale points.

How sure are we at this time?

1	2	**3**	4	5
Hint	Suggestive	**Trending**	Substantial	Solid

Discussion

There is a science of scaling from many years of research on how scales work in the hands of real raters. There are three considerations in selecting points on a general rating scale. The first is that the research says that most people can make about three distinctions on performance or competencies, with a few people able to make more. The second is the observation of human behavior. In general, people are not comfortable using the extremes of a rating scale. They are a bit more reluctant to use the lowest extreme point than the highest extreme point. Also, most raters tend to rate higher than their actual feelings. So most ratings are a bit higher than what is really true. The third issue is a statistical finding that the usefulness of rating scales decreases significantly after 7 points.

So the answer is somewhere between 3 and 7 rating points. Because of the above, in order to get a decent 3 point rating result, you would have to use more than 3 points. Therefore, in order to get three real categories—lower than the rest, higher than the rest, and those in between—you would probably be best off with 5 points, fully expecting that few will use the lowest point and some might use the highest point and you have to allow for rating inflation (about .75 on a five-point scale—too many 4s, not enough 3s and 2s). These additional points help raters express shades of meaning. The 2 needs to be there for people to be comfortable using the 1, and the 4 needs to be there for people to use the 5 choice. Misses expectations is stark—a 1, and very few people will use it. Misses some expectations is more believable—a 2 response. Very few employable people would miss expectations totally on any key result area. Similarly, always exceeds expectations (a 5 rating) is unlikely anywhere the bar is set high. Individuals simply don't have that kind of unilateral control at work. Very few people are comfortable giving that sort of rating.

With a bias toward the simplest possible scale, there is not much gain in statistical clarity moving to 6 or 7 points unless there is a specific situation calling for a finer distinction—the ability to pilot a fighter jet; the ability to withdraw plutonium rods from the reactor safely. The rating distribution will spread out a bit, but the extra complexity is probably not worth the increased spread. Fewer choices are more economical and easier to use. Eliminating the midpoint argument generally doesn't hold water. The fact is that a large percentage of the people on any competency are in the middle. They are a 3 on a five-point scale or a 4 on a seven-point scale. So forcing people to get off the middle fence and shift up or down will probably result in a false shift up because of the tendency to inflate ratings.

The three-point scale is very popular today among simplicity focused people. The script is intellectually compelling. You only need three points. Either they meet expectations, exceed expectations, or miss expectations. Sounds right. What could be easier? What more do you need to know? Simplicity achieved. Unfortunately, such a scale does not produce the kind of information needed for development or performance measurement. There is usually not enough spread and differentiation. People shy away from missed expectations and too many ratings would migrate up. It's common to see 95 percent or more of ratings in the top two categories.

So, people generally use a three-point decision model, seeing people as higher than others, lower than others, or somewhere in between, but you need a five-point scale to capture this. Basically, most people use 2s, 3s and 4s when they rate with a five-point scale—with more using a 5 than a 1.

Selected Research

- While literature identifies five primary types of rater error in evaluating performance—severity or leniency, halo effect, central tendency effect, restriction of range, and inter-rater reliability—research by Engelhard and Stone (1998) have demonstrated that the statistics obtained from the Rasch Model can be used to measure these five types of error. They found that central tendency, which reflects reluctance by raters to use extreme ends of the rating scale, can significantly affect results.

- Likert (1932) did not consider the number of choices to be an important issue, stating only that "If five alternatives are used, it is necessary to assign values from one to five with the three assigned to the undecided position." (It is implied that the actual number of choices may be left to the tastes of individual researchers. In practice, researchers often do assign the number of choices arbitrarily according to personal taste or past convention.)

- Research by Murphy and Likert (1938) concludes that the optimum number of alternatives is likely to depend on the application and the number of items in the instrument. Further, they found that as the number of choices is increased, the rounding errors decrease—at first rapidly and then more slowly. The maximum rounding error is always half the distance between adjacent choices. As the number of choices increases, this distance shrinks geometrically.

• Research by Munshi (1990) argues that the precision and accuracy of the instruments used determine the extent to which measurement errors can be avoided; an instrument with low precision can cause Type II errors by failing to detect real effects, while those with low accuracy may detect spurious effects that do not exist.

• According to research by Green and Vithala (1970), the error imposed by a scale with a fixed number of choices is the round-off error committed when the assumed continuous response is converted into a scale choice. All this means is that the precision of the scale necessarily increases with the number of choices used. And the induced measurement error asymptotically approaches zero (asymptotically = a straight line associated with a curve such that as a point moves along an infinite branch of the curve the distance from the point to the line approaches zero and the slope of the curve at the point approaches the slope of the line).

• Pemberton (1933) sought to find "how coarse a scale we could use without lowering reliability below a minimum acceptable value." He found that the reliability did not always increase with the number of scale points but rose to a maximum of 0.82 at seven intervals and thereafter decreased. If too few choices, like three, are provided on the scale, then the subject may wish to select a nonexistent choice in between two consecutive choices. Since such a choice does not exist, the response will likely be assigned to the higher of the adjacent existing choices. Clearly, such a random assignment of choices will lower the correlation between items that are, in truth, highly correlated. The loss in correlation helps to explain the improvement in reliability with finer scale construction mentioned above. On the other hand, if the scale has too many choices, then the subject will be indifferent between two or more consecutive choices that represent a single internal level. Being forced to select only a single choice rather than a range, the subject randomly assigns the response to one of the choices within this range. Once again, the random assignment reduces correlation and all measures of reliability and consistency.

• Kaiser et al. (2002) have experimented with a scale that takes into account that people rarely use the negative end of a scale in many practical applications. Their first point is negative; the second, adequate; and the remaining three, various shades of effectiveness. They also try to scare people away from the top rating by anchoring it as "among the best in the world." The authors report they got more of a normal distribution curve than is typically the case with many instruments and more variation. Hay-McBer uses a similar approach which has only one negative point and spreads out degrees of effectiveness.

So what difference do these findings make?

• In general, use a five-point scale. Use a seven-point scale when greater precision is needed and/or when the raters are more sophisticated on the behavior being rated, as in Olympic judging where each successful move is awarded a set value and each error a specific deduction. Even-numbered scales seem to be harder to devise due to the lack of a midpoint.

• If making your own scale, make sure the scale has anchors on each end and numbers in between. For example, "To what extent does this person: *A little* 1 2 3 4 5 *Greatly*" rather than words. People may interpret words differently, so using numbers leads to more consistency in responses. Unless you are a professional test developer, you may bias the answer by the words you choose to describe the scale points. If you want to have all scale points described with words or phrases, use a standard scale developed by psychometricians. There are many of these.

Some Key Sources

Engelhard, G., Jr., & Stone, G.E. (1998). Evaluating the quality of ratings obtained from standard-setting judges. *Educational and Psychological Measurement, 58* (2), 179–196.

Green, P.E., & Vithala, R.R. (1970, July). Rating scales and information recovery: How many scales and response categories to use? *Journal of Marketing, 34,* 33–39.

Kaiser, R.B., Craig, S.B., Kaplan, R.E., & McArthur, C.G. (2002, April). Practical science and the development of Motorola's leadership standards. In K.B. Brookhouse (Chair), *Transforming leadership at Motorola.* Practitioner forum presented at the 17th Annual Conference of the Society for Industrial and Organizational Psychology, Toronto, Ontario.

Likert, R. (1932, June). A technique for the measurement of attitudes. *Archives of Psychology, 140.*

Munshi, J. (1990). *A method for constructing Likert Scales.* Research report, Sonoma State University, CA. http://www.munshi.sonoma.edu/likert.html

Murphy, G., & Likert, R. (1938). *Public opinion and the individual: A psychological study of student attitudes on public questions with a re-test five years later.* New York: Harper Books.

Pemberton, E. (1933). A technique for measuring the optimum rating scale for opinion measures. *Sociology and Social Research, 17,* 470–472.

DIVERSITY

71.

What effect have affirmative action plans and programs had on producing diversity in universities?

SELECT ONE:

☐ A. While many remedies have been tried, very little progress has been demonstrated.

☐ B. There is proven learning and practical benefit for those universities that are more successful with their affirmative action efforts.

☐ C. While affirmative action has been effective in increasing representation of protected classes, no learning environment benefit has been documented.

☐ D. More diverse universities are actually at a disadvantage because managing diversity is more difficult.

☐ E. Diversity on campus only matters if the students apply for private sector jobs.

71. What effect have affirmative action plans and programs had on producing diversity in universities?

The correct answer is B: There is proven learning and practical benefit for those universities that are more successful with their affirmative action efforts.

How sure are we at this time?

1	2	**3**	4	5
Hint	Suggestive	**Trending**	Substantial	Solid

Discussion

While you can always argue about whether the pace is satisfactory, substantial evidence exists that, as a result of a whole host of affirmative action programs, there is steady increase in the representation of women and covered minorities on campuses. Those universities with stronger affirmative action programs have shown the most progress. Additionally, there is some evidence that diversity increases the quality of learning and the nature of the social environment (see the Michigan Supreme Court case), with projected benefits once the students graduate and enter the work environment.

Selected Research

- Research by Bowen and Bok (1998) demonstrates that affirmative action has increased student body diversity in higher education. There is also data to support that students, institutions, and society in general benefit from this diversity.

- Gurin, Dey, Hurtado, and Gurin (2002) collected data from over 10,000 students at a variety of colleges and universities to test the benefits of diversity. They found that students who experience the most racial diversity in and out of the classroom demonstrate the greatest growth in intellectual motivation and in academic skills.

- According to Gurin (1999), attending a university with a diverse student body increases the likelihood of group interaction. He concludes that this introduction to diversity motivates students to seek out more integrated communities after graduation and that this tendency to seek out diversity significantly predicts the extent of cross-racial interactions five years after graduation.

- Research by Orfield et al. (1999) points out that Gurin's findings are especially revealing because most students do not live in racially diverse neighborhoods or attend diverse schools. They summarize by saying that diversity in the college experience could play a significant role in creating more racial integration in our society.

So what difference do these findings make?

- Aside from the moral aspects of affirmative action, well-thought-through and executed programs addressing university and college admissions are reaping multiple benefits and deserve support.

- Students hired from universities with strong affirmative action programs should have, in general, better sensitivities to managing differences.

Some Key Sources

Bowen, W., & Bok, D. (1998). *The shape of the river: Long-term consequences of considering race in college and university admissions.* Princeton, NJ: Princeton University Press.

Gurin, P. (1999). In *The compelling need for diversity in higher education.* University of Michigan. Retrieved from http://www.umich.edu/~urel/admissions/legal/expert/gurintoc.html

Gurin, P., Dey, E.L., Hurtado, S., & Gurin, G. (2002). Diversity and higher education: Theory and impact on educational outcomes. *Harvard Educational Review, 72,* 330–366.

Orfield, G. (1999, December 10). Affirmative action works—But judges and policy makers need to hear that verdict. *Chronicle of Higher Education,* p. B7.

COMPETENCIES

72.

What is the relationship between being creative and moving an idea from spark to market?

SELECT ONE:

☐ A. There is very little relationship between the two.

☐ B. There is a strong relationship; you have to be creative in order to manage innovation.

☐ C. There is a strong relationship for technical creativity but less for the arts.

☐ D. There is a negative relationship; being too creative gets in the way of managing innovation.

☐ E. Creativity is actually part of the definition of managing innovation, so they are perfectly related.

72.   What is the relationship between being creative and moving an idea from spark to market?

The correct answer is A: There is very little relationship between the two.

How sure are we at this time?

1	2	**3**	4	5
Hint	Suggestive	**Trending**	Substantial	Solid

Discussion

There is not much relationship between being creative and managing innovation. Managing innovation (moving an idea, new service, or product through an organization and then to market) takes political skills, planning, positioning skills, presentation skills, and patience, and also personal power and influence. Generally, a highly creative person doesn't possess many of those skills. It's possible that a facile innovation manager could have average personal creativity. It's also possible that a highly creative person might have passable innovation skills. It's not likely that you could be high on both.

Personal creativity is only the first step of the innovation process. Innovation requires someone with an idea or unique insight, but it also requires the capacity to turn the idea into reality, which requires skills other than creativity.

Selected Research

- Although conventional wisdom says "when the pressure's on, people produce," social psychologist Teresa Amabile, PhD, the Edsel Bryant Ford Professor of Business Administration at Harvard Business School, says it's not the recipe for producing creative ideas. In her studies of creativity in corporate America, she has found that the more workers feel crunched, the less likely they are to solve a tricky problem, envision a new product line, or have other such "Aha!" experiences that qualify as innovation. In a 2002 APA Annual Convention talk, Amabile noted that her studies of 177 highly educated employees in seven U.S. chemical, high-tech, and consumer-products companies revealed that time pressure quashes creativity and that intrinsic motivation (personal passion for one's work) is a critical creativity stimulator that can be squashed by extrinsic constraints. In her workplace study of the employees, published in the *Harvard Business Review* (Vol. 80, No. 8), it turned out employees were 45 percent less likely to think creatively on high-pressure days than they were on low-pressure days. Surprisingly, though, they reported feeling *more* creative under higher time pressure (Murray, 2002).

- A research study by Hammerschmidt (1996) found that creative style does impact how people approach, solve, and communicate problems. The study tracked the problem solving success rates of teams formed using the Kirton Adaption Innovation Inventory (KAI) and found that those teamed with similar KAI types significantly increased group success rates and those teamed outside their role preference had lower success rates.

- A study that explored the relationship between a measure of creative style and a measure of creative climate (Isaksen & Kaufmann, 1990) found that "adaptors and innovators held different perceptions of the creative climate." Specific results revealed that adaptors perceived more challenge than innovators, and innovators perceived significantly more conflict than adaptors. It seems that these differences in styles speak to the difference between the creative person and the innovation manager type person.

- Another study that looked at entrepreneur's adaptor-innovator styles and related behaviors found that entrepreneurs tend to be more innovative than their managerial counterparts in large organizations; the more innovative entrepreneurs tend to start more new business ventures than their adaptive colleagues; the more adaptive entrepreneurs tend to actively run their businesses longer than their innovative colleagues; and the more adaptive entrepreneurs spend more time than do innovators in administrative activities which fit their preferred problem solving style (Buttner & Gryskiewicz, 1993).

- Research by Schwarz-Gescha (1994) on creativity and innovation management in Japanese society found that corporate culture, including group-oriented communication and decision making, and individual flexibility have a positive effect on creativity. The research also demonstrated a link between Japanese creativity (observed to be adaptive, cultivated, and intuitive) and successful production.

- William Shockley described the process of inventing the transistor at Bell Labs as "creative failure methodology." A multidiscipline Bell Labs team was formed to invent the MOS transistor and ended up instead with the junction transistor and the new science of semiconductor physics. These developments eventually led to the MOS transistor and then to the integrated circuit and to new breakthroughs in electronics and computers (Iannone, 2003).

- Lombardo and Eichinger (2003) found both creativity and innovation management to be consistently related to both performance and promotion for managers.

So what difference do these findings make?
- Both managing innovation and creativity can be important for performance and potential for the future and need to

be assessed separately because of the lack of relationship between the two.

- Innovation can be assessed by examining an individual's ability to move ideas into action. This might include competencies in engaging people, presenting ideas, working with different constituencies in an organization, and being persistent in accomplishing a goal.

- Creativity can be assessed by lateral thinking, or the ability to see novel and new solutions to old problems.

- Since there isn't much if any relationship between the two, they should not be combined in a competency statement such as "Should be creative and innovative."

Some Key Sources

Buttner, E.H., & Gryskiewicz, N. (1993, January). Entrepreneur's problem solving styles: An empirical study using the KAI Theory. *Journal of Small Business Management*, 23–31.

Hammerschmidt, P.K. (1996). The Kirton Adaption Innovation Inventory and group problem solving success rates. *Journal of Creative Behavior, 30* (1), 61–74.

Howard, A., & Bray, D.W. (1988). *Managerial lives in transition: Advancing age and changing times.* New York: Guilford Press.

Iannone, D. (2003, February 1). *Invention of the transistor—The benefits of "Creative Failure Methodology."* Examples of the use of planned serendipity. Economic development futures: Information and insights about where economic development is headed. Retrieved May 6, 2003 from http://www.saskschools.ca/~ischool/paasurvey/entre/Content/appr.htm

Isaksen, S.G., & Kaufmann, G. (1990). Adaptors and innovators: A discriminant analysis of the perceptions of the psychological climate for creativity. *Studia Psychologica: The Journal of Basic Research, 32* (3), 129–141.

Lombardo, M., & Eichinger, R. (2003). *The LEADERSHIP ARCHITECT® norms and validity report.* Minneapolis: Lominger Limited, Inc.

Murray, B. (2002, November). A ticking clock means a creativity drop. *Monitor on Psychology, American Psychological Association, 33* (10). Print version p. 24.

Schwarz-Gescha, M. (1994). Creativity in Japanese society. *Creativity and Innovation Management, 3* (4), 229–232.

MEASUREMENT

73.

How many core dimensions of personal dispositions or personality traits are there?

SELECT ONE:

☐ A. Four—like the Myers-Briggs Type Indicator or the Firo-B.

☐ B. Five to seven.

☐ C. Sixteen—like in the 16PF or the CPI.

☐ D. Probably somewhere around 20—most personality questionnaires have about 20 scales.

☐ E. There are over 30 personality characteristics that many questionnaires measure.

BEST PEOPLE PRACTICES FOR MANAGERS & HR

73. How many core dimensions of personal dispositions or personality traits are there?

The correct answer is B: Five to seven.

How sure are we at this time?

1	2	3	**4**	5
Hint	Suggestive	Trending	**Substantial**	Solid

Discussion

Over the past 35 years, a number of researchers have investigated how many real, consistent, fundamental, and predictive personality characteristics there are. They have reviewed all of the studies of personality over the years and statistically combined and compared them and have come to the conclusion that there are five to seven core stable universal personality characteristics. Most other so-called personality characteristics can be derived from combinations of the five. These results are variously called the "Big Five" or the "Big Seven." We probably know for sure there aren't four and unlikely to be nine. The Big Five or Norman's Big Five are Extraversion, Emotional Stability, Agreeableness, Conscientiousness, and Openness to Experience.

While this construct is very useful, some have further divided extraversion into two traits: ambition and sociability—therefore becoming the Big Six.

Consequently, the best choice is B, that there are five to seven core dispositions that seem to hold across cultures, depending on whether or not you wish to further divide extraversion into "ambition" and "sociability."

The presence of the Big Five factor model has been demonstrated in many well-known personality inventories, including the popular MBTI and EPI.

Selected Research

- Norman (1963) identified five core personality dimensions: Extraversion, Emotional Stability, Agreeableness, Conscientiousness, and Openness to Experience.

- In a meta-analysis of 117 studies using the Big Five, (Barrick & Mount, 1991), conscientiousness "showed consistent relations with all job performance criteria for all occupational groups; extraversion was a valid predictor for managers and sales." The researchers also found that "other personality dimensions were valid predictors for some occupations and some criterion types."

- Three comprehensive studies examined the generality of the five factor model (Big Five) using 1,431 trait adjectives, 479 common terms, and analysis of 100 clusters derived from 339 trait terms. All three studies found that the five factor model of personality holds and accounts for most of the variance in how people differ (Goldberg, 1990).

So what difference do these findings make?

- The Big Five still hold (Norman; Goldberg). Norman came up with the Big Five traits almost 40 years ago and researchers ever since have been validating his results. The Big Five are somewhat related or predictive of managerial success.

- Matching the competence to the job (Barrick). Since extraversion is a valid predictor for managers and sales, it only makes sense to use these to evaluate these types of positions. The same is true of openness to experience and extraversion since both are valid predictors of the training proficiency criterion across all professions. Conscientiousness is related to most jobs.

- When you need to describe people in personality terms, use the Big Five or Big Seven. That's as complex as it needs to be. Tests like the Myers-Briggs or FIRO-B should be framed as part of this Big Five or Big Seven set of personality traits.

- Providing individuals feedback on their personality, particularly feedback from others, helps individuals learn and adapt their predispositions.

Some Key Sources

Barrick, M.R., & Mount, M.K. (1991). The Big Five personality dimensions and job performance: A meta-analysis. *Personnel Psychology, 44,* 1–26.

Goldberg, L.R. (1990). An alternative description of personality: The Big Five factor structure. *Journal of Personality and Social Psychology, 59,* 1216–1229.

Norman, W.T. (1963). Toward an adequate taxonomy of personality attributes: Replicated factor structures in peer nomination personality ratings. *Journal of Abnormal and Social Psychology, 66,* 574–583.

CAREER DEVELOPMENT

What is the most likely outcome of people focusing exclusively on developing their strengths and doing only those jobs that match those strengths?

SELECT ONE:

74

☐ A. It would only work well for those with the right strengths to begin with.

☐ B. People would be happier and more productive because they wouldn't have to worry about weaknesses.

☐ C. The strengths would get stronger, overwhelming any weaknesses that might get in the way.

☐ D. Strengths are likely to be overdone or not balanced, and unaddressed weaknesses would become blind spots.

☐ E. More people would become strong performers over time.

74. **What is the most likely outcome of people focusing exclusively on developing their strengths and doing only those jobs that match those strengths?**

The correct answer is D: Strengths are likely to be overdone or not balanced, and unaddressed weaknesses would become blind spots.

How sure are we at this time?

1	2	3	**4**	5
Hint	Suggestive	Trending	**Substantial**	Solid

Discussion

The best evidence for working on both strengths and weaknesses comes from the derailment research (CCL, Sears) and the Kaplan and Kaiser studies on versatility. Studies of what happens to people with promising careers show that without feedback, strengths can become weaknesses. People become more focused on what they do well to the exclusion of or even knowing about their downsides. By the time they derail, a strength (say, intelligence) tips over into a weakness (a know-it-all) or a weakness (poor team building) that suddenly matters.

A lack of self-awareness is the big crippler here. People don't know what they don't know and tend to overestimate their skills dramatically, especially their interpersonal skills and impact on others. Lombardo and Eichinger (2003) found that the higher the self-rating compared to that of other rater groups, the more likely a person is to be eventually fired due to overused strengths and weaknesses that begin to matter.

However, research has also shown that successful leaders have a few strengths, not 20. When looking at successful leaders,

Zenger and Folkman (2002) found that, if leaders could be high in 4 or 5 competencies on a 360, they were rated around the 90th percentile in effectiveness as long as the weaknesses were near neutral and they addressed their fatal flaws. McClelland reported a tipping point of 6 strengths to be successful.

Common sense also argues against working on strengths only. Who among us really believes that our strengths will carry us throughout a total career? Who believes they have not developed a significant new skill or neutralized a weak one? The soundest argument is to reinforce strengths, develop in new areas, and be aware of and neutralize weaknesses and flaws. No one is suggesting that a truly conflict-averse person can become a conflict master. However, that person can learn to deal in a straightforward fashion with conflict situations (i.e., understanding the other side; asking more questions; making clear, unemotional statements).

Selected Research

- Kaplan and Kaiser (2003) found that overdoing strengths was common in executives and that the more effective executives were more versatile. By this, they mean the executives were able to combine seemingly opposites in behavior—being forceful but also enabling others to act. They were definitely not one-sided, exclusively focusing on their natural strengths. The authors note that overspecializing is favored by organizations, and that contributes to this problem by exploiting an individual's talents.

- Lombardo and Eichinger (2002) note that low-performing executives seem to have much more difficulty learning to do anything differently as a result of their experiences. They tend to repeat past patterns of successful behavior and fail to adapt by developing in new areas. These executives had virtually no pattern of learning from jobs. Their learning appeared to be virtually random. They also underestimated the newness of the demands, seeing them as just another version of what they had done before.

• Zenger and Folkman (2002) argue that much development should focus on strengths, backed up by neutralizing or making irrelevant weaknesses, and dealing with fatal flaws such as failure to learn from mistakes. They conclude that strengths only hurt a person's effectiveness when not counterbalanced. They advocate combining skills such as drive for results and interpersonal savvy to enhance overall effectiveness.

• In the CCL studies, McCall et al. (1988) found that "successful executives had a strong and similar pattern of learning from key job assignments." This learning primarily resulted from developing in new areas triggered by unfamiliar and stressful job assignments. Executives were forced to go against their natural proclivities in order to succeed.

• In a companion study (McCall & Lombardo, 1983), one of the key reasons cited for derailment was being blocked to new learning. Though successful and unsuccessful executives had many of the same experiences, the "right stuff" of the successful executives in the study seemed to be an ability to "make the most of your experience" (p. 122).

• In studies that have dealt with success and derailment, failure to learn to do something differently in order to make key transitions has figured prominently in the results. Additionally, lack of self-awareness and a tendency to overrate oneself have been found to be crippling. In contrast, successful people learned more new behavior and were more self-aware (Spreitzer et al., 1997; Lombardo & Eichinger, 2000; Shipper & Dillard, 2000; Lombardo & Eichinger, 2003).

So what difference do these findings make?

- It is so appealing to focus on strengths only. No more bad news. Like most solutions that are too good to be true, this one borders on irresponsibility. Focusing on strengths alone leads to not dealing with change, not growing or changing, and being blindsided by weaknesses.

- Is it a good idea to focus on strengths? Of course. That's what accounts for much of our success. We should focus on the strengths we've been given, leverage them, and use those strengths (i.e., planning) to attack a weakness (i.e., slow to take action). People can plan an attack on a problem in a few minutes, then commit to action.

- Knowing yourself is still the best option—strengths, averages, weaknesses, and untested areas. Successful people don't have all possible skills. Their edge is in fully knowing themselves—developing where they can and neutralizing weak areas where they will never be strong.

- Working on strengths alone also negates the chance all of us have to move from competent to strong in an area. If we are already average (skilled) in an area, we have a track record of some success to fall back on and some indication we might excel in some of these areas. Much research indicates that via training in how more successful managers plan, for example, that people can move well on the way from average to superior.

- The bottom line is that everyone needs to know themselves completely—the good, the bad, and the ugly. Then choose what to do about it. Those who decide to stick with their strengths will be limited in the future. Those who decide to enhance their strengths and be aware of their weaknesses and work on them or around them will be more successful.

Some Key Sources

Kaplan, R.E., & Kaiser, R.B. (2003). Developing versatile leadership. *MIT Sloan Management Review, 44* (4), 19–26.

Lombardo, M., & Eichinger, R. (2000). High potentials as high learners. *Human Resource Management, 39* (4), 321–330.

Lombardo, M., & Eichinger, R. (2004). *The leadership machine.* Minneapolis: Lominger Limited, Inc.

Lombardo, M., & Eichinger, R. (2003). *The LEADERSHIP ARCHITECT® norms and validity report.* Minneapolis: Lominger Limited, Inc.

McCall, M.W., & Lombardo, M. (1983). What makes a top executive? *Psychology Today, 17* (2), 26–31.

McCall, M.W., Lombardo, M., & Morrison, A. (1988). *The lessons of experience: How successful executives develop on the job.* Lexington, MA: Lexington Books.

Shipper, F., & Dillard, J. (2000). A study of impending derailment and recovery of middle managers across career stages. *Human Resource Management, 39* (4), 331–347.

Spreitzer, G.M., McCall, M.W., & Mahoney, J.D. (1997). Early identification of international executive potential. *Journal of Applied Psychology, 82* (1), 6–29.

Zenger, J., & Folkman, J. (2002). *The extraordinary leader: Turning good managers into great leaders.* New York: McGraw-Hill.

360 DEGREE FEEDBACK

75.

What would happen if the ratings of people's strengths and weaknesses or their performance ratings in a 360 degree multi-rater event were made public and shared with the boss?

SELECT ONE:

☐ A. Nothing—people rate very much the same in both private and public formats.

☐ B. The ratings would go up a bit but would still be related to job performance.

☐ C. The ratings go up and would be less related to job performance.

☐ D. Strengths and weaknesses would stay the same but performance ratings would go up.

☐ E. The ratings would all go down a bit because bosses would see them.

75

75. **What would happen if the ratings of people's strengths and weaknesses or their performance ratings in a 360 degree multi-rater event were made public and shared with the boss?**

The correct answer is C: The ratings go up and would be less related to job performance.

How sure are we at this time?

1	2	3	**4**	5
Hint	Suggestive	Trending	**Substantial**	Solid

Discussion

Studies have shown that accuracy decreases as confidentiality is breached. When raters are easier to identify, or the boss or others in the organization get a copy of the report, or there are mandatory sharing requirements, the average scores go up, and the spread (lowest to highest score) goes down. Studies show that confidentiality and anonymity increase the chances of honesty. 360 for development works best when the results are confidential, the raters are guaranteed anonymity, and the information is owned and controlled by the target person. Anything less than that will compromise accuracy. Giving anonymous feedback is easier than face-to-face. That is, the same people who are reluctant to deliver critical feedback face-to-face will do it more on a confidential 360 degree questionnaire. This may be because giving critical feedback anonymously invites us to be honest.

One reason we are using 360 degree feedback is because it is difficult for peers, direct reports, managers, and executives to engage in straight talk with people about weaknesses. So any decrease in real or perceived confidentiality will be accompanied by a decrease in accuracy. The majority of people do not want their bosses to have their actual data. If that is a requirement, they and their raters will inflate their ratings and not include as many critical notes.

Selected Research

- Lombardo and Eichinger (2003) report that "when raters did not request anonymity, their ratings were significantly higher and unrelated to job performance. When they requested confidentiality, scores went down and were related to job performance."

- In a survey by Rogers et al. (2000), almost one-half of the bosses had access to the reports and about one-third of the HR groups did.

- One study of upward feedback (ratings of the supervisor by direct reports only) found that direct reports whose ratings were not anonymous felt less comfortable and rated their managers significantly higher than direct reports whose ratings were anonymous (Antonioni, 1994).

- CCL's research on data from a multi-rater questionnaire assessing a variety of leadership skills in which a boss's responses were not anonymous, found that boss ratings tend to be higher, on average, than ratings from peers or from direct reports (Lombardo & McCauley, 1994).

- Scores go up and accuracy goes down when the people doing the rating know they will be identified (Jawahar & Williams, 1997). In a study of 58,000 appraisals, scores went up significantly in public appraisal processes. "When raters' responses are not anonymous or when adequate safeguards have not been developed to protect the anonymity of rater identity, fears of retribution may arise and may result in a lack of candor in their responses or, in fact, to complete nonresponse."

So what difference do these findings make?

- Issues related to confidentiality and anonymity are issues of trust and safety. The effective use of 360 degree feedback for development or for appraisal depends on creating an environment that is seen as supportive of individuals, respectful of their needs for privacy, and concerned about their development.

- To guard against inflated single supervisor ratings (which are often displayed separately from peers and direct reports), it may be feasible to create more anonymity for supervisor ratings by collecting responses from several people who are in a more indirect supervisory relationship to the manager or from a past boss as well as the present boss.

- The immediate concern of many practitioners is that the value of the feedback for learning and development is compromised if conditions of psychological safety such as feedback confidentiality and rater anonymity are removed. A 360 degree instrument can only be effective if the data are accurate, and in order for this to happen the program must provide for the anonymity of respondents.

- Even mandatory sharing of the results with a boss is a violation of the confidentiality pledge. Most people (depending upon the culture of the organization) will share anyway. Mandatory sharing will decrease accuracy.

- Share developmental needs, not results. The individual has a responsibility to acknowledge and work on leveraging strengths, neutralizing downsides, and stretching into new areas. A candid discussion of this can occur by keeping the discussion at this level. Actual feedback results can remain private, but one's needs aren't private. One's raters have suggested them.

- The individual receiving the 360 feedback should be given an opportunity to make personal development plans prior to the feedback being tied to compensation, promotion, or other rewards. Many companies want to assess both results and behaviors for employees as part of their performance appraisal and compensation. Results are assessed through some form of objective setting and results attaining. Behaviors, or how those results are attained, often come from 360 feedback forms. Behaviors can still be assessed through a 360 and honest data can be collected if assessor results are combined into groups without individual ratings reported.

Some Key Sources

Antonioni, D. (1994). The effects of feedback accountability on upward appraisal ratings. *Personnel Psychology, 47,* 349–356.

Jawahar, I.M., & Williams, C.R. (1997). Where all the children are above average: The performance appraisal purpose effect. *Personnel Psychology, 50* (4), 905–925.

Lombardo, M., & Eichinger, R. (2003). *The LEADERSHIP ARCHITECT® norms and validity report.* Minneapolis: Lominger Limited, Inc.

Lombardo, M., & McCauley, C.D. (1994). *Benchmarks®: A manual and trainer's guide.* Greensboro, NC: Center for Creative Leadership.

Rogers, E., Metlay, W., Kaplan, I., & Barriere, M. (2000). *Multisource feedback: A state of the art and practice report.* Unpublished manuscript.

76.

Do women get tough jobs or developmental opportunities at the same rate as men?

SELECT ONE:

☐ A. Not in the past but they are now equal.

☐ B. No, women receive significantly fewer tough developmental assignments.

☐ C. Not yet, but it's getting better; there is now only a slight difference.

☐ D. Because of the increased sensitivity, women are now receiving slightly more tough developmental assignments than their male counterparts.

☐ E. Because of the increased sensitivity, women are now receiving significantly more tough developmental assignments than their male counterparts.

76. Do women get tough jobs or developmental opportunities at the same rate as men?

The correct answer is B: No, women receive significantly fewer tough developmental assignments.

How sure are we at this time?

1	2	3	**4**	5
Hint	Suggestive	Trending	**Substantial**	Solid

Discussion

Review of research on the selection and development of the talent pool reveals a bias against women for tough and developmental jobs. There are different standards for women and stereotypical beliefs about women.

While statistics show improvement with salaries, promotions, and positions for women, it's important to look beyond the statistics to the types of positions, responsibilities, and exposure they are getting. Research shows that the improvement is lagging where it matters—with start-ups, fix-its, turnarounds, or jobs with profit-loss responsibilities.

Selected Research

- According to research by Morrison et al. (1987, rev. 1992), "men were three times more likely to report that the major developmental jobs that season managers most are start-ups, fix-its or turnarounds, and having a large jump in scope (moving into a complex, well-functioning organization)." An unpublished study by the Center for Creative Leadership found the same results (*Lessons of a Diverse Workforce Project,* 2000).

- Research by Lyness and Thompson (2000) showed that women have fewer moves, narrower experiences, jobs with less authority, and are less likely to say that mentoring facilitated their advancement.

- Loden (1985) reports on a Gallup survey that showed that 71 percent of women interviewed stated they do not think they have had the same chance for promotions to top executives and that this belief leads them to identify less than White males do with their organization and to look elsewhere more often.

- Findings of one study show that male decision makers tend to choose men for promotions because of a "perceived comfort level, and they choose women for the personal strength they exhibit or the familiarity (tenure) and continuity they already have in a particular job situation" (Ruderman et al., 1997).

- In their research, VanVelsor and Hughes (1990) conclude that the lessons that executives reported had changed their leadership permanently differed remarkably between men and women, with women not getting the leadership-building experiences that men were getting.

- Mueller et al. (1989) found that a double standard exists. "Women and African Americans may, in fact, have to perform better to get ahead than men do. There is probably a double standard. This would be typical of any out-group working its way into the dominant culture."

So what difference do these findings make?

- There is, still today, a bias against women in key developmental jobs. There are few women in the boardrooms and few at the top. While progress is certainly being made, women are currently being underselected for the types of jobs that we know build leaders.

- It's jobs, jobs, jobs. Challenging jobs are the engine of personal growth. Without them, all your diversity efforts will amount to nothing. Tough jobs will prepare future leaders because some will succeed and some will fail. It is important to give women and minorities opportunities to succeed, fail, and learn from these tough assignments. Without them, women will be less prepared for the leadership jobs they receive.

Some Key Sources

Center for Creative Leadership. (2000, June). *Lessons of a diverse workforce project.* Working report.

Loden, M. (1985). *Feminine leadership, or how to succeed in business without being one of the boys.* New York: Times Books.

Lyness, K.S., & Thompson, D.E. (2000). Climbing the corporate ladder: Do male and female executives follow the same route? *Journal of Applied Psychology, 85* (1), 86–101.

Morrison, A., White, R., & VanVelsor, E. (1987, rev. 1992). *Breaking the glass ceiling: Can women reach the top of America's largest corporations?* Reading, MA: Addison-Wesley.

Mueller, C.W., Parcel, T.L., & Tanaka, K. (1989). Particularism in authority outcomes of Black and White supervisors. *Social Science Research, 18,* 1–20.

Ruderman, M.N., Ohlott, P.J., & Kram, K.E. (1997, April). Managerial promotion: The dynamics for men and women. *HR Magazine.*

VanVelsor, E., & Hughes, M.W. (1990). *Gender differences in the development of managers: How women managers learn from experience* (Report No. 145). Greensboro, NC: Center for Creative Leadership.

CAREER DEVELOPMENT

77.

What's the best developmental path for high potentials to follow?

SELECT ONE:

☐ A. Go through a disciplined set of business and functional rotational assignments so that they are exposed to as much of the organization as possible.

☐ B. Be assigned a senior mentor early and attend high-quality programs along the way attended by other international high potentials.

☐ C. Go through a set of experiences that are challenging and require new and different skills.

☐ D. Stay in significant jobs long enough to get the learnings; high potentials move too often.

☐ E. Go through mostly strategically important jobs where they can best learn the business.

77

77. What's the best developmental path for high potentials to follow?

The correct answer is C: Go through a set of experiences that are challenging and require new and different skills.

How sure are we at this time?

1	2	3	**4**	5
Hint	Suggestive	Trending	**Substantial**	Solid

Discussion

The best course to follow is to put ambitious people with potential through a series of challenging, new, unique, and different experiences, the content of which builds the projected skills needed to lead in the future.

Studies across 50 years support the predictive power of some combination of key traits and personal history. Studies reveal that a combination of certain traits and key experiences which shaped the managers over their careers was required for managerial success. Without those challenging leadership experiences, talented young managers might atrophy or not mature as leaders.

Selected Research

- Bray et al. (1974) argue that much if not most managerial leadership development takes place on the job rather than in seminars or classrooms and that early leadership experiences are among the key influences on career development.

- In describing their research on executives, McCall et al. (1988), conclude that it is "critical to executive effectiveness for individuals to have experience with a wide variety of managerial roles; and that this diversity is not correlated with the number or frequency of promotions, rather with moves across problem domains."

- A fundamental conclusion of the McCall et al. (1988) study is that on-the-job learning is most likely to occur when managers are faced with challenging situations. The study results also revealed that "what was learned from challenging on-the-job experiences was not technical in nature but consisted of leadership attributes, such as handling relationships, temperament, basic values, and personal awareness" (in McCauley et al., 1994).

- A research model by Locke & Latham (1990) called the High Performance (HPRF) Cycle, found that "success (in job satisfaction, which engenders commitment to the organization and its goals) is a combination of high challenge or difficult goals mixed with high expectations for success, feedback, adequate ability, and low situational constraints."

- Yukl's research (1994), noted in his comprehensive book on leadership in organizations, revealed that many of the skills learned by corporate managers are based on experience rather than formal education. He argues that "managers are more likely to learn relevant leadership skills and values if they are exposed to a variety of developmental experiences on the job, with appropriate coaching and mentoring by superiors and peers" (p. 456).

So what difference do these findings make?
- New, different, challenging and unique with content that matches the skills needed now and in the future is the best program to develop future leaders.

There are many ways to develop people through assignments. Below is a list from Lombardo and Eichinger (2002).

What are the most developmental jobs?

Cross Moves: Changing to a very different set of activities. Typical examples would be: Changing divisions or functions, field/HQ shifts, country switch, or changing line of business.

Fix-its/Turnarounds: Cleaning up a mess where this is the last chance to fix it, usually accompanied by serious people and morale problems. Typical examples: Failed business/unit, disasters like bungled labor negotiations, strikes, thefts, fraud, obsolete staff, restructuring, product liability events, system/process breakdowns.

Heavy Strategic Demands: Requires new or significant strategic redirection; visible and watched by senior people. Typically part of a major job switch.

Influencing Without Authority: Significant challenge where one has the responsibility but not the authority. Typical examples: Planning project, installing new systems, troubleshooting systems problems, negotiating with outside parties, working in a staff group.

International Assignment: First time working in the country. Usually features new language, business rules, different cultural norms, assigned for more than a year.

Line to Staff Switch: Visible role in a staff function, often at headquarters. Typical examples: Business/strategic planning role, heading a staff department, assistant to senior executive, head of a task force, human resources role.

Projects/Task Forces: One-time, short-term events usually lasting from a few weeks to a year. Much of the work in today's flatter, less hierarchical organizations can be classified as project work. Also e-commerce start-ups are almost entirely day-to-day project work. Typical examples: Implementing new ideas, product launches, systems development, acquisitions, joint ventures, one-time events like business crises, reorganizations.

Scale (size): Jump in the size of a job in same area for the person. Typically involves much more budget, volume of business, people, layers of the organization.

Scope (complexity) Change: Managing substantially more breadth. Typically involves new areas of business, increase in visibility, complexity. Typical scope jobs: Moving to a new organization, adding new products or functions or services, moving from staff to line, and numerous first-time jobs such as first-time manager, managing managers, executive, or team leader.

Significant People Demands: Involves a sizable increase in either the number of people managed or the complexity of the people-challenges faced. Typical examples are: Going to team-based management structures, changing to a quality format for work, and working with groups not worked with before.

Start-Ups: Starting something new for the organization. Typical examples are: Building a team, creating new systems or facilities or products, heading something new, establishing branch operation, and moving a successful program from one unit to another.

Some Key Sources

Bray, D.W., Campbell, R.J., & Grant, D.L. (1974). *Formative years in business: A long-term AT&T study of managerial lives.* New York: Wiley.

Locke, E.A., & Latham, G.P. (1990, July). Work motivation and satisfaction: Light at the end of the tunnel. *Psychological Science, 1* (4), 240–246.

McCall, M.W., Lombardo, M., & Morrison, A. (1988). *The lessons of experience: How successful executives develop on the job.* Lexington, MA: Lexington Books.

McCauley, C.D., Ruderman, M.N., Ohlott, P.J., & Morrow, J.E. (1994). Assessing the developmental components of managerial jobs. *Journal of Applied Psychology, 79,* 544–560.

Yukl, G. (1994). *Leadership in organizations* (3rd ed.). Englewood Cliffs, NJ: Prentice Hall.

SUCCESS PREDICTION

How predictive are intelligence and technical/functional skills for individual contributors and professionals?

SELECT ONE:

☐ A. They are the key attributes in these roles; nothing else comes close to accounting for effective performance.

☐ B. They are important attributes in these roles along with many other nontechnical and nonintellectual competencies.

☐ C. They don't correlate much with differences in performance, but they do predict who is promoted and successful later in a management job.

☐ D. Intelligence and technical/functional skills are very minor predictors of success for individual contributors and professionals unless the job is very technical.

78

☐ F. Intelligence and technical/functional skills account for very little or no differences in performance; it's mostly interacting with people skills that make the difference.

78. **How predictive are intelligence and technical/functional skills for individual contributors and professionals?**

   The correct answer is B: They are important attributes in these roles along with many other nontechnical and nonintellectual competencies.

How sure are we at this time?

1	2	3	**4**	5
Hint	Suggestive	Trending	**Substantial**	Solid

Discussion

Intelligence, technical learning, and functional/technical skills are significant skills in most individual contributor/professional roles. No doubt of that. But other skills matter as much or more—results orientation, learning on the fly (learning quickly from job experience), creativity, and organizing to name a few. We often focus too much on technical or skill-based competencies that are obviously nice to have, without paying enough attention to what else might drive performance.

Even though requirements change rather dramatically with level, few people are developed on much besides technical job skills in most organizations. Individual contributors perform the best because they are at least hired to do what they end up doing.

Selected Research

- Research by Howard and Bray (1988) showed a significant correlation between intelligence, or cognitive ability, and later advancement. Correlations of factors with management potential were highest for administrative skills (.62), interpersonal skills (.57), and intellectual ability (.61). The researchers conclude "some individual contributors will grow to be seasoned professionals in very valuable technologies. Although they may never manage anyone, both they and the organization benefit when jobs are seen as sets of challenges requiring competencies as well as sets of challenges requiring technical proficiencies."

- According to research by Howard and Bray (1988), the best predictors of later on-the-job adjustment were measures of personality and motivation. A study of self-esteem, affability, positiveness, leadership motivation, and impulsivity showed that intellectual aptitude and accomplishments "run at cross-purposes in terms of advancement in management and high personal adjustment. The most astute thinkers were, at best, only moderate in adjustment."

- According to research by Simonton (1987), "intelligence is a necessary but not sufficient cause of adulthood success in careers that demand creativity or leadership." Further findings reveal that excessive intelligence seems to hurt, with the most effective people being "somewhat smarter than the average for their group, but not too much smarter."

- In Sternberg et al. (1995), the correlations reported in studies of practical intelligence rival those of IQ in relating to performance, potential, or a number of other organizational measures, such as salary. Their measure of practical intelligence (which they also refer to as learning from experience) "added 32 percent to the variance explained by IQ alone, and was the single best predictor of managerial performance."

- Further research by Sternberg (1996) concludes that scores on a measure of learning from experience were unrelated to IQ scores. Sternberg found that "almost everyone starts as an individual contributor—with some foundation skills that lead to their first management job. Development is development. Even if a person wanted to or just remained an individual contributor his or her whole life, some adjustments in skill would be necessary. Adjusting old skills or building new ones follow all the traditional development logic research. A target. Feedback. Development plan. Skill building. Practice. Blending. Individual contributors benefit most when jobs are developmental, especially early in a career."

So what difference do these findings make?

• Even for individual contributors, where intelligence and technical/functional skills do help predict who will be the most successful, there are other noncognitive characteristics that predict just as well. Look to relationship skills and organization savvy characteristics along with the willingness and the ability to learn new behaviors to prepare for other roles, especially management jobs.

• Hiring people with technical competencies is like ante in poker. They assure that the people hired will be "in the game," but they do not assure that the people will help win the game. Since technical competencies are often more apparent, they get too much attention in hiring. We often measure what is easy to count, and we hire what is easy to see, and both are dangerous.

Some Key Sources

Howard, A., & Bray, D. (1988). *Managerial lives in transition: Advancing age and changing times.* New York: Guilford Press.

Simonton, D.K. (1987). Developmental antecedents of achieved eminence. *Annals of Child Development, 4,* 131–169.

Sternberg, R.J. (1996). *Successful intelligence: How practical and creative intelligence determine success in life.* New York: Simon & Schuster.

Sternberg, R.J., Wagner, R.K., Williams, W.M., & Horvath, J.A. (1995). Testing common sense. *American Psychologist, 50* (11), 912–927.

DIVERSITY

79.

***When trying to help overweight employees,
the most realistic view and approach is:***

SELECT ONE:

☐ A. Being overweight is all genetics. You're just born
with it. With a few exceptions, it's best to counsel overweight employees to just adjust to their
condition and try to maintain where they are.

☐ B. They just plain lack impulse control and
discipline; it's just a matter of eating less and
exercising more; anyone can do it and many do.
The best suggestion would be to start a diet
plan and join an exercise club.

☐ C. The largest reason people are seriously
overweight is genetics. People inherit a set
point weight determined by frame size, Basic
Metabolism Rate, and activity level. It takes great
effort for most to lose weight and maintain the
loss. The best advice is to eat as smart as
possible, increase activity, and get help as a
family unit for support.

☐ D. We really don't know. The research is confusing
and contradictory.

☐ E. The majority of overweight people lack self-
discipline and just find excuses for their
condition. For a few, there might be physical
issues that would have to be solved medically.
The best advice is to join Overeaters Anonymous
and get serious about helping themselves.

79

79. When trying to help overweight employees, the most realistic view and approach is:

The correct answer is C: The largest reason people are seriously overweight is genetics. People inherit a set point weight determined by frame size, Basic Metabolism Rate, and activity level. It takes great effort for most to lose weight and maintain the loss. The best advice is to eat as smartly as possible, increase activity, and get help as a family unit for support.

How sure are we at this time?

1	2	3	**4**	5
Hint	Suggestive	Trending	**Substantial**	Solid

Discussion

More than half of Americans are 3 to 5 percent above their ideal weight, and at least 8 million people weigh at least 100 pounds more than ideal. Despite the fact that weighing "too much" is common, research shows that job discrimination against people of size is common, subtle, and generally ignored.

Most studies show that, in our culture being thin means more than good health, it symbolizes self-control, hard work, ambition, and success in life. Positive attributes are accorded to thin people, but those with less than the perfect body are blamed and thought to be self-indulgent, lazy, or even irresponsible and immoral.

The role of biology in body weight regulation must be placed in perspective. Overstating the role of genetics and metabolism may create hopelessness and may discourage lifestyle change that could ultimately improve health. At the same time, the role of biology can be understated when individuals believe that weight is entirely a matter of personal control, leading to self-blame when a discrepancy exists between actual and ideal body shapes.

Selected Research

- Twin studies have shown that whether identical twins are reared together or apart, they resemble their twin in weight much more than fraternal twins. In other adoption studies, children's obesity was most strongly correlated to their biological parents' weight, not their adoptive parents' weight (Stunkard et al., 1986).

- For studies that detail the genetic aspects of obesity, see Comuzzie and Allison (1998) and Gura (1998).

- An experiment conducted by Maddox et al. (1968) showed that 76 percent agreed that "a man with a flabby body" was personally responsible for his poor shape, and 84 percent said a woman was accountable for her condition.

- In a series of experiments, DeJong (1986) found that obese women are viewed very differently, depending on how responsible they are thought to be for their condition. Specifically, when told women had a thyroid condition, first impressions were much more favorable toward them.

- Brownell's research showed that physical abnormalities such as endocrine gland malfunction account only for a very small percentage of weight disorders. Biological realities are what ultimately shape the degree to which our weight is behaviorally malleable (Brownell, 1991)

So what difference do these findings make?

- Education of managers and supervisors can help promote acceptance of different body shapes and sizes, with the aim of alleviating the need to seek a rigidly lean and contoured body. Society accepts variation in many physical attributes (eye and hair color, etc.) and should do the same with shape and weight.

• The evaluations of overweight employees may be skewed downward. You need to take caution when comparing two equally qualified employees, one lean and trim and the other overweight, for unintended bias.

• Overweight people are more likely to lose weight and keep it off when they personalize their diet and lifestyle. Hinting, imposing, or suggesting that they change only creates defensiveness and increases shame. Encouraging, supporting, and listening help overweight people make better lifestyle choices.

Some Key Sources

Brownell, K.D. (1991). Personal responsibility and control over our health: When expectation exceeds reality. *Health Psychology, 10* (5), 303–310.

Comuzzie, A.G., & Allison, D.B. (1998). The search for human obesity genes. *Science, 280,* 1374.

DeJong, W., & Kleck, R.E. (1986). The social psychological effects of overweight. In C.P. Herman, M.P. Zanna, & E.T. Higgins (Eds.), *Physical appearance, stigma, and social behaviour: The Ontario Symposium.* Hillsdale: Lawrence Erlbaum.

Gura, T. (1998). Uncoupling proteins provide new clue to obesity's causes. *Science, 280,* 1369.

Maddox, G.L., Back, K., & Liederman, V. (1968). Overweight as social deviance and disability. *Journal of Health and Social Behavior, 9,* 287–298.

Stunkard, A.J., Foch, T.T., & Hrubec, Z. (1986). A twin study of human obesity. *Journal of the American Medical Association, 256,* 51–54.

HR EFFECTIVENESS

80.

What are the key skills that lead to success as an HR professional in order of importance?

SELECT ONE:

☐ A. Personal credibility with customers, knowledge of HR practices, understanding the business, strategic contribution, HR technology.

☐ B. Knowledge of HR practices, strategic contribution, understanding the business, personal credibility with customers, HR technology.

☐ C. Personal credibility with customers, strategic contribution, knowledge of HR practices, understanding the business, HR technology.

☐ D. Strategic contribution, knowledge of HR practices, understanding the business, personal credibility with customers, HR technology.

☐ E. Understanding the business, knowledge of HR practices, personal credibility with customers, strategic contribution, HR technology.

80

80. What are the key skills that lead to success as an HR professional in order of importance?

The correct answer is C: Personal credibility with customers, strategic contribution, knowledge of HR practices, understanding the business, HR technology.

How sure are we at this time?

1	2	3	**4**	5
Hint	Suggestive	Trending	**Substantial**	Solid

Discussion

The successful HR professional has to influence by expertise and relationship, not by power. The relationship comes from personal credibility with clients. This credibility comes from HR professionals forming relationships of trust, communicating well, and earning respect by delivering on results. With credibility, HR professionals must then contribute to the strategic direction of the business. To do this, they must know the business and how HR practices affect the business. Knowing the HR technology is not yet a significant factor.

Being successful as an HR professional and helping the business perform are two different issues. The Michigan research (Brockbank & Ulrich, 2000, 2002) found that personal credibility was the most important thing for HR professionals to be personally successful, but when it comes to helping the business deliver results, the ability to make a strategic contribution was most important.

These results on HR competencies that affect personal success likely apply to other staff groups like IT, finance, legal, and facilities. Having personal credibility is central to staff influence, but making a strategic contribution is central to business success.

Selected Research

- In a series of studies ranging over 15 years, Ulrich and Brockbank (2000, 2002) studied the effectiveness of 27,000 HR professionals across diverse firms on four continents. They asked customers to evaluate the HR professionals on a number of skills and also asked for an overall evaluation of their effectiveness. The study divided the most effective from the least effective and looked at what competency clusters made the most difference. In the 2002 run of the study, the results were:

Personal Credibility = 33 percent.

Strategic Contribution = 25 percent.

HR Practices = 22 percent.

Know the Business = 12 percent.

HR Technology = 8 percent.

So what difference do these findings make?

- HR effectiveness is more about the person than knowledge of HR practices or even knowledge of the business. The ability to influence and persuade are key. Using the influence and persuasion skills in the strategic areas of change and culture are what HR's customers are looking for most.

- Personal credibility becomes very important. It is divided into two factors:

Factor 1: Achieves Results With Integrity

Demonstrates high integrity.

Meets commitments.

Has earned trust.

Has track record of results.

Has "chemistry" with key constituents.

Instills confidence in others.

Factor 2: Contributes to Business Decisions

Provides candid observations.

Asks important questions.

Frames complex ideas in useful ways.

Takes appropriate risks.

Provides alternative insights on business issues.

When HR professionals engage in these behaviors, they gain respect and credibility from their clients. Their personal credibility allows them to have influence and impact on the business.

Some Key Sources

Brockbank, W., & Ulrich, D. (2000, 2002). *The new HR agenda: Human Resource Competency Study* (HRCS). Ann Arbor: The University of Michigan Business School.

Brockbank, W., & Ulrich, D. (2003). *Competencies for the new HR*. Washington DC: Society for Human Resource Management.

Which two characteristics are most associated with success out of one's home country?

SELECT ONE:

☐ A. Learning agility and cultural sensitivity.

☐ B. Knowing the language and international business skills.

☐ C. Knowing the language and one previous international assignment.

☐ D. Working with people previously from that country and learning the language.

☐ E. Pre-assignment travel to that country and international business skills.

81. Which two characteristics are most associated with success out of one's home country?

The correct answer is A: Learning agility and cultural sensitivity.

How sure are we at this time?

1	2	3	**4**	5
Hint	Suggestive	Trending	**Substantial**	Solid

Discussion

Development is the land of the first time and the difficult. People who succeed usually have survived and learned from unique and diverse developmental experiences. The first time working outside one's home country means a new language, new business rules, and different cultural norms. In the special case of serving outside one's home country, adaptability or learning agility coupled with cultural sensitivity seem to be the best overall predictors of performing well. While learning agility is well documented as a predictor of domestic success in many countries, cultural sensitivity is relatively unique to expatriate assignments.

Selected Research

- According to research by Black and Gregersen (1999), between 10 and 20 percent of all U.S. managers sent on international assignments returned early because of problems in adjusting to a foreign country. And, of those who stayed to complete the assignment, almost one-third didn't perform up to the expectations set for them. Another discovery was that "25 percent of those who completed an assignment left their company, often to join a competitor, within one year after repatriation—a turnover rate double that of managers who did not go abroad."

- Dalton et al. (2002) studied the special case of global managers who have responsibility for international operations but aren't technically expatriates. Their research, based on a three-year study with 211 global and local managers, shows that cultural cross-study training is as important to their role as it is to expatriates. From their research, the authors have identified "pivotal capabilities for global management" that are what they refer to as a specific skill set for effective international leadership development based on their experience with hundreds of global managers. The four pivotal capabilities they've identified include "international business knowledge, cultural adaptability, perspective-taking, and the ability to play the role of innovator."

- An in-depth study of 101 global leaders from 36 countries (McCall & Hollenbeck, 2002) found that there is a "critical difference between business-crossings and culture-crossings" and that development to master the complexities of the business-crossings pales in comparison to getting a true understanding of the cultural and human aspects of leading in a global society.

- Based on years of research assessing successful and unsuccessful leadership development methods, McCall (1998) summarizes successful efforts by linking them to the business goals of the organization. Results of his research show a clear strategic advantage for organizations that invest heavily in development—noting that the "ten most admired" companies in America are also considered to be "benchmark companies for developing talent."

- Studies of a learning agility measure found that it related to performance or potential as well for German or British managers as it did for U.S. residents. Spreitzer's work related performance as an expatriate to learning. Expatriate jobs contain a high portion of performing under first-time and tough changing conditions. A major finding was that curiosity, learning adventuresomeness, and more effective learning from experience differentiated high potentials from average performers (Spreitzer et al., 1997).

- Lombardo and Eichinger (2002) note a company that reported its success rate on international placements went from 50 to 95 percent once it instituted learning agility as its primary selection criteria.

- Research by Stone (1991) emphasizes the need to identify personal characteristics and success factors like adaptability, customer sensitivity, risk taking, personal integrity, and flexibility to predict successful offshore candidate profiles.

- A study of derailment in the United States and Europe found that "there are not great differences in factors related to derailment when U.S. and European managers are compared" (Leslie & VanVelsor, 1996).

- Research by Wilson and Dalton (1998) suggests that a combination of technical/functional, professional, managerial, business and cross-cultural expertise and developmental experiences is the difference between success and failure for senior expatriate managers. Specifically, extensive language and cultural training—that teach the customs and etiquette of the country—can make a significant difference. The authors say it's not necessarily the language proficiency itself that makes the difference but that the attempt to learn another language represents a basic, and necessary, courtesy.

- One firm with international operations in more than 100 countries used the same competency model and the same derailment prevention techniques everywhere. In an empirical study of successful versus failed international managers, the competency factors that differentiated the two groups were: handling business complexity; directing, motivating, and developing direct reports; integrity; drive for excellence; organizational savvy; composure; sensitivity to others; and staffing (Lombardo et al., 1988).

- In their book about how two disparate generations approach leadership, Bennis and Thomas (2002) argue that leaders have all been through what they call a "crucible"— explained as a defining event or series of events. According to the authors, that defining event is often an expatriate assignment, because the assignments teach integrity, adaptability or learning agility, courage, and judgment.

So what difference do these findings make?

- Expatriate Selection: When looking at candidates for out of home country assignments, especially for the first one, look for evidence of learning agility and adaptability in past first-time and diverse situations, plus look for cultural sensitivity and prior foreign exposures (study or travel, language training, rooming with foreign students, diversity of educational experiences, foreigners among friends, foreigners among relatives, interest in things foreign, willingness to learn language, etc.).

- Expatriate Preparation: Learning agility can be enhanced. In a number of studies it has been shown that many can significantly enhance their openness to learning new things. Most studies say that cultural orientation or training in the country and culture of the foreign assignment can enhance success once they get there. Studies have also shown that adjustment of the family is as important as the person, so including the whole family in the cultural-awareness training is beneficial.

- Expatriate Success: There is a higher short- and long-term failure rate for first-time foreign assignments. It is usually due to the inability or unwillingness to adapt to a new culture and the unique set of business conditions it presents. Assigning someone to be available and to monitor early experiences would be helpful and increase the chances of success.

- Expatriate Retention: Studies have shown a higher turnover rate for expatriates upon return, so special attention should be paid to managing the return process.

Some Key Sources

Bennis, W.G., & Thomas, R.J. (2002). *Geeks and geezers: How eras, values and defining moments shape leaders.* Boston: Harvard Business School Press.

Black, J.S., & Gregersen, H.B. (1999, March/April). The right way to manage expats. *Harvard Business Review,* 52–63.

Dalton, M., Ernst, C., Deal, J., & Leslie, J. (2002). *Success for the new global manager: What you need to know to work across distances, countries, and cultures.* San Francisco: Jossey-Bass and Greensboro, NC: Center for Creative Leadership.

Leslie, J.B., & VanVelsor, E. (1996). *A look at derailment today: North America and Europe.* Greensboro, NC: Center for Creative Leadership.

Lombardo, M., & Eichinger, R. (2004). *The leadership machine.* Minneapolis: Lominger Limited, Inc.

Lombardo, M., Ruderman, M.N., & McCauley, C.D. (1988). *The dynamics of management derailment.* Greensboro, NC: Center for Creative Leadership.

McCall, M.W. (1998). *High flyers: Developing the next generation of leaders.* Boston: Harvard Business School Press.

McCall, M.W., & Hollenbeck, G.P. (2002). *Developing global executives: The lessons of international experience.* Boston: Harvard Business School Press.

Spreitzer, G.M., McCall, M.W., & Mahoney, J.D. (1997). Early identification of international executive potential. *Journal of Applied Psychology, 82* (1), 6 29.

Stone, R.J. (1991). Expatriate selection and failure. *Human Resource Planning, 14* (1).

Wilson, M.S., & Dalton, M.A. (1998). *International success: Selecting, developing, and supporting expatriate managers.* Greensboro, NC: Center for Creative Leadership.

TEAM PERFORMANCE

82.

When putting groups and teams and taskforces together:

SELECT ONE:

☐ A. Slightly overstaffing gets the best results because people can cover for one another.

☐ B. The natural size of a team is seven and usually leads to the best results.

☐ C. The more complex the task, larger teams are better; larger teams solve problems better because there is more input and diversity of viewpoint.

☐ D. Smaller teams outperform larger teams.

☐ E. Always have one more member than is needed to anticipate weakness in one member.

82. **When putting groups and teams and taskforces together:**

The correct answer is D: Smaller teams outperform larger teams.

How sure are we at this time?

1	**2**	3	4	5
Hint	**Suggestive**	Trending	Substantial	Solid

Discussion

Although managers sometimes form teams too small to accomplish the task, the far more common and dangerous mistake is overstaffing them. Managers sometimes add staff to compensate for projects running late or they staff politically (everyone gets on the team so no one gets rejected).

The right size team depends on the project, but generally a team of five produces high results. Larger teams often break into sub-teams and they become more complex inter-personally. Smaller teams lack the range of skills necessary to solve problems.

Each member on the team should bring a unique skill to the team task. Each member should be able and committed to performing the task at a high level.

Selected Research
• Having researched the effectiveness of team processes for over 20 years, Hackman (2002) concludes that over-manning (referring to settings that have too many team participants) is a greater risk for team performance than is undermanning (having too few team participants).

- An exercise by Hackman and Vidmar (1970) studied groups that ranged in size from two to seven members to assess the impact of size on group processes and performance for various kinds of intellective tasks. After completion of the tasks, the group was asked if there were too few or too many to complete the tasks. Although neither group thought their group was too small or too large, when a perpendicular line was dropped at the point the two groups crossed, it came up with 4.6 members. The study was just an exercise, but the researchers conclude that a team may actually function better when it has slightly fewer members than the task actually requires.

- Research by Lipton and Lorsch (1992) suggests that seven or eight directors is the optimum size on a corporate board. Almost all *Fortune 500* boards are larger than eight.

- Approaching it from another perspective, Hackman (2002), citing research by Morrison (1991), argues that even a six-member team has 15 two-person combinations among members; a seven-member team has 21; and so on. The increased dynamics of the additional pairs can bog down any team.

- Myers and Norris (1968) report findings of an air traffic control research study designed to resolve a conflict between two separate groups—one group who wanted a three-person crew on a Boeing 737 and one group who wanted a two-person crew. The pilots' group felt a three-person crew would add safety, and United Airlines wanted to save labor costs by using a two-person crew. The researchers found that the pilots' fears were unfounded and that there were "no more potentially conflicting air traffic incidents with a two-person crew than there were with a three-person crew."

- Cusumano (1997) notes that, by taking a modular approach to large projects—often with just a project manager and three to eight developers—even Microsoft, as large as it is, has found a way to have large teams work like small teams.

So what difference do these findings make?

• Smaller is better. Undermanning is better than over-manning. Less is more. Asking people to stretch is better than allowing them to atrophy.

• In the movement over the last decade of flattening the organization, many supervisors and managers have more than the usual seven reporting to them. By taking layers out of the organization, team size has increased. Care should be taken to monitor and assist team performance.

• Taskforces probably have too many members in the typical situation. Ask yourself, "What unique skills does this person bring to this team?" If the skills are shared with others, remove one of the people so that each person on the team feels obligated to fully engage. Do not let people be freeloaders on teams. This will reduce their effectiveness and the team's performance. Do not have political appointees. Everyone must bring something to the party.

Some Key Sources

Cusumano, M.A. (1997, Fall). How Microsoft makes large teams work like small teams. *Sloan Management Review*, 9–20.

Hackman, J.R. (2002). *Leading teams: Setting the stage for great performances.* Boston: Harvard Business School Press.

Hackman, J.R., & Vidmar, N. (1970). Effects of size and task type on group performance and member reactions. *Sociometry, 33,* 37–54.

Lipton, M., & Lorsch, J. (1992). A modest proposal for improved corporate governance. *Business Lawyer, 48,* 59–77.

Myers, I.A., & Norris, R.E. (1968). *Summary of results: B-737 crew complement evaluation.* Elk Grove Village, IL: United Airlines.

SUCCESS PREDICTION

83.

What is the best selection variable for predicting the future long-term success of campus hires?

SELECT ONE:

☐ A. All grades.

☐ B. Grades in major.

☐ C. Grades in all job-related courses.

☐ D. Extracurricular activities like sports participation, clubs, sorority/fraternity participation, leadership positions.

☐ E. Scores on school entrance exams plus all grades.

83. What is the best selection variable for predicting the future long-term success of campus hires?

The correct answer is D: Extracurricular activities like sports participation, clubs, sorority/fraternity participation, leadership positions.

How sure are we at this time?

1	2	**3**	4	5
Hint	Suggestive	**Trending**	Substantial	Solid

Discussion

Research that explored five different aspects of college life that might relate to later business success—level of education, grades, the quality of the undergraduate institution, major field of study, and extracurricular activities—revealed: Grades related specifically to intellectual ability and motivation to do quality work; the better-quality schools seemed to produce nonconformity, which often translates into leadership abilities; humanities and social science majors had the best overall performance, with particularly good interpersonal skills; and engineers and math and science majors lacked many important managerial skills. But most studies point to a variety of extracurricular studies as being the most predictive of success.

Selected Research

- Howard's (1986) research found there was either no or very little relationship between grades and managerial success. Using the AT&T studies as a framework, Howard found significant relationships between extracurricular involvement and several career attainment and performance variables.

- According to research by Howard and Bray (1988), the best predictors of later on-the-job adjustment were measures of personality and motivation. A study of self-esteem, affability, positiveness, leadership, motivation, and impulsivity showed that intellectual aptitude and accomplishments "run at cross-purposes in terms of advancement in management and high personal adjustment. The most astute thinkers were, at best, only moderate in adjustment."

- Results of a study of college students by Talbot (1990) found that previous high school achievement and preferences for complex explanations of behavior were the best correlates with persistence and achievement.

- Research by Rubin et al. (2002) found that participation in extracurricular activity is linked to interpersonal skill performance. A study of 618 business students measured the relationship of their extracurricular involvement to four interpersonal skills and found that the extracurricular index score is significantly associated with each of the four interpersonal skill dimensions—communication skills, initiative, decision making, and teamwork.

- Boone, Kurtz, and Fleenor (1988) found that those who became CEOs had considerably higher involvement in extracurricular activity during their college years than did other students.

- Goleman's work (1998) reports on an analysis of 181 jobs in 121 organizations worldwide and notes that "intellectual capability (IQ), knowledge and technical expertise are threshold competencies, while emotional intelligence (EQ) is the differentiating factor in success."

- When the Center for Creative Leadership studied "derailed executives," the researchers found that these executives failed most often because of "an interpersonal flaw" rather than a technical inability (Epperson et al., 1995).

- A study of 1,300 U.S. Air Force recruiting personnel compared high- and low-performers (Handley, 1998) and in the process debunked two long-held beliefs: The study found that those who scored highest on emotional intelligence skills performed the best, regardless of the geographic location; and, that the highest performers worked the fewest hours, perhaps because their higher emotional intelligence traits or "street smarts" made recruiting easier for them than for their less-skilled counterparts.

So what difference do these findings make?

- When evaluating campus candidates, grades are just the starting point. Given two students with equal grades and the same courses, select the one who has had the most variety of out-of-the-classroom experiences along the way.

- Look for patterns of extracurricular activity: Did the candidate do things that required stretch learning and new skills? Did the candidate take personal initiative in some of the extracurricular activities? What roles did the candidate play in the extracurricular activities? What relationships did the candidate engender in the activities? What did the candidate learn from the activities?

Some Key Sources

Boone, L.E., Kurtz, D.L., & Fleenor, C.P. (1988). CEOs: Early signs of a business career. *Business Horizons, 31* (5), 20–25.

Epperson, S.E., Mondi, L., Graff, J.L., & Towle, L.H. (1995, October 2). The EQ factor. *Time Magazine*, p. 66.

Goleman, D. (1998). *Working with emotional intelligence.* New York: Bantam Books.

Handley, R. (1998). *Leveraging corporate performance through human capital profiling.* Unpublished paper.

Howard, A. (1986). College experiences and managerial performance. *Journal of Applied Psychology Monograph, 71* (3), 530–552.

Howard, A., & Bray, D. (1988). *Managerial lives in transition: Advancing age and changing times.* New York: Guilford Press.

Rubin, R.S., Bommer, W.H., & Baldwin, T.T. (2002, Winter). Using extracurricular activity as an indicator of interpersonal skill: Prudent evaluation or recruiting malpractice? *Human Resource Management, 41* (4), 441–454.

Talbot, G.L. (1990, Fall). Self-regulated learning, effort awareness and management in college students: Are they aware of how they act on learning tasks and their learning skills? *Journal of Research & Development in Education, 24* (1), 53–57.

OUTSOURCING

84.

Which of the following is most true about outsourcing?

SELECT ONE:

☐ A. Outsourcing has been proven to be a very cost effective and successful resource and talent management strategy.

☐ B. At this point, with outsourcing being fairly new, about 50% has been successful.

☐ C. Outsourcing works for benefits processing and IT, but little else so far.

☐ D. Outsourcing, like almost anything else, has been shown to be only 25% to 33% cost effective and successful. Most organizations have pulled back from outsourcing.

☐ E. The jury is still out; we really don't know yet.

84. Which of the following is most true about outsourcing?

The correct answer is E: The jury is still out; we really don't know yet.

How sure are we at this time?

1	**2**	3	4	5
Hint	**Suggestive**	Trending	Substantial	Solid

Discussion

Taking HR as an example, the HR world can be divided in half. One half of the HR world is traditional administrative work. This includes routine, standardized transactions, such as payroll, benefits, and training administration. This work has generally consumed more than half of the HR resources. Today, HR is finding new ways to do this work. It is being done through service centers where telephone operators can answer an employee's questions. It is being done through technology where employees are self-sufficient in their administrative duties. It is also being outsourced. Many firms are outsourcing pieces of the HR transaction work to vendors (e.g., payroll to one vendor, benefits administration to another). Increasingly, large firms are outsourcing their entire HR administrative duties to external vendors like Exult. These outsourcing firms become partners for the HR function and sometimes accomplish the administrative work better, faster, and cheaper. The driving goal for the transactional half of the HR world is parity. Doing administrative things better, faster, and cheaper will not lead to a competitive advantage but should get parity in the market.

The second half of HR is transformation work, where the HR professional is charged with turning business strategies into results. This work requires HR professionals who are coaches, facilitators, architects, designers, and leaders. This work requires that HR professionals understand how to identify and create organization capabilities. This work means forming partnerships with line managers, understanding external customers, and serving investors.

By doing outsourcing well, HR departments can spend more time and attention to the more strategic transformational work.

Another example is IT. Companies are outsourcing part or all of IT to vendors like EDS and CSC. Those vendors manage and run IT, and in some cases the employees actually are converted and become employees of the vendor.

There isn't much research work published on outsourcing effectiveness. We might anticipate mixed results. All other major attempts for transition and change (mergers, acquisitions, TQM, Six Sigma, reinventing the organization, etc.) show that less than half are successful. Outsourcing might join that list.

Selected Research

- Kessler (2001), drawing on data from surveys carried out following a major outsourcing effort, warns against "a simplistic view of worker perceptions and outsourcing and suggests that they are likely to be embedded in a set of specific organizational circumstances and a range of situational factors."

- An MIT Management Review White Paper (Sweetman, 2001) found that moving the IT function outside the company resulted in a turnover rate of only 10 percent in the previous year, about half of what would be expected from similar groups.

- According to research by Pfeffer (2001), the free-agent mentality generates high turnover, with turnover estimates ranging from 20 percent to more than 30 percent annually.

- In her research, Kaye (1996) found significant correlation between companies who outsource functions previously performed in-house and career movement for workers who see this as eliminating internal opportunities.

- Jeannette Swist (1997), reporting on a broad-based survey, noted that 94 percent of survey respondents said their companies had implemented recent changes, and 34 percent of survey respondents report a significant increase in outsourcing.

So what difference do these findings make?
- Be smart with outsourcing. Try to measure the real costs. Especially look at the costs of not developing internal talent in the outsourced areas and retention of other key talent. Make sure to measure customer satisfaction. Be on the lookout for best practices. Watch the industry leaders.

- Don't outsource sources of competitive advantage. Realize that if you outsource something, you are going for industry average, not differentiation.

- Form partnerships with outsourcing vendors. Do not have these relationships be arm's length because they will become critical to your success over time.

- Create clear contracts with outsourcing vendors that define what is expected, and offer incentives for performance.

Some Key Sources
Kaye, B. (1996, February). Up is not the only way. *Training and Development, 50* (2), 48–53.

Kessler, I. (2001). Outsourcing and the employee perspective. *Human Resource Management Journal, 9* (2).

Pfeffer, J. (2001, Spring). What's wrong with management practices in Silicon Valley? A lot. *MIT Sloan Management Review, 42* (3), 102.

Sweetman, K. (2001, Summer). Spreading IT expertise throughout the company. *MIT Sloan Management Review, 42* (4), 13.

Swist, J. (1997). *Addressing the challenges of executing change.* Published as a White Paper through the Society for Human Resource Management. Copyright© 1997–1999, *Applied Resource Management.*

DIVERSITY

85.

Being a member of a protected class alone . . .?

SELECT ONE:

☐ A. Can impact performance negatively.

☐ B. Cannot affect performance unless there is overt or covert discrimination.

☐ C. Cannot affect performance unless there is an overt act of prejudice.

☐ D. Can affect performance if there has been demonstrated bias in the same environment.

☐ E. Can affect performance if he or she is the only member of the protected class present.

85. Being a member of a protected class alone . . .?

The correct answer is A: Can impact performance negatively.

How sure are we at this time?

1	**2**	3	4	5
Hint	**Suggestive**	Trending	Substantial	Solid

Discussion

There is a relatively new concept being added to the long list of potential threats to equal opportunity. The new threat is sometimes named "stereotype threat." Basically, it means that if you are a member of a stereotyped class, that alone, can lead to poorer performance since you expect it to happen. This can cause anxiety or it can lead to increased levels of disengagement—in essence, giving up before you start. It is similar to the Pygmalion effect. The Pygmalion effect in education found that if teachers were given false data about the mental abilities of students, the teacher treated each according to the false data, and the students subsequently performed according to the false data. Expectations affect behavior.

Selected Research

- Research on "stereotype threat" (Steele, 1997; Steele & Aronson, 1995) demonstrates that a person only has to know he or she is a potential target of a negative stereotype for it to have an effect, even if people outside of their stereotyped group don't actually display any prejudicial behavior.

- A study by Quinn and Spencer (2001) found evidence to support the role anxiety plays in stereotype threat. Women in one commonly known stereotype threat situation performed less well on a math test than men or than women in a low-threat condition. These same women were more likely to say they "could not formulate a strategy to solve the problems."

- Research by Schmader, Major, and Gramzow (2001) found evidence that Blacks are less affected than Whites by positive or negative feedback on intelligence tests. The research showed a relationship between the perceived injustices of being in a particular ethnic group and the tendency to discount academic feedback for Blacks and Latinos/as but not for Whites.

So what difference do these findings make?

- If things were not precarious enough, mere membership in a protected class with a history of stereotyped expectations is enough to make it partially come true.

- It's important to continually counter the myths of stereotyping, not only to those who stereotype but also to those who are stereotyped.

- On a personal note, if you are a member of a minority group, try to avoid doing the behaviors included in the stereotype. Try to focus on doing your job and living your life. For example, if you are deeply religious and people have stereotyped expectations of you, it may not make sense to try to proselyte at work and bring up religion in every conversation. This will only affirm a stereotype and turn colleagues against you. This does not mean you need to hide from your beliefs, but let them emerge naturally rather than forcing the issue.

Some Key Sources

Quinn, D.M., & Spencer, S.J. (2001). The interference of stereotype threat with women's generation of mathematical problem solving strategies. *Journal of Social Issues, 57* (1), 55–71.

Schmader, T., Major, B., & Gramzow, R.H. (2001). Coping with ethnic stereotyping in the academic domain: Perceived injustice and psychological disengagement. *Journal of Social Issues, 57* (1), 93–111.

Steele, C.M. (1997). A threat in the air: How stereotypes shape intellectual identity and performance. *American Psychologist, 52,* 613–629.

Steele, C.M., & Aronson, J. (1995). Stereotype threat and the intellectual performance of African Americans. *Journal of Personality and Social Psychology, 69,* 797–811.

MEASUREMENT

86.

If a study reported that the correlation between grades in college and performance as a manager five years later was .50 and was significant beyond the .01 level, what would that mean?

SELECT ONE:

☐ A. 50% of the people who have high grades also are the best managers.

☐ B. 50% of the highest scoring grade getters are also the best managers.

☐ C. 25% of the difference in manager performance could be explained by differences in grades.

☐ D. 50% of the people have both high grades and good managerial performance.

☐ E. If you have grades in the upper 50% of the group, you have a 50% chance of being a good manager.

86

86. **If a study reported that the correlation between grades in college and performance as a manager five years later was .50 and was significant beyond the .01 level, what would that mean?**

The correct answer is C: 25% of the difference in manager performance could be explained by differences in grades.

How sure are we at this time?

1	2	3	4	**5**
Hint	Suggestive	Trending	Substantial	**Solid**

Discussion

A correlation shows the relationship of two measures—to interpret it as a percent, it must be squared. This is because you have to multiply together the two variables being related. This yields 25 percent for a correlation of .50. So the above finding would mean that 25 percent of the difference between managers would be accounted for by differences in grades. The remaining 75 percent would be due to other factors. **This fictitious finding is also not true.** There is actually little relationship between grades and subsequent performance as a manager.

Selected Research

- A correlation is a measure of the association or relationship between two variables. The two most popular correlation coefficients are: Spearman's correlation coefficient rho and Pearson's product-moment correlation coefficient. When calculating a correlation coefficient for ranked data (such as the standings in a golf tournament), select Spearman's technique. For interval (such as one to five performance rating scale) or ratio-type data (such as percent of sales against plan), use Pearson's technique. Pearson's is the most commonly used correlational method. An example would be if you want to find out if boss ratings on competencies relate to independent measures of performance.

- The value of a correlation coefficient can vary from -1 to +1. A -1 indicates a perfect negative correlation, while a +1 indicates a perfect positive correlation. A correlation of zero means there is no relationship between the two variables. When there is a negative correlation between two variables, as the value of one variable increases, the value of the other variable decreases, and vice versa. If productivity goes up when absenteeism goes down, there is a negative correlation between the two. When there is a positive correlation between two variables, as the value of one variable increases, the value of the other variable also increases. The variables move together. If the ratings of strategic thinking go up as performance ratings go up, then there would be a positive correlation between the two. However, the fact that a relationship exists doesn't mean the relationship is noteworthy. The significance (probability) of the correlation coefficient is determined from the t-statistic, which essentially looks at the odds that the relationship occurred by chance. Ordinarily, you should have at least 30 pairs before using a correlation coefficient.

So what difference do these findings make?

- When you see a correlation coefficient reported as part of a study, square it to get the percent difference the relationship would account for.

- Be aware that in the social sciences, correlations of .40 to .60 are generally quite high. This means that 16 to 36 percent of something is explained by these results. Social science is still as much of an art as a science, but

20 to 40 percent explanations are profound and worth paying attention to.

Some Key Sources

Johnson, R.A., & Wichern, D.W. (2001). *Applied multivariate statistical analysis.* Englewood Cliffs, NJ: Prentice Hall.

Weiss, N.A. (1999). *Introductory statistics* (5th ed.). Reading, MA: Addison-Wesley.

EMPLOYEE DEVELOPMENT

87.

How skilled are managers, in general, at being good coaches and helping others develop their long-term careers?

SELECT ONE:

☐ A. Managers, in general, are outstanding at coaching and helping their people develop.

☐ B. Managers, in general, are strong at coaching and helping their people develop.

☐ C. Managers, in general, are about average in their ability to develop their people.

☐ D. Managers, in general, are not very skilled in helping their people in career development.

☐ E. Managers, in general, are very poor at coaching and developing their people.

87. How skilled are managers, in general, at being good coaches and helping others develop their long-term careers?

The correct answer is E: Managers, in general, are very poor at coaching and developing their people.

How sure are we at this time?

1	2	3	4	**5**
Hint	Suggestive	Trending	Substantial	**Solid**

Discussion
This is one thing that almost everyone agrees upon—that helping people with long-term career development is important and that few do it well. No wonder the leadership bench isn't filled with a lot of skilled people. Companies know they have to build and develop the talent pool but, for many reasons, they're simply not doing it. The science and technology is known, the best practices agreed to, but implementation and execution is still poor. There are few companies that are trying to help their managers become better coaches.

Selected Research
- Normative data (Lombardo & Eichinger, 2002) indicate that developing others is 67th of 67 possible competencies in rated competence. The data were collected across six years, in over 140 diverse organizations and involved over 50,000 raters.

- According to the McKinsey Heir Apparent study (Grossman, 1999) only 7 percent of firms hold managers accountable in any direct way for the development of their people.

Grossman notes that "according to McKinsey's War for Talent study, only 3 percent of firms said they did a good job filling the bench with viable candidates for increased responsibilities."

- Research by Kotter (1988) argues that organizations with superior leadership focus on "working to make younger managers visible to senior management and creating a wealth of challenging leadership development opportunities."

- In the Sears Credit research reported in *HR Magazine* (Joinson, 2001), "the company realigned its incentive system to recognize excellent people-management as the most significant factor in promotions. It also created specialized project management positions to do high-value work and developed career paths for both team managers and project managers. Now, the team manager's goal (measured by their managers on associate development logs) is to spend 80 percent of their contact time with associates developing them, primarily through coaching."

- Hogan et al. (1994) found that the base rate for managerial incompetence in America is between 60 and 75 percent.

- Lombardo and Eichinger (2002) argue that "companies suffer an enormous cost by not acting on the negative influence of underperformers. Underperformers are unable to attract top talent, do not develop the people below them, block opportunities for those around them, undermine the morale of the group they lead, and ultimately cause better performers to leave the company."

- As early as 1991 (Barrick et al., 1991), research indicated that a high performing executive was 15 percent better than an average one, or worth $25 million after taxes for a *Fortune 500* company.

- Studies by Goleman and Cherniss (2001) reported that top performers exceeded revenue targets by 15 to 20 percent.

- In another large study (Hunter et al., 1990), top performers had 19 to 48 percent higher output than average performers.

- Spencer and Spencer (1993) found that, with sales jobs, top performers routinely outperform the lowest performers by 100 percent.

- Spencer (2001) found that "among computer programmers, superb performers were 1,272 percent better than average performers and superior account managers produced 600 percent more revenue than average account managers."

So what difference do these findings make?

- Relying exclusively on line managers to coach and develop their people for the long-term is a losing strategy. Typical line managers aren't good at it, don't have much motivation to do it, are terminally busy and don't have or make quality time for it, and are not rewarded for it when the few do actually do it.

- Best practice is a coordinated process driven by professional HR and passionately supported by top management, with the cooperation and involvement of line managers and the people themselves. No one group has enough skill or time or motivation to get it done.

- Be careful, however, of the growing "coaching" profession. Often, former executives label themselves "coaches" without much training or experience. A good coach is someone who has a variety of experiences, not just in one company; who knows the research on managerial excellence, not just the practice; who is able to adapt research to each unique situation, not just apply the same tools over and over again; is able to form relationships of trust by caring about the person being coached and giving honest and direct feedback; and is constantly learning to be a more effective coach.

Some Key Sources

Barrick, M.R., Day, D.V., Lord, R.G., & Alexander, R.A. (1991). Assessing the utility of executive leadership. *Leadership Quarterly, 2* (1), 9–22.

Goleman, D., & Cherniss, C. (Eds.). (2001). *The emotionally intelligent workplace: How to select for, measure, and improve emotional intelligence in individuals, groups, and organizations.* San Francisco: Jossey-Bass.

Grossman, R.J. (1999). McKinsey study reported in "Heirs Unapparent." *HR Magazine 44* (2), 36-44.

Hogan, R., Curphy, G.J., & Hogan, J. (1994, June). What we know about leadership: Effectiveness and personality. *American Psychologist, 49* (6), 493–504.

Hogan, R., Raskin, R., & Fazzini, D. (1990). The dark side of charisma. In K.E. Clark & M.B. Clark (Eds.), *Measures of leadership* (pp. 343–354). West Orange, NJ: Leadership Library of America.

Hunter, J.E., Schmidt, F.L., & Judiesch, M.K. (1990). Individual differences in output variability as a function of job complexity. *Journal of Applied Psychology, 75* (1), 28–42.

Joinson, C. (2001, May). Employee sculpt thyself, with a little help. *HR Magazine, 46* (5).

Kotter, J.P. (1988). How leaders grow leaders. *Across the Board, 25,* 38–42.

Lombardo, M., & Eichinger, R. (2004). *The leadership machine.* Minneapolis: Lominger Limited, Inc.

Spencer, L. (2001). The economic value of emotional intelligence competencies and EIC-based HR programs. In D. Goleman & C. Cherniss (Eds.), *The emotionally intelligent workplace: How to select for, measure, and improve emotional intelligence in individuals, groups, and organizations.* San Francisco: Jossey-Bass.

Spencer, L., & Spencer, S. (1993). *Competence at work.* New York: John Wiley & Sons, Inc.

DIVERSITY

What is the effect of formal diversity training programs?

SELECT ONE:

☐ A. There is little impact; prejudice in, prejudice out.

☐ B. There is some impact but not much.

☐ C. There is moderate impact; there is noticeable improvement.

☐ D. The impact on the organization is actually better than on individuals; just having a diversity training program makes a difference because it signals the importance of diversity.

☐ E. There is actually a reverse effect; people get more convinced of their opinions.

88. What is the effect of formal diversity training programs?

The correct answer is B: There is some impact but not much.

How sure are we at this time?

1	2	3	4	**5**
Hint	Suggestive	Trending	Substantial	**Solid**

Discussion

Studies have shown mixed but some positive impact of formal diversity training. Some people break free of past negative views and prejudices and many get a bit more sensitive. A direct bottom-line impact has yet to be demonstrated. As in everything like this, those programs that are better designed and executed work better.

Selected Research

- A five-year BOLD (Business Opportunities for Leadership Diversity) initiative begun in 1997 examined the relationships between gender and racial diversity and business performance (Kochan et al., 2003). They found few direct effects of diversity on performance—either positive or negative.

- Research by Bezrukova and Jehn (2001) revealed that diversity training initiatives in organizations rarely lead to long-term changes in attitudes or behaviors.

- A review of the literature (Richard & Johnson, 1999; Richard et al., 2002; Williams & O'Reilly, 1998) shows that few organizations have conducted research that demonstrates the impact of diversity or diversity management practices on financial success.

- One exception to the above is a study that compared companies who have well-laid-out diversity management programs with those who have paid legal damages to settle discrimination lawsuits. The companies with exemplary diversity programs also performed better as measured by their stock prices (Wright et al., 1995). This, the researchers point out, doesn't make a direct connection. "It may just mean that better-managed companies perform better and have better people programs, including diversity."

- Research by Williams and O'Reilly (1998) reports that diverse groups, teams, or business units don't necessarily perform better, feel more committed to their organizations, or experience higher levels of satisfaction. Instead, the evidence suggests that diversity may produce more conflict and employee turnover, as well as more creativity and innovation.

- Conflicting research that examined diversity in top management teams in the banking industry found in one study (Bantel & Jackson, 1989) that diversity in top management was associated with greater innovation within bank branches. In another study, diversity was associated with higher rates of turnover among top management team members (Jackson et al., 1991).

So what difference do these findings make?

- Efforts to create and manage diverse workforces have generally paid off by eliminating some of the potentially negative effects of diversity on group processes and performance documented previously in research and popular literature. There are some conditions where diversity, if managed well, may even enhance performance.

Suggestions for best practices:

- Modify the business case. Since research doesn't seem to support the direct business case for diversity, some recommend "success [in diversity efforts] is facilitated by a perspective that considers diversity to be an opportunity for everyone in an organization to learn from each other how better to accomplish their work and, on occasion, that requires a supportive and cooperative organizational culture." Diversity also encourages innovation, where people have different approaches and ideas and thus find new ways of doing things.

- Look beyond the business case. If there isn't a business case that says diversity makes for better or worse results, look beyond that to "diversity is both a labor-market imperative and societal expectation and value."

- Support experimentation and evaluation. Create new interventions that have the potential to demonstrate a positive link between diversity and performance.

- A challenge of all training programs is to turn what is learned in the classroom into practice. Diversity training may raise awareness, but if it does not change behavior, it is not effective. Changing behavior is difficult, particularly when some causes of behavior are deep-seated biases or prejudices. Ongoing feedback becomes a critical factor in behavioral change. After a diversity training course, the follow-up is critical: What are people doing differently? Who is holding participants accountable for their actions? What are the incentives for changing behaviors?

Some Key Sources

Bantel, K.A., & Jackson, S.E. (1989). Top management and innovations in banking: Does the composition of the top team make a difference? [Special issue]. *Strategic Management Journal, 10*, 107–124.

Bezrukova, K., & Jehn, K.A. (2001). *The effects of diversity training programs.* Unpublished manuscript, The Wharton School, University of Pennsylvania, Philadelphia, PA.

Jackson, S.E., Brett, J.F., Sessa, V.I., Cooper, D.M., Julin, J.A., & Peyronnin, K. (1991). Some differences make a difference: Individual dissimilarity and group heterogeneity as correlates of recruitment, promotions, and turnover. *Journal of Applied Psychology, 76*, 675–689.

Kochan, T., Bezrukova, K., Ely, R., Jackson, S., Joshi, A., Jehn, K., Leonard, J., Levine, D., & Thomas, D. (2003, Spring). The effects of diversity on business performance: Report of the Diversity Research Network. *Human Resource Management, 42* (1), 3–21.

Richard, O.C., & Johnson, N.B. (1999). Making the connection between formal human resource diversity practices and organizational effectiveness: Beyond management fashion. *Performance Improvement Quarterly, 12*, 77–96.

Richard, O.C., Kochan, T.A., & McMillan-Capehart, A. (2002). The impact of visible diversity on organizational effectiveness: Disclosing the contents in Pandora's black box. *Journal of Business and Management, 8,* 1–26.

Williams, K.Y., & O'Reilly, C.A., III. (1998). Demography and diversity in organizations: A review of 40 years of research. In B.M. Staw & L.L. Cummings (Eds.), *Research in organizational behavior* (Vol. 20, pp. 77–140). Greenwich, CT: JAI Press.

Wright, P., Ferris, S.P., Hiller, J.S., & Kross, M. (1995). Competitiveness through management of diversity: Effects on stock price valuation. *Academy of Management Journal, 38*, 272–287.

GENDER

89.

Research has shown that women who have to play multiple roles, like mother, spouse, and management professional . . .:

SELECT ONE:

☐ A. Have more trouble dealing with all of the cumulative stress.

☐ B. Are able to only do well in one or maybe two of the three roles.

☐ C. Actually cope better than those women who only play one role.

☐ D. Tend to do poorly in all three roles.

☐ E. Select one to excel in and marginally hold the other two together.

89

89. **Research has shown that women who have to play multiple roles, like mother, spouse, and management professional . . .:**

The correct answer is C: Actually cope better than those women who only play one role.

How sure are we at this time?

1	2	3	**4**	5
Hint	Suggestive	Trending	**Substantial**	Solid

Discussion

Much research has shown that women who have to play multiple roles simultaneously actually cope better than childless or single women managers. The studies show that the multiple-role women are able to derive emotional benefits from all of the roles they play. Studies have also indicated that they get better at multitasking, which helps them in their managerial careers. And they have more points of support they can rely on during tough times.

Selected Research

• Where popular media and prior organizational studies address conflict between work and family in terms of dysfunction, Ruderman, Ohlott, Panzer, and King (2002) found the opposite to be true. Their study reports that the roles women play in their personal lives actually enhance their effectiveness in the management role. The researchers point specifically to the psychological benefits, emotional advice and support, and practice multitasking as helpful in building interpersonal and task-related managerial skills.

- Research by Barnett (1998) found similar results, suggesting the psychological and sociological benefits of multiple roles for women.

- According to research by Tharenou et al. (1994), women advance more slowly in corporations than married men with children.

- Along this same vein, research by Marks and MacDermid (1996) suggests a new method of looking at the concept of the benefits of multiple roles in determining management success. Their research looks at personal resources as generating more rather than less energy and that these resources can be shared among the various roles.

So what difference do these findings make?

- While much is written in the popular literature about the awful plight of women who have the seemingly impossible job of playing multiple roles and more roles than male counterparts or childless or single colleagues, the research says it's not all bad. We still need to support all of the various subgroups of employees, each with their special needs. In the case of multiple-role female professionals, day care support, time flexibility, and assignment timing seem called for. Supporting these female professionals during the child-raising and management years would seem to yield above average managers once they are empty nesting.

- One company focused hiring on post-child-rearing women. They found that these women who were competent in child rearing and active in social responsibilities (e.g., head of parent-teacher association or active in neighborhood groups) are a good source of managerial talent.

Some Key Sources

Barnett, R.C. (1998). Toward a review and reconceptualization of the work/family literature. *Genetic, Social, and General Psychology Monographs, 124* (2), 125–182.

Marks, S.R., & MacDermid, S.M. (1996). Multiple roles and the self: A theory of role balance. *Journal of Marriage and the Family, 58,* 417–432.

Ruderman, M.N., Ohlott, P.J., Panzer, K., & King, S.N. (2002). Benefits of multiple roles for managerial women. *Academy of Management Journal, 45* (2), 369–386.

Tharenou, P., Latimer, S., & Conroy, D. (1994). How do you make it to the top? An examination of influence on women's and men's managerial advancement. *Academy of Management Journal, 37,* 899–931.

EAP

90.

When it comes to suggesting, recommending, or buying therapy directly or through an employee assistance program (EAP):

SELECT ONE:

☐ A. In efficacy studies of all types of therapeutic techniques across a wide range of problems gainfully employed people have, Behavior Modification and Rational Cognitive Behavioral techniques show the best long-term results. It's best to use therapists who use those methods and let them refer out issues handled better by other methods.

☐ B. In studies of the effectiveness of different schools of therapy, there is a specific type of therapy for each specific kind of problem. Relationship problems are best addressed with Rogerian and Psychodrama methods, self-esteem issues are best dealt with by Psychodynamic techniques, values conflicts by either Gestalt or Logo methods, and so on. Most mental health professionals know which method best fits which problem type. It's best to leave that decision with them.

☐ C. The method of therapy isn't as important as the quality of the therapist. Rogerian, Adlerian, Gestalt, Psychodynamic, Logo, Existential, Behavior Modification, etc. are all about equal across most light problems employees face. Best to find good people regardless of the method they use.

☐ D. We really don't know. The research is contradictory and confusing.

☐ E. All major schools of therapy that have been around a long time (more than 20 years) are equally effective on adult-employed populations.

90

90. **When it comes to suggesting, recommending, or buying therapy directly or through an employee assistance program (EAP):**

   The correct answer is A: In efficacy studies of all types of therapeutic techniques across a wide range of problems gainfully employed people have, Behavior Modification and Rational Cognitive Behavioral techniques show the best long-term results. It's best to use therapists who use those methods and let them refer out issues handled better by other methods.

How sure are we at this time?

1	2	3	**4**	5
Hint	Suggestive	Trending	**Substantial**	Solid

Discussion

Cognitive therapy is considered the most heavily researched form of psychotherapy. Research points to the fundamental ideas behind cognitive behavior therapy as the primary reasons to recommend this method over others: the approach is a collaborative relationship between the client and the therapist; holds the premise that psychological distress is largely a function of disturbances in cognitive processes; focuses on changing cognitions to produce desired changes in behavior; and is generally time-limited and focused on specific and structured target problems. In an adult-employed population, it is the best.

Other therapeutic techniques have had less research, so while they may prove to be effective in the future, at the present time, the research is not as clear.

Selected Research

- According to the National Institute of Mental Health (NIMH), CBT or cognitive behavioral therapy generally lasts about 12 weeks—with evidence that, after treatment, the beneficial effects of CBT last longer than those of medications for either panic disorder or social phobia (Beck, 2001, NIMH Web site).

- In the third edition of *Barlow's Handbook of Psychological Disorders* (2001), he notes the results of effective and ineffective treatments: "Cognitive-behavioral treatment for panic disorder and agoraphobia are highly effective; a combination of exposure therapy and cognitive restructuring therapy (such as CBGT) is an effective intervention for Social Anxiety Disorder; and depressed clients treated with cognitive therapy have lower relapse rates than those treated with medication."

- A review of multiple studies by Wright and Beck (1995) shows that cognitive therapy is an effective treatment for depression, panic disorder, and social phobia.

- Butler and Beck (2000) reviewed 14 meta-analyses that have investigated the efficacy of cognitive therapy with a total of 9,138 subjects in 325 studies involving 465 specific comparisons. They found that one year after treatment discontinuation, depressed patients who had been treated with cognitive therapy had half the relapse rate of depressed patients who had been treated with antidepressant medication (30 percent versus 60 percent). They also found cognitive therapy was equally effective as behavior therapy in the treatment of adult depression and obsessive-compulsive disorder.

- Findings by Butler and Beck (2000) demonstrate the effectiveness of cognitive and cognitive behavioral therapies (CBT). In particular, the researchers found "these therapies are substantially superior to no-treatment, wait list, and placebo controls for adult and adolescent depression, generalized anxiety disorder, panic disorder with or without agoraphobia, social phobia, and childhood depressive and anxiety disorders."

- Schmidt and Woolaway-Bickel (2000) found evidence that the quality of patients' efforts at self-help—that the more frequently patients try cognitive therapy skills, the more likely they are to increase competency in their use and derive greater benefits in the form of reduced symptoms and better functioning—is a better predictor of outcome in cognitive therapy than is the quantity of those efforts.

So what difference do these findings make?

- Cognitive behavior therapy would be the first-choice recommendation for most employed adults with problems.

- It's faster and more cost effective because it's generally time-limited and focuses on specific and structured target problems.

- It's less disruptive to the organization—again, the goals are to have the employee "learn to minimize emotional disturbances and self-defeating behaviors, acquire more realistic philosophies of life, reduce blame of self and others for problems in life, learn ways to deal with future difficulties, and learn to examine and change some basic values that cause disturbances." The method focuses on learning how to dispute irrational beliefs, not the emotional and behavioral consequences.

- Finding qualified therapists who do cognitive behavioral therapy is worth the time and effort. It will assure that employees find help that is the most helpful.

- While medication may seem like a quick fix, it does not have the same long-term effect as cognitive behavioral therapy.

Some Key Sources

Barlow, D.H. (2001). *Clinical handbook of psychological disorders* (3rd ed., pp. 49, 120, 268). New York: Guilford Press.

Beck, J.S. (2001, June 13). *Cognitive-behavioral and behavioral therapy.* National Institute of Mental Health: www.nimh.nih.gov

Butler, A.C. (2000). Meta-analysis findings favour cognitive therapy for many disorders. *Cognitive Therapy Today, 5* (1), 3–5.

Butler, A.C., & Beck, J.S. (2000). Cognitive therapy outcomes: A review of meta-analyses. *Journal of the Norwegian Psychological Association, 37.*

Schmidt, N.B., & Woolaway-Bickel, K. (2000). The effects of treatment compliance on outcome in cognitive-behavioral therapy for panic disorder: Quality versus quantity. *Journal of Consulting and Clinical Psychology, 68* (1), 13–18.

Wright, J.H., & Beck, A.T. (1995). Cognitive therapy. In R.E. Hales, S.E. Yudofsky, & J.A. Talbott (Eds.), *American Psychiatric Press textbook of psychiatry* (2nd ed., pp. 1083–1114.90). Washington, DC: American Psychiatric Press.

91.

What is the single best predictor of who will climb to higher levels in organizations and perform well once there?

SELECT ONE:

☐ A. Grades in major.

☐ B. Past performance.

☐ C. Intelligence (cognitive ability).

☐ D. Learning agility.

☐ E. Functional and technical skills.

91. **What is the single best predictor of who will climb to higher levels in organizations and perform well once there?**

The correct answer is D: Learning agility.

How sure are we at this time?

1	2	3	**4**	5
Hint	Suggestive	Trending	**Substantial**	Solid

Discussion
The best way to forecast leadership is to use a weighted combination of cognitive ability, personality, simulation, role play, learning agility, and multi-rater assessment instruments and techniques evaluating strengths and weaknesses. But the single best predictor, used alone, is learning agility. It has the strongest relationship to performance in new and different jobs and potential to successfully perform in new and different jobs. Adding and deploying new skills on the fly is what plays most in first-time conditions.

Selected Research
- Research by Wagner and Sternberg (1990) found tacit knowledge (an applied form of intelligence—or street smarts) to be a predictor of executive success.

- In the CCL studies (McCall et al., 1988), successful executives had a strong and similar pattern of learning from key job assignments. In a companion study (McCall & Lombardo, 1983), one of the key reasons cited for derailment was being blocked to new learning.

- In studies that have dealt with success and derailment, failure to learn to do something differently in order to make key transitions has figured prominently in the results.

Additionally, lack of self-awareness and a tendency to overrate oneself have been found to be crippling. In contrast, successful people learned more new behavior and were more self-aware, etc. (see Spreitzer et al., 1997; Lombardo & Eichinger, 2000; Shipper & Dillard, 2000; Lombardo & Eichinger, 2003).

- Research from Yale by Robert Sternberg states that scores on a measure of learning from experience were unrelated to IQ scores, and that the best predictor of level attained was a measure of learning from experience (Sternberg et al., 1995).

- One study (McCauley & Brutus, 1998) that included tests for intelligence, personality, cognitive, preference for innovation, job satisfaction, and orientation in interpersonal relations found that the test of tacit knowledge (experience learned) was the single best predictor of performance (.61 correlation versus .38 for IQ correlation).

- In numerous studies of successful leaders, researchers at the Center for Creative Leadership (CCL) in Greensboro, NC have determined that developmental learning occurs primarily through work experiences, less in formal training programs, and that successful corporations emphasize job challenge for developing managers (McCauley et al., 1994).

- In a study that related learning agility, IQ, and Big Five personality measures to job performance and measures of promotability, learning agility was by far the most related to both criterion measures. The other measures added very little to the regression equations (Connolly & Viswesvaran, 2002).

- Lombardo and Eichinger (2003) found that the best predictors of actual promotion were competencies measuring learning agility and drive for results (achievement motivation).

- Lombardo and Eichinger (2003b) found that after promotion, people with higher learning agility scores performed significantly better than those with moderate or low learning agility scores. Of the 155 men and women who were promoted, all the highest performers were in the high-scoring learning agility group.

- Research by Boyatzis (1982) showed that, among managers and executives, top performers are able to balance their drive and ambition with emotional self-control, harnessing their personal needs in the service of the organization's. The research also showed self-confidence as the competency that distinguishes average from star performers.

- Stogdill (1948) reviewed research on personality and emergent leadership in a variety of unstructured groups. He concluded that measures of "dominance, extraversion, sociability, ambition or achievement, responsibility, integrity, self-confidence, mood and emotional control, diplomacy, and cooperativeness were positively related to emergent leadership."

- In the AT&T Managerial Assessment Project, Howard and Bray (1988) found that the performance dimensions that were predictive of success included need for advancement, behavior flexibility, creativity, organizing and planning—which correspond to the Big Five dimensions of surgency, conscientiousness, emotional stability, and intellect.

- In McClelland's (1998) analysis of the competencies that distinguish star performers from average ones, he found a tipping point effect when people exhibited excellence in six or more competencies. McClelland argues that a critical mass of competencies above the tipping point distinguishes top from average performers. "In life—and particularly on the job people exhibit these competencies in groupings, often across clusters, that allow competencies to support one another. Emotional competencies seem to operate most powerfully in synergistic groupings, with the evidence suggesting that mastery of a 'critical mass' of competencies is necessary for superior performance."

So what difference do these findings make?

- If you only had one thing you could assess to predict future success, use learning agility. Of all the things you measure people on, how well they learn from experience is probably the one most important for predicting future performance and potential. There are several well-established measures of acquiring new learning/behaviors. So the lesson is to be sure to assess learning agility and combine the results with other assessments of other skills, abilities, and experiences.

- Learning agility is the ability to reflect on experience and then engage in new behaviors based on those reflections. Learning agility requires self-confidence to honestly examine oneself, self-awareness to seek feedback and suggestions, and self-discipline to engage in new behaviors. It comes from a constant thirst for improvement and a capacity to have new insights from almost every job experience.

- Since scores on measures of learning from experience are not very related to IQ and grades, this means that additional assessment must be done on how smart they are. Grades in school and scores on cognitive ability tests can be used to assess intelligence.

Some Key Sources

Boyatzis, R. (1982). *The competent manager: A model for effective performance.* New York: John Wiley and Sons, Inc.

Connolly, J.A., & Viswesvaran, C. (2002, April). *Assessing the construct validity of a measure of learning agility.* A presentation at the Seventeenth Annual Conference of the Society for Industrial and Organizational Psychology, Toronto, Canada.

Howard, A., & Bray, D. (1988). *Managerial lives in transition: Advancing age and changing times.* New York: Guilford Press.

Lombardo, M., & Eichinger, R. (2000). High potentials as high learners. *Human Resource Management, 39* (4), 321–330.

Lombardo, M., & Eichinger, R. (2003). *The LEADERSHIP ARCHITECT® norms and validity report.* Minneapolis: Lominger Limited, Inc.

Lombardo, M., & Eichinger, R. (2003b). *Learning agility as an aspect in promotion.* Minneapolis: Lominger Ltd., Inc.

McCall, M.W., & Lombardo, M. (1983). What makes a top executive? *Psychology Today, 17* (2), 26–31.

McCall, M.W., Lombardo, M., & Morrison, A. (1988). *The lessons of experience: How successful executives develop on the job.* Lexington, MA: Lexington Books.

McCauley, C.D., & Brutus, S. (1998). *Management development through job experiences: An annotated bibliography.* Greensboro, NC: Center for Creative Leadership.

McCauley, C.D., Ruderman, M.N., Ohlott, P.J., & Morrow, J.E. (1994). Assessing the developmental components of managerial jobs. *Journal of Applied Psychology, 79,* 544–560.

McClelland, D.C. (1998). Identifying competencies with behavioral-event interviews. *Psychological Science, 9* (5), 331–340.

Shipper, F., & Dillard, J. (2000). A study of impending derailment and recovery of middle managers across career stages. *Human Resource Management, 39* (4), 331–347.

Spreitzer, G.M., McCall, M.W., & Mahoney, J.D. (1997). Early identification of international executive potential. *Journal of Applied Psychology, 82* (1), 6–29.

Sternberg, R.J., Wagner, R.K., Williams, W.M., & Horvath, J.A. (1995). Testing common sense. *American Psychologist, 50* (11), 912–927.

Stogdill, R.M. (1948). Personal factors associated with leadership: A survey of the literature. *Journal of Personality, 25,* 35–71.

Wagner, R.K., & Sternberg, R.J. (1990). Street smarts. In K.E. Clark & M.B. Clark (Eds.), *Measures of leadership* (pp. 521–534). West Orange, NJ: Leadership Library of America.

MANAGERIAL COMPETENCIES

92.

How common are the competencies necessary to be successful in typical jobs and job families across companies?

SELECT ONE:

☐ A. There are more competencies in common than there are ones that are different.

☐ B. Each company and each industry is unique; there are more unique competencies than there are competencies in common.

☐ C. There are really no unique competencies across organizations, just differences in wording and emphasis.

☐ D. Competencies within industries are mostly common, but there are significant differences between industries.

☐ E. It's about half and half, 50% are in common and 50% are unique.

92. How common are the competencies necessary to be successful in typical jobs and job families across companies?

The correct answer is A: There are more competencies in common than there are ones that are different.

How sure are we at this time?

1	2	3	**4**	5
Hint	Suggestive	Trending	**Substantial**	Solid

Discussion

It appears about 85 percent of individual contributor, manager, and executive competencies are in common across organizations and across the world. That means the same competencies generally predict effectiveness and success anywhere you study them. So the same robust competency library will apply across organizations, industries, and even across countries. Emphasis on individual competencies will vary but the basic competency won't. Listening skills are listening skills. How important that is might be unique, not the fact that it exists.

This, however, does not mean there is a set of competencies that can be used to describe any organization, function, or job, only that careful selecting from a standard list will yield a useful description. The key competencies for an IT professional may have nothing in common with those of a salesperson, but all can be located in a single competency library. There's no need to reinvent the wheel.

Standard research-based behavioral (not job technical skills) competency models and libraries are robust across organizations and across jobs. Personal and managerial competencies have a higher correlation with performance than technical skills; hence the case for building custom models is weak. No one has discovered any new competencies in a long, long time—we simply give them different names and different emphasis. Most people who have looked across organizations have found about 85 percent in common.

This is not to say that no modification should be done—the competency model for one organization or job will not be exactly the same as for the next. But you can get 85 percent of the way there with a standard model, tested empirically to see which competencies matter most for a particular situation.

Of course, the competencies required may vary depending on the strategy of your organization. If your organization is working to grow globally, it may require different competencies than if the strategy is to reduce costs in a local market. Being able to tie competencies to business strategy is an important issue.

Selected Research

- According to research by Spencer and Spencer (1993), a common set of competencies can be used to describe 85 percent of job types. The book gives the example of the Hay-McBer competency studies, where the same set of 21 competencies are used to describe superior performance across 286 situations, entrepreneurs, technical, professional, sales, human service, and managerial jobs. They argue that "unique competencies ranged from 2 to 20 percent of competency measurement, so 80 to 98 percent used the standard set."

- Wusteman (2000) notes that DDI's (Development Dimensions Incorporated) taxonomy of competencies, in development for 30 years, uses the same 70 competencies worldwide to describe all jobs.

- Findings of a 1999 study concluded that 60 percent of companies giving 360 degree feedback to their employees were developing custom models that were based on a competency model; only 21 percent were tailored from generic models (Linkage Annual 360 Degree Conference, 1999).

- Lombardo and Eichinger (2002) argue that "essentially, there is little difference in any of these [competency] models. Some are oriented higher and some lower, they are all worded differently, and they use somewhat different indicators (such as planning). But they end up measuring the same underlying competencies."

So what difference do these findings make?

- It's a case of no need to buy new when used will do. In this business, used is better. The longer a competency has been identified and used, the more we will know about it, how to assess it, how to develop it, and how it works across jobs. There are several research-based and experience-tested competency models and libraries on the market. All are basically equivalent, aside from size of competency and wording. Some are more oriented toward selection and others more toward development. It is a waste of organization resources and shareholder's money to build a competency model or library from scratch. The most intelligent practice is to select one of the commercial libraries, apply the 85 percent that best fits your specific situation, and then do some additional work to find the unique 15 percent.

- If you have no internal research and you do not have the time, skills, or resources to study what leads to success in your organization, using any of the respected models or libraries "off-the-shelf" will provide at least 85 percent coverage. Better to be that correct than to be random.

Some Key Sources

Linkage Third Annual Assessment of 360 Degree Assessment Survey (1999, September). Linkage Annual 360 Degree Conference.

Lombardo, M., & Eichinger, R. (2004). *The leadership machine.* Minneapolis: Lominger Limited, Inc.

Spencer, L., & Spencer, S. (1993). *Competence at work.* New York: John Wiley & Sons, Inc.

Wusteman, L. (2000). New dimensions to competencies: An interview with Bill Byham. *Competency and Emotional Intelligence Quarterly, 8* (1).

SUCCESS PREDICTION

93.

What is the relationship between the national ranking of colleges and later success as a manager and executive?

SELECT ONE:

☐ A. There is very little relationship between the two.

☐ B. There is a strong relationship; the better the ranking of the college attended, the more likely you will be successful later on.

☐ C. There is a moderate relationship; primarily because the higher the ranking, the better the student is to begin with.

☐ D. There is a negative relationship; people from lower-ranked colleges actually do better.

☐ E. People from private colleges outperform those from public colleges.

93. **What is the relationship between the national ranking of colleges and later success as a manager and executive?**

    The correct answer is A: There is very little relationship between the two.

How sure are we at this time?

1	2	3	4	**5**
Hint	Suggestive	Trending	Substantial	**Solid**

Discussion

There is no evidence that the national ranking of the college or university one attends has much to do with later success. Success is probably better predicted by the level of experience one has in the college years, regardless of which institution it is. Variety and diversity of experience during college years has more to do with success than grades or quality of instruction.

The ranking of the college attended may not predict managerial performance either. Although recruiting profiles continue to feature it, there is only mixed evidence that it predicts anything beyond performance in the early years of employment. What it predicts very well, however, is how intelligent people are. Just 10 universities attract more than 30 percent of the highest scorers on the SAT-Verbal (Herrnstein & Murray, 1994).

Selected Research

* The jury is still out on college quality. The McKinsey studies support it as a hiring criteria (Chambers et al., 1998), but a large empirical study, Howard (1986), did not.

- Pascarella and Terenzini (1991) reviewed over 2,500 research studies conducted over a 20-year period and concluded "one of the most inescapable and unequivocal conclusions we can make is that the impact of college is largely determined by the individual's quality of effort and level of involvement in both academic and nonacademic activities. Such a conclusion suggests that the impact of college is a result of the extent to which an individual student exploits the people, programs, facilities, opportunities, and experiences that the college makes available" (pp. 610–611).

- According to research by Howard and Bray (1988), the best determinants of overall management effectiveness were college major, extracurricular activities, and higher education (including field of graduate education).

- Using the AT&T studies as a framework, Howard (1986) found significant relationships between extracurricular involvement and several career attainment and performance variables. Specific correlations were found between extracurricular activities and administrative and interpersonal abilities as well as motivation.

- Howard (1986) also noted that the job emphases themselves should determine what kind of college experiences to look for. So if administrative skills are a strong requirement, those with MBAs and a lot of related extracurricular activities would be a good choice. If interpersonal skills are critical requirements, humanities and social science majors are generally better than engineers or math majors. And, if intellectual ability requirements are critical, getting a master's degree and having good grades would be selection criteria. (College major is also a good indicator here with humanities majors stronger in verbal and written skills and engineers and math majors stronger in quantitative skills.) Certain types of extracurricular activities point to leadership abilities and high priority for work activities, and, finally, grades point to high inner work standards.

- Research by Rubin et al. (2002) found that participation in extracurricular activity is linked to interpersonal skill performance. A study of 618 business students measured the relationship of their extracurricular involvement to four interpersonal skills and found that the extracurricular index score is significantly associated with each of the four interpersonal skill dimensions—communication skills, initiative, decision making, and teamwork. The researchers note that the implications for HR practitioners include considering extracurricular involvement when interviewing for roles requiring refined interpersonal skills.

So what difference do these findings make?
- Recruiting at better schools will get you smarter people on average, but smarts is not as predictive of success as depth of experience, which you can get on any large campus. Look for the learning agile person, not the school.

- Some companies have a best practice where they target second-tier schools, but the top candidates at those schools. The top candidates at the second-tier schools are probably comparable to the better candidates at the top schools. But the candidates from the second-tier schools are generally cheaper and more open to learning.

Some Key Sources
Chambers, E.G., Foulon, M., Handfield-Jones, H., Hankin, S.M., & Michaels, E.G. (1998). The war for talent. *The McKinsey Quarterly,* Number 3, 44–57.

Herrnstein, R.J., & Murray, C. (1994). *The bell curve.* New York: Free Press.

Howard, A. (1986). College experiences and managerial performance. *Journal of Applied Psychology Monograph, 71* (3), 530–552.

Howard, A., & Bray, D. (1988). *Managerial lives in transition: Advancing age and changing times.* New York: Guilford Press.

Pascarella, E.T., & Terenzini, P.T. (1991). *How college affects students: Findings and insights from twenty years of research.* San Francisco: Jossey-Bass.

Rubin, R.S., Bommer, W.H., & Baldwin, T.T. (2002, Winter). Using extracurricular activity as an indicator of interpersonal skill: Prudent evaluation or recruiting malpractice? *Human Resource Management, 41* (4), 441–454.

MERGERS AND ACQUISITIONS

94.

Overall, what portion of mergers and acquisitions are deemed successful, meaning they performed up to the goals announced before the event?

SELECT ONE:

☐ A. Most are successful against the targets and goals set forward at the time of the event.

☐ B. Mergers are two times more successful than acquisitions.

☐ C. Less than 50% of mergers and acquisitions are successful.

☐ D. Acquisitions are two times more successful than mergers.

☐ E. About 50% are successful with a third very successful.

94. **Overall, what portion of mergers and acquisitions are deemed successful, meaning they performed up to the goals announced before the event?**

The correct answer is C: Less than 50% of mergers and acquisitions are successful.

How sure are we at this time?

1	2	3	4	**5**
Hint	Suggestive	Trending	Substantial	**Solid**

Discussion

Less than half of mergers and acquisitions are successful when measured against the targets and standards set forth before the event. It might even be that only about one-third are successful. There are differences depending upon what kind of merger or acquisition it is. The success percentages generally follow the research on major change events in organizations, like trying to implement TQM or Six Sigma. It appears that less than half of all major change attempts, including mergers and acquisitions, are successful. Aside from bad due diligence, the major culprit tends to be clashing cultures post-merger or acquisition. Failure to resolve cultural conflict is oft stated as the number one reason for failure.

Selected Research

*   Several studies (Mueller, 1995) covering M&A activity in the past 75 years have concluded that well over half failed to create their expected value. In many cases, value was destroyed. Company performance after the deal was significantly below what it had been before the deal.

- James Quella, director of Mercer Management Consulting, Inc., looked at 150 deals over $500 million. He said about half destroyed shareholder value and another third contributed only marginally (Zweig et al., 1995).

- Sirower (1997) studied 131 deals over $500 million between 1994–1997 in the U.S., Europe, and Asia. For 59 percent, market value went down on announcement (45 percent were still down 12 months after announcement), and 71 percent were negative 12 months after the deal.

- Porter (1987) states there is "...strong evidence that mergers and acquisitions...over the last 35 years...have hurt more than helped companies." He argued that most would-be deal synergies are never realized.

- A *BusinessWeek* (Henry & Jespersen, 2002) analysis shows that 61 percent of buyers destroyed shareholder wealth. Fully 17 out of the 21 "winners" in the heady merger Spring of 1998 became busts for investors who owned their shares. Similar patterns appeared across the 302 major mergers from July 1, 1995 to August 31, 2001. The magazine looked at deals worth at least $500 million. A year after their deals, the losing 61 percent had an average return 25 percentage points below their industry peers. The gains of the winning minority couldn't make up for the buyers' losses, making the average return for all buyers 4.3 percent below their industry peers and 9.2 percent below the S&P 500. The analysis shows that there has been no improvement in CEOs' deal-making skills since 1995, when *BusinessWeek's* major survey of mergers in the early 1990s found that 50 percent were failures. Since then, an army of consultants and bankers has tried to help CEOs improve their success rate. But they've failed.

- *BusinessWeek* (Zweig et al., 1995) studied why mergers don't work. They concluded that there were six reasons:

  1. Inadequate due diligence by acquirer or merger partner.

  2. Lack of a compelling strategic rationale.

  3. Unrealistic expectations of possible synergies.

  4. Paying too much.

  5. Conflicting corporate cultures.

  6. Failure to move quickly to meld the two companies.

- Bower (2001) argues that all of the above numbers need to be looked at in the light of five different kinds of mergers and acquisitions. He says there are five types: 1. The Overcapacity M&A; 2. The Geographic Roll-Up M&A; 3. The Product/Market Extension M&A; 4. The M&A as R&D; and 5. The Industry Convergence M&A.

  1. The Overcapacity M&A, which accounts for 37 percent of M&A activity, is one where the acquiring company will eliminate costs, gain market share, and create more efficient operations. In an Overcapacity M&A, you must decide what activities and assets to eliminate quickly, and integrate internal processes, cultures, and values. The two management groups typically fight for control. These tend to be very big one-time events, are the toughest to pull off, and the ones most likely to fail. Examples would be Chemical Bank buys Manufacturers Hanover and Daimler-Benz buys Chrysler.

  2. The Geographic Roll-Up M&A (9 percent) is one where a company wants to expand what it does to a broader geography. Integration can go slowly. Culture integration can be gradual. It is usually a win-win and

goes smoothly. Examples are Bank One buying lots of smaller banks.

3. The Product/Market Extension M&A (36 percent) is one where the companies want to expand product lines or extend to international markets. In these, the farther away from home the worse. Cultural and government integration is usually a problem. In terms of success, the bigger the better and the more you do of these the better. Examples would be Quaker buys Snapple; Compaq buys Tandem and DEC, then HP buys Compaq.

4. The M&A as a substitute for R&D (1 percent) is used in lieu of in-house R&D to build a market position quickly. This has been used a lot in Internet firms. The integration must go fast and often leaves a lot of culture damage behind. Talent retention is key. These M&As usually involve much smaller acquisitions. A prime example would be when Cisco bought 62 smaller companies.

5. In the Industry Convergence M&A (4 percent), the acquiring company makes a bet on an allied but different industry. Most of the time they leave the acquisition alone and only integrate where no noise would be created. An example would be when Viacom bought Paramount and Blockbuster.

Bower also commented that companies usually pay too much, stock deals do better, friendly deals work better, CEOs can't let go of a deal once it is proposed, cultural integration is hard to do, and most fail.

- Kroger, Habeck, and Tram (2000), after studying failed mergers and acquisitions, concluded by offering a seven-step plan for doing it right:

1. Thorough due diligence.

2. Settle leadership issues first before forming integration task groups.

3. Merge or acquire for growth, not synergy and cost avoidance (because growth mergers outperformed synergy mergers).

4. Get early wins to motivate the workforce and please investors.

5. Create a new culture. Don't just meld or pick one of the two. Actually create a new culture in line with the new business proposition.

6. Overcommunicate.

7. Prioritize; you can never do it all.

So what difference do these findings make?

- Proceed with caution. Mergers and acquisitions are a slippery slope.

- Do more and earlier soft due diligence. The key is to spot and prevent unproductive culture clashes.

- Merge or acquire for growth more than for cost savings.

- The type of merger matters greatly. Each has different issues and different chances of success. Know which one you are involved in.

- There is no shortage of good advice and best practices material available. Make sure all decision makers are up to speed on the best ways to make mergers and acquisitions work.

- Have a careful plan for merger integration. This plan generally starts by getting out costs and redundancies. In this phase, move quickly and boldly. Get it over with. Be clear about what you are doing and why. In the next phase, find ways to leverage the merger. Find ways to share products, customers, or technology to grow the business. Do not jump to the growth without some consolidation, but get there as soon as you can.

- Have HR issues be a part of pre-merger talks. In particular, examine cultural differences and costs associated with changing the culture. Cultural differences should not stop a merger, but the cost of their integration should be considered.

Some Key Sources

Bower, J.L. (2001, April 2). Not all M&As are alike—And that matters. *Harvard Business Review.*

Henry, D., & Jespersen, F.F. (2002, May 1). Mergers: Why most big deals don't pay off. *BusinessWeek.*

Kroger, F., Habeck, M.M., & Tram, M R (2000) *After the merger: Seven rules for successful post-merger integration.* Pearson Education.

Mueller, D.C. (1995). Mergers: Theory and evidence. In G. Mussati (Ed.), *Mergers, markets and public policy* (pp. 9–43). Dordrecht: Kluwer Academic Publishers.

Porter, M. (1987, May 1). From competitive advantage to corporate strategy. *Harvard Business Review.*

Sirower, M. (1997). *The synergy trap.* New York: Free Press.

Zweig, P.L., Kline, J.P., Forest, S.A., & Gudridge, K. (1995, October 30). The case against mergers. *BusinessWeek.*

HR EFFECTIVENESS

95.

What HR role is most asked for by top management but HR is the least skilled at doing?

SELECT ONE:

☐ A. Operating partner.

☐ B. Strategic partner.

☐ C. HR excellence in HR best practices.

☐ D. HR management of e-HR.

☐ E. The cost effectiveness of HR programming and practices.

95

95. What HR role is most asked for by top management but HR is the least skilled at doing?

The correct answer is B: Strategic partner.

How sure are we at this time?

1	2	3	**4**	5
Hint	Suggestive	Trending	**Substantial**	Solid

Discussion

With all the attention on HR issues, researchers have started to clarify the roles HR professionals have played and need to play. The criteria for defining HR roles has varied from a focus on activities (what do HR people do) to time (where do HR people spend time) to metaphors (what identity do HR people have) to value creation (what value do HR people create). There has been a general call by top management for HR to step up and play a more strategic role in the organization. That strategic role is one of linking all that HR does to the mission and strategy of the enterprise as well as to the bottom line.

Selected Research

- Within the field of strategic HRM, Dyer and Reeves (1995), in their review of research on the value of "bundling" HR practices, proposed four types of organizational performance measurement: (1) HR outcomes: turnover, absenteeism, job satisfaction; (2) organizational outcomes: productivity, quality, service; (3) financial accounting outcomes: ROA, profitability; and (4) capital market outcomes: stock price, growth, returns.

- In his research, Walker (1994) noted that there seems to be a continuum of four roles around what people do—

support, service, consulting, and leadership—with most HR practitioners spending time in the support and service roles rather than the consulting and leadership roles, which is what the companies want to emphasize.

- According to Schuler (1994), "linking HR strategy and business strategy is a major role for Human Resources today." He argues that HR's new role is to "act as a partner with line management" and that "they can add the most value by using their expertise to link internal organization and management practices to external business requirements."

- Wiley (1992) classifies the HR role under three headings— the strategic process, the legal aspects, and the operational aspects. "The strategic process includes these roles: consultant, assessor, diagnostician, innovator/change agent, catalyst, business partner, and cost manager. Legal roles include auditor/controller, consultant, provider, and conciliator. And operational roles include firefighter, innovator/change agent, employee advocate, facilitator, policy formulator, and consultant."

- A research study conducted with 256 mid- to upper-level human resource executives from mid- to large-sized companies measured four key HR roles—strategic partner, change agent, employee champion, and administrative expert—and found high scores for the employee champion and administrative expert roles and lower scores for strategic partner and change agent roles (Conner & Ulrich, 1996).

- Watson Wyatt's survey of 1,000 senior executives for its 1999 Leadership in the Global Economy study (in Axelrod et al., 2001) cited leadership development as the single most important human resource issue facing their companies. The study also found a statistically significant relationship between leadership development and financial success in four areas: shareholder return, growth in market share, growth in net income, and return on sales.

- Eichinger and Ulrich (1996) reported discouraging findings from interviews with line executives: "Individual members of the HR team are not strong enough or credible enough personally to help HR succeed, much less the business."

So what difference do these findings make?

- The drive for major change in the HR function. For more than a decade, Human Resources management has recognized the need to act as a business partner to line leaders. Many HR organizations are discovering how difficult it is to implement breakthrough change in the role of the function, especially on a worldwide basis. The irony is difficult to miss, given the pressing need for change management expertise to support continuous and radical change in the business. It is clear that HR leaders must demonstrate high degrees of change management skills to change themselves. One observation is that HR professionals are better at advocating change than engaging in it. Line managers develop cynicism when they hear HR professionals cajoling and coaching them to change, when the HR department has been slow to adapt to change.

- There seems to be consensus that HR, aside from its more traditional roles, needs to have the strategic skills necessary to link HR initiatives with the bottom line, the business environment, and organization strategy.

- HR professionals who act as partners in a business must master the ability to coach (provide one-on-one counseling and direction), facilitate (manage the processes in organizations), architect (conceive of new approaches to solve problems), design and deliver (make HR programs happen), and model in their own function what they want from others.

Some Key Sources

Axelrod, E.L., Handfield-Jones, H., & Welsh, T.A. (2001). The war for talent: Part two. *The McKinsey Quarterly,* Number 2.

Conner, J., & Ulrich, D. (1996). Human resource roles: Creating value, not rhetoric. *Human Resource Planning, 19* (3).

Dyer, L., & Reeves, T. (1995, May 31–June 4). *Human resource strategies and firm performance: What do we know and where do we need to go?* Paper presented at the 10th World Congress of the International Relations Association, Washington, DC.

Eichinger, R., & Ulrich, D. (1996). Are you future agile? *Human Resource Planning, 18* (4), 30–41.

Schuler, R.S. (1994). *The changing role of human resource: Systematically linking with the business.* Unpublished paper.

Walker, J.W. (1994). *Integrating the human resource function with the business?* Unpublished paper.

Wiley, C. (1992, November/December). A comprehensive view of roles for human resource managers in industry today. *Industrial Management,* 27–29.

TRAINING

96.

New Employee Orientation (NEO) is:

SELECT ONE:

☐ A. Nice to do but has little benefit that can be documented.

☐ B. A highly used but little measured program.

☐ C. Mostly done in only large companies.

☐ D. Generally too elementary to do any real good.

☐ E. A cost-justified program with documented benefits.

96

96. New Employee Orientation (NEO) is:

The correct answer is E: A cost-justified program with documented benefits.

How sure are we at this time?

1	2	3	**4**	5
Hint	Suggestive	Trending	**Substantial**	Solid

Discussion

Many companies provide some sort of introductory training or orientation for most of their new employees. It may take the form of an older employee assigned to show the new employee "the ropes." Or it may be left to the HR department or the individual's new supervisor to show them where the coffee pot is and how to apply for time off and fill out other forms.

Many organizations, especially in government and academia, have created new employee training that is designed, exclusively or primarily, to provide mandated safety familiarization.

Some companies in highly competitive industries recognize the value in New Employee Orientation (NEO) that goes much farther. They require several weeks or even months of training to familiarize every new employee with the company, its products, its culture and policies, even its competition. Employees in these companies generally are more productive because they know more about the context of the company and their role within it.

Selected Research

- Results of a study by Klein and Weaver (2000) that examined the impact of attending a voluntary, organizational-level new employee orientation training program on six content dimensions of organizational socialization revealed that "employees attending the orientation training were significantly more socialized on three of the six socialization content dimensions (goals/values, history, and people) than employees who did not attend the training."

- A two-year long study (Cable & Parsons, 2001) examined how firms' NEO tactics help establish person/organization fit between newcomers and the existing organization. The findings indicated that newcomers' personal fit perceptions, as well as changes in their values, were associated with two types of NEO tactics: (1) content— what was communicated, and (2) social aspects—how it was done.

- One survey (Arthur, 1998) revealed that 98 percent of those surveyed said the supervisor's role was very critical to the success of new employee orientation but only 28 percent said supervisory support was "great," 66 percent said there was "some" support, and 14 percent said there was "little" support for orientation.

- In her book on employee orientation, Jerris (1993) notes that one of the most interesting trends she's found is the increase in organizations that measure the results of NEO for bottom line results. Sixteen percent review turnover statistics, 6 percent review accident/safety records, and 6 percent review increased productivity indicators, with 2 percent tracking grievance statistics.

- In her research, Nelson (1990) suggests that organizations "need strategies for newcomers and for the organization itself that can ease the transition for both parties. For newcomers, these strategies include making a realistic job choice and seeking out social support from others. For organizations, strategies include providing early job challenges, flexible scheduling, and timely feedback to newcomers."

So what difference do these findings make?

• New employee orientation is a proven winner and cost justified. (Increased commitment means less turnover, which means less money spent in replacement and less money spent due to lost productivity or get-up-to-speed time.)

• Get the supervisors involved. The research is showing that everyone thinks the supervisor's role is critical to success with new employees, yet most aren't participating.

• In a new employee orientation, employees are taught more than administrative procedures. They are taught about the heritage of the company and reasons the company is what it is; about the culture of the company and the identity the firm wants to be known for by targeted customers; about competitors and how the firm is positioned to win; and about the company's current strategic focus and organization capabilities.

Some Key Sources

Arthur, D. (1998). *Recruiting, interviewing, selecting and orienting new employees.* New York: AMACOM.

Cable, D.M., & Parsons, C.K. (2001, Summer). Socialization tactics and person-organization fit. *Personnel Psychology, 54* (1).

Jerris, L.A. (1993). *Effective employee orientation.* New York: AMACOM.

Klein, H.J., & Weaver, N.A. (2000, Spring). The effectiveness of an organizational-level orientation training program in the socialization of new hires. *Personnel Psychology, 53* (1).

Nelson, D.L. (1990). Adjusting to a new organization: Easing the transition from outsider to insider. *Prevention in Human Services, 8* (1), 61–86.

97.

About what percent of supervisor, manager, and executive jobs were held by women in 2002 in the United States?

SELECT ONE:

☐ A. 25%.

☐ B. 30%.

☐ C. 35%.

☐ D. 40%.

☐ E. 50%.

97

97. **About what percent of supervisor, manager, and executive jobs were held by women in 2002 in the United States?**

The correct answer is E: 50%.

How sure are we at this time?

1	2	3	4	**5**
Hint	Suggestive	Trending	Substantial	**Solid**

Discussion

According to the 2000 Census, 46 percent of all management jobs in the United States were held by women. The percentage decreases as jobs increase in height in the organization, with about 5 percent of board membership now female. According to Catalyst surveys, 25 to 30 percent of MBA graduates are women. Women comprise over 15.7 percent of corporate officers.

Selected Research

- According to the U.S. Census Bureau (2003), almost 46 percent of management positions were filled by women in 2002, up from only about a third in 1983 but virtually unchanged from the record high set in 2001. Women also hold almost 55 percent of the jobs in professional specialty fields, which include education and medicine, and have held a majority of those positions for over a decade. Overall, women comprised 51 percent of the country's 282.1 million people in March 2002. Men outnumber women in the workforce 53 percent to 47 percent. Nearly one-quarter of the 63.6 million employed women aged 16 and older worked in administrative or clerical positions in 2002, larger than any other field. Another 19 percent of women worked in professional specialty fields. The next two most popular areas for women were jobs related to services and management/executive positions. Last September the Bureau also reported that "median earnings for women who worked full time rose 3.5 percent to $29,215 compared with $38,275 for men. Put another way, women earned 76 cents for every dollar a man earned, surpassing the previous high of 74 cents to the dollar recorded in 1996."

• According to an article in the *New York Times* (Walsh, 2002), Catalyst, a New York-based nonprofit that tracks female clout in the *Fortune 500*, reported that the proportion of top female officers since 1995 has nearly doubled, from 8.7 percent to 15.7 percent. That translates to 2,140 female executives out of 13,600. That was up slightly from 12.5 percent in 2000. Catalyst found that men continued to dominate the line officer positions. Women held just 9.9 percent of these jobs, a slight increase from 7.9 percent in 2000.

• A 2002 article in the *Wall Street Journal* references the same Catalyst study and reports that women hold one out of six corporate officer positions at *Fortune 500* companies, or nearly 16 percent. In 1995, when Catalyst first started counting, women held 8.7 percent of corporate officer posts. As of March 31, 2002—the cutoff date for the survey—429 companies, or nearly 86 percent, have at least one woman corporate officer. Two-thirds of companies have two or more female corporate officers, up from 64 percent in 2000 and 44 percent in 1995. Sixty companies, or 12 percent, have one-quarter or more female officers, up from 10 percent in 2000 and 5 percent in 1995. Sixteen companies, or 3.2 percent, have one-third or more female corporate officers.

• As women continue to climb the corporate ladder in greater numbers, senior executive women are becoming less assertive, more formal, and more risk-averse. These findings are the results of a nationwide research study of *Fortune 500* executives and other senior executives with salaries of $150,000 and above. The study shows that "a woman's ascent in the corporate world is often accompanied by a dramatic and unexpected shift in her behavior—a shift that may prove detrimental to future career advancement" (Shepard, 2003).

• A study of male and female pay at the uppermost levels of corporate America lends evidence to both sides of the hotly debated question of whether women are paid less than men. Top female executives in large U.S. companies are paid about 45 percent less on average than their male counterparts, according to a study by Kevin F. Hallock at the University of Illinois and Marianne Bertrand at the University of Chicago. But as much as 75 percent of the gap can be accounted for by the fact that women manage relatively smaller companies and are much less likely to be the chair or chief executive officer of the company. Another reason is that women hold only 10 percent of more highly paid line officer jobs (Hallock & Bertrand, 2002).

So what difference do these findings make?
• We seem to have reached gender parity as far as total numbers are concerned. Additionally, with over 50 percent of supervisory jobs being women, we should be able to increase the number who are considered high potentials and eventually reach parity at all levels of management.

Some Key Sources
Hallock, K.F., & Bertrand, M. (2002). *The gender gap in top corporate jobs.* Working paper by K.F. Hallock at the University of Illinois & M. Bertrand at the University of Chicago.

Shepard, M.D. (2003, January/February). Women experience changes at the top. *Women in Business, 55* (1), 24.

U.S. Census Bureau. (2003, March 24). *Women closing the gap with men in some measures, according to Census Bureau.* www.census.gov/Press-Release/www/2003/cb03-53.html

Walsh, M.W. (2002, November 19). Number of women in upper ranks rises a bit. *The New York Times.*

Women are holding more corporate posts. (2002, November 19). *The Wall Street Journal.*

CAREER DEVELOPMENT

98.

What is the dominant source of the necessary lessons to be an effective and successful manager or executive?

SELECT ONE:

☐ A. Formal schooling.

☐ B. Jobs.

☐ C. Mentors and bosses.

☐ D. Peers and role models.

☐ E. All of the above are about equal in influence.

98

98. What is the dominant source of the necessary lessons to be an effective and successful manager or executive?

The correct answer is B: Jobs.

How sure are we at this time?

1	2	3	4	5
Hint	Suggestive	Trending	Substantial	**Solid**

Discussion

Most (70 percent or so in various studies) of the critical lessons, competencies, and skills that managers and executives need to be successful come from jobs. Successful executives report that roughly 70 percent of key learning comes from jobs, 20 percent from other people, and 10 percent from courses and self-study. The figure is lower for women, who often lack major developmental job experiences.

Selected Research

- Baldwin and Padgett (1993) note that it's the post-school job assignments people have that make a difference. Results of research they've done on learning in leaders reveal that the most important lessons are learned from on-the-job experiences.

- McCall et al. (1988) found that most of the lessons executives reported learning came from challenging job assignments. They point out the importance of managers developing into effective leaders by "making the most of job assignments" and taking the initiative to learn from every experience.

- According to Sternberg et al. (1995), the tacit-knowledge aspect of practical intelligence can be "effectively measured and predicts success and level attained as a manager." They define tacit knowledge as action-oriented knowledge, which is typically acquired without direct help from others and which allows individuals to achieve goals they personally value. Various studies they've completed showed correlations "between tacit-knowledge scores and criteria such as salary, years of management experience, and whether the manager worked for a company at the top of the *Fortune 500*." Another study revealed that tacit knowledge was significantly correlated with managerial compensation and level within the company. Tacit knowledge also correlated, but not as much, with job satisfaction.

- One study (McCauley & Brutus, 1998) that included tests for intelligence, personality, cognitive, preference for innovation, job satisfaction, and orientation in interpersonal relations found that the test of tacit knowledge (learning from experience) was the single best predictor of performance (.61 correlation versus .38 for IQ correlation).

- One significant finding came from the AT&T studies where 61 percent of those predicted (in assessment centers) to fail to make middle management succeeded in doing so if they had high job challenge. In contrast, only 30 percent of those predicted to make it to middle management made it if job challenge was low (Bray et al., 1974).

So what difference do these findings make?
- It's jobs that develop future leaders. Putting people with talent and potential into jobs that teach the mission critical lessons needed for future service is the key to filling the bench with top candidates.

- And it's not just any jobs but very specific jobs. The jobs that are needed to assure success are to some extent the same for everyone—jobs like start-ups, fix-its, and international assignments—but also different. The jobs depend upon what the person is missing.

Some Key Sources

Baldwin, T.T., & Padgett, M.Y. (1993). Management development: A review and commentary. In C.L. Cooper & I.T. Robertson (Eds.), *International review of industrial and organizational psychology* (1993, Vol. 8, pp. 35–85). Chichester, England: John Wiley & Sons, Ltd.

Bray, D.W., Campbell, R.J., & Grant, D.L. (1974). *Formative years in business: A long-term AT&T study of managerial lives.* New York: Wiley.

McCall, M.W., Lombardo, M., & Morrison, A. (1988). *The lessons of experience: How successful executives develop on the job.* Lexington, MA: Lexington Books.

McCauley, C.D., & Brutus, S. (1998). *Management development through job experiences: An annotated bibliography.* Greensboro, NC: Center for Creative Leadership.

Sternberg, R.J., Wagner, R.K., Williams, W.M., & Horvath, J.A. (1995). Testing common sense. *American Psychologist, 50* (11), 912–927.

E-LEARNING

99.

What is the effectiveness of e-Learning compared with classroom learning?

SELECT ONE:

☐ A. e-Learning is more effective than classroom learning because learners can go at their own pace.

☐ B. Classroom learning is more effective because people can learn from each other.

☐ C. e-Learning is superior for technical learning but classroom is more effective for everything else.

☐ D. For the purpose of knowledge training, e-Learning and classroom are about equal.

☐ E. It really all depends upon the learner; younger people learn better electronically, and older people learn better in the classroom setting.

99

99. What is the effectiveness of e-Learning compared with classroom learning?

The correct answer is D: For the purpose of knowledge training, e-Learning and classroom are about equal.

How sure are we at this time?

1	**2**	3	4	5
Hint	**Suggestive**	Trending	Substantial	Solid

Discussion

Many organizations are starting and operating e-learning networks and distance learning. It is cheaper, faster and more flexible, and capable of delivering around the world. There are now conferences dedicated to e-learning. Its effectiveness is just now starting to be evaluated. We know that experience develops best when it comes to learning new behaviors, but the jury is out about learning technical knowledge. At this moment, it looks like for the purposes of transferring knowledge, e-learning is as effective as classroom.

Selected Research

- A study by Navarro and Shoemaker (2000) compared the performance and perception of cyberlearners to that of traditional learners and found that "cyberlearners learn as well as, or better than, traditional learners regardless of characteristics such as gender, ethnicity, academic background, computer skills, and academic aptitude. And that they do so with a high degree of satisfaction."

- Brown (2001), who conducted a study of 78 technical employees who volunteered to take a problem solving course over the Intranet at the corporate training facility of a *Fortune 500* manufacturing company, found that the employees who learn most from computer-based training are those who complete more of the practice activities and take more time to complete them. He concludes "the e-learning experience depended upon the learning orientation of the students."

- A study by Berge and Muilenburg (2000) found 10 barriers to distance education. The 10 factors found were:

    1. Administrative structure.

    2. Organizational change.

    3. Technical expertise.

    4. Social interaction and quality.

    5. Faculty compensation and time.

    6. Threat of technology.

    7. Legal issues.

    8. Evaluation/effectiveness.

    9. Access.

    10. Student-support services.

    All of these need to be addressed before e-learning can truly experience its potential.

- Research shows that development of a competency will be about 70 percent from on-the-job experiences, 20 percent from feedback or working around good and bad examples or role models of the need, and 10 percent from courses and reading (Lombardo & Eichinger, 1989).

- In a meta-analysis of the effectiveness of training across 70 studies, Burke and Day (1986) identified behavior modeling training (a type of training based on social cognitive theory which suggests that effective performance will be enhanced if the learner has first had an opportunity to observe others performing the behavior) and role playing as methods associated with positive results for skill-based training.

- An ASTD survey on using electronic learning technologies systems of 275 HRD executives from U.S. organizations (Van Buren, 1998) revealed that "investing in learning technologies is important to both HRD executives (92 percent) and top executives (82 percent)" but that survey respondents differed significantly on the degrees of importance of this type of investment. Almost 70 percent of HRD executives said learning-technology investments were "very important," but only 26 percent of top executives felt the same way. And, although it has increased since that time, HRD executives reported that only 1 percent of their 1997 budget was allocated to developing e-learning and other new learning technology systems.

- According to Harris (2003), it's fairly easy to determine "hard savings" a company realizes by replacing its dependence on the classroom with a distance learning operation (the standard ROI equation calculates Return = Benefits ÷ Cost of the System). Measurable savings include reduction in training budgets and materials, travel, instructors, physical facilities, administrative time, and hours of lost productivity. The author points out that "soft savings" like improved productivity and proficiency, learning curve and employee retention, and satisfaction and morale are very difficult to measure. ASTD research points to recommendations that feature blended learning solutions.

- An *InformationWeek* research survey of 200 IT managers revealed that, although most of the managers prefer traditional training methods, observers "predict strong growth in Web-based training as more companies develop Intranets with training applications and senior executives realize cost savings over conventional classroom and paper methods" (Violino, 1998).

* Research on Web-based training (Rosen, 2000) from International Data Corp., a technology research firm in Framingham, MA, predicted that corporate spending on e-learning would exceed $9 billion by 2002, up from $1.5 billion in 1999.

So what difference do these findings make?
* It looks like e-learning is real and helpful. Users would be advised to go slowly and follow the research and best practice reports to get the best out of this new technology.

* Lots of innovation is going on with e-learning. This includes what types of skills are better or worse taught through e-learning and what e-learning methods have the most impact.

Some Key Sources
Berge, Z.L., & Muilenburg, L.Y. (2000, June 7–9). *Barriers to distance education as perceived by managers and administrators.* In the Proceedings of the Distance Learning Administration 2000 Conference, Callaway Gardens, GA. Retrieved April 18, 2001, from http://www.emoderators.com./barriers/man_admin.shtml

Brown, K.G. (2001, Summer). Using computers to deliver training: Which employees learn and why? *Personnel Psychology, 54 (2).*

Burke, M.J., & Day, R.R. (1986). A cumulative study of the effectiveness of managerial training. *Journal of Applied Psychology, 71 (2),* 232–245.

Harris, P. (2003, February 18). ROI of e-learning: Closing in. *Learning Circuits* (ASTD's online magazine all about e-learning). Retrieved from http://www.learningcircuits.com/2003/feb2003/roi.html

Joinson, C. (2001, May). Employee sculpt thyself, with a little help. *HR Magazine, 46* (5).

Lombardo, M., & Eichinger, R. (1989). *Preventing derailment: What to do before it's too late.* Greensboro, NC: Center for Creative Leadership.

Morrow, C., Jarrett, M., & Rupinski, M. (1997). An investigation of the effect and economic utility of corporate-wide training. *Personnel Psychology, 50* (1), 91–120.

Navarro, P., & Shoemaker, J. (2000). Performance and perceptions of distance learners in cyberspace. In M.G. Moore & G. Cozine (Eds.), *Web-based communications, the Internet and distance education* (pp. 1–15). Pennsylvania State University.

Rosen, M. (2000, July 31). Specific needs influence type of Web-based training. *Puget Sound Business Journal.*

Van Buren, M. (1998, January/February). Mainstreaming learning technologies. *Technical Training Magazine.*

Violino, B. (1998, July 18). Web training catches on. *InformationWeek Online.* http://www.informationweek.com/691/91iutra.htm

DERAILMENT

100.

Why do previously successful managers fail in new assignments?

SELECT ONE:

☐ A. Lack of fresh, up-to-date functional and technical skills.

☐ B. Lack of sufficient intelligence for the new job.

☐ C. An overriding flaw or weakness that suddenly matters.

☐ D. Lack of specific experience in the area.

☐ E. A poor team that can't be turned around in time.

100. Why do previously successful managers fail in new assignments?

The correct answer is C: An overriding flaw or weakness that suddenly matters.

How sure are we at this time?

1	2	3	**4**	5
Hint	Suggestive	Trending	**Substantial**	Solid

Discussion

Leaders fail for a variety of reasons that are not personal—product lines no longer interest customers, services are no longer required, significant competitors arise and companies reorganize and downsize. Nevertheless, a number of leaders fail for personal rather than structural or economic reasons. They may be skilled in a particular area, such as accounting, engineering, or sales. They fail because they can no longer rely solely on their own skills and effort; that is, they have been promoted into positions that require them to work through others to be successful. Because they are unable to build a team, their management careers come to a halt. Many so-called derailment studies show that previously successful managers all fail for the same small number of reasons. The general finding is that they had weaknesses in the past that did not play in their success or failure and that the new job challenges made their weaknesses suddenly matter. Their strengths could no longer carry them because other skills were required.

Selected Research

- Bentz (1985) essentially founded modern derailment research while analyzing the correlates of executive performance at Sears. He reported that "among the persons with the appropriate positive characteristics (i.e., intelligence, confidence, ambition), a subset failed." Bentz catalogued the themes associated with failure (e.g., playing politics, moodiness, dishonesty) and concluded that the failed executives had an "overriding personality defect or character flaw that alienated their subordinates and prevented them from building a team."

- Research on managerial incompetence at the Center for Creative Leadership has come to similar conclusions: Many managers who are bright, hardworking, ambitious, and technically competent fail (or are in danger of failing) because they are perceived as arrogant, vindictive, untrustworthy, selfish, emotional, compulsive, over-controlling, insensitive, abrasive, aloof, too ambitious, or unable to delegate or make decisions (Peterson, 1993).

- In his research, Sweeney (1999) found that collaboration is particularly crucial to the success of higher level managers; a deficit in the ability to work cooperatively with peers was, in one survey, the most common reason managers failed or were fired.

- In her research, Millikin-Davies (1992) found that the two most common complaints from direct reports concerned managers' unwillingness to exercise authority (e.g., "is reluctant to confront problems and conflict"; "is not as self-confident as others") and managers tyrannizing their subordinates (e.g., "manages his/her employees too closely, breathes down their necks"; "treats employees as if they were stupid"), both of which were also found in the CCI studies.

- According to Hogan et al. (1990), managerial derailment is now well understood; it is caused by flawed interpersonal skills that prevent a person from being able to build a team. These sources suggest that the base rate for flawed leadership in corporate America is above 50 percent, which means that the majority of employed adults work for someone with seriously diminished leadership skills. He argues that "if current estimates of the base rates of bad management are realistic, then organizations in which 60 percent of the managers are incompetent will likely be at a serious competitive disadvantage."

- Low-performing executives seem to have much more difficulty learning from experience...tending to form preconceived and general notions of, for example, how to develop others. The derailed executives, all of whom had been successful for many years before derailing and who had gone through many of the same key assignments as the successful executives, had virtually no pattern of learning from jobs. Their learning appeared to be virtually random. Derailed executives quit learning, thought they were infallible, became legends in their own minds, or couldn't make the transition to a different job or way of behaving. They relied on what had gotten them to where they were, ironically, becoming victimized by their past successes. They got locked into standard ways of thinking and acting that didn't really meet the new demands. They also underestimated the newness of the demands, seeing them as just another version of what they had done before (Lombardo & Eichinger, 2002).

- In the CCL studies (McCall et al., 1988), successful executives had a strong and similar pattern of learning from key job assignments. In a companion study (McCall & Lombardo, 1983), one of the key reasons cited for derailment was being blocked to new learning.

- In studies that have dealt with success and derailment, failure to learn to do something differently in order to make key transitions has figured prominently in the results. Additionally, lack of self-awareness and a tendency to overrate oneself have been found to be crippling. In contrast, successful people learned more new behavior, were more self-aware, etc. (Spreitzer et al., 1997; Lombardo & Eichinger, 2000; Shipper & Dillard, 2000; Lombardo & Eichinger, 2003).

So what difference do these findings make?

- People succeed for a variety of reasons, but previously successful people fail for a smaller number of reasons.

- People who later derail have common characteristics leading up to the derailment event. Derailment can be prevented by early assessment of the danger signs.

- Knowing yourself is still the best option—strengths, averages, weaknesses, and untested areas. Successful people don't have all possible skills. Their edge is in fully knowing themselves—developing where they can and neutralizing weak areas where they will never be strong.

Some Key Sources

Bentz, V.J. (1985, August). *A view from the top: A thirty year perspective of research devoted to discovery, description, and prediction of executive behavior.* Paper presented at the 93rd Annual Convention of the American Psychological Association, Los Angeles.

Hogan, R., Raskin, R., & Fazzini, D. (1990). The dark side of charisma. In K.E. Clark & M.B. Clark (Eds.), *Measures of leadership* (pp. 343–354). West Orange, NJ: Leadership Library of America.

Lombardo, M., & Eichinger, R. (2000). High potentials as high learners. *Human Resource Management, 39* (4), 321–330.

Lombardo, M., & Eichinger, R. (2004). *The leadership machine.* Minneapolis: Lominger Limited, Inc.

Lombardo, M., & Eichinger, R. (2003). *The LEADERSHIP ARCHITECT® norms and validity report.* Minneapolis: Lominger Limited, Inc.

McCall, M.W., & Lombardo, M. (1983). What makes a top executive? *Psychology Today, 17* (2), 26–31.

McCall, M.W., Lombardo, M., & Morrison, A. (1988). *The lessons of experience: How successful executives develop on the job.* Lexington, MA: Lexington Books.

Millikin-Davies, M. (1992). *An exploration of flawed first-line supervision.* Unpublished doctoral dissertation, University of Tulsa, Tulsa, OK.

Peterson, D.B. (1993). Measuring change: A psychometric approach to evaluating individual training outcomes. In V. Arnold (Chair), *Innovations in training evaluation: New measures, new designs.* Symposium conducted at the Eighth Annual Conference of the Society for Industrial and Organizational Psychology, San Francisco.

Shipper, F., & Dillard, J. (2000). A study of impending derailment and recovery of middle managers across career stages. *Human Resource Management, 39* (4), 331–347.

Spreitzer, G.M., McCall, M.W., & Mahoney, J.D. (1997). Early identification of international executive potential. *Journal of Applied Psychology, 82* (1), 6–29.

Sweeney, P. (1999, February 14). Teaching new hires to feel at home. *The New York Times.*

Author Index

Chapter Number Referenced

Key Word Index

Chapter Number Referenced

In addition to

100 Things You Need to Know:
Best people practices for managers and HR

Lominger International: A Korn/Ferry Company offers these publications:

The Leadership Machine
FYI For Your Improvement™
(available in English, French, German, Italian, Spanish, Chinese
Traditional, Chinese Simplified, and Japanese)
FYI for Teams™
CAREER ARCHITECT® Development Planner

To order, visit our Web site at:
www.lominger.com

Want to learn more about the LEADERSHIP ARCHITECT® Suite?

☐   Yes, I would like to be on your mailing list to learn more about special offers and events.

Name _____

Title _____

Company _____

Address _____

City _____ State _____ ZIP _____

Country _____

Telephone _____ FAX _____

E-mail _____

I work for:
☐ A corporation
☐ A consulting organization
☐ An educational institution

Complete and FAX to: 952-345-3601

or mail to:
Lominger Limited, Inc.
5051 Highway 7, Suite 100
Minneapolis, MN 55416-2291

LOMINGER
International
A KORN/FERRY COMPANY

Fold out this answer sheet
to record your answers
on the 100 Things test.

	correct answer		correct answer
1. A B C D E	_____	26. A B C D E	_____
2. A B C D E	_____	27. A B C D E	_____
3. A B C D E	_____	28. A B C D E	_____
4. A B C D E	_____	29. A B C D E	_____
5. A B C D E	_____	30. A B C D E	_____
6. A B C D E	_____	31. A B C D E	_____
7. A B C D E	_____	32. A B C D E	_____
8. A B C D E	_____	33. A B C D E	_____
9. A B C D E	_____	34. A B C D E	_____
10. A B C D E	_____	35. A B C D E	_____
11. A B C D E	_____	36. A B C D E	_____
12. A B C D E	_____	37. A B C D E	_____
13. A B C D E	_____	38. A B C D E	_____
14. A B C D E	_____	39. A B C D E	_____
15. A B C D E	_____	40. A B C D E	_____
16. A B C D E	_____	41. A B C D E	_____
17. A B C D E	_____	42. A B C D E	_____
18. A B C D E	_____	43. A B C D E	_____
19. A B C D E	_____	44. A B C D E	_____
20. A B C D E	_____	45. A B C D E	_____
21. A B C D E	_____	46. A B C D E	_____
22. A B C D E	_____	47. A B C D E	_____
23. A B C D E	_____	48. A B C D E	_____
24. A B C D E	_____	49. A B C D E	_____
25. A B C D E	_____	50. A B C D E	_____

practices for managers and HR Answer Sheet

Instructions and Scoring

This answer sheet folds out so you can record your answers. A blank line follows each A–E choice to note the correct answer.

An average score should be about 57 correct, the lowest score should be about 26 correct, and the best score should be about 86 correct according to the findings of Rynes et al. in their article entitled "HR Professionals' Beliefs About Effective Human Resource Practices: Correspondence Between Research and Practice."

100 Things You Need to Know:
Best people practices for managers & HR

Volume 1

Robert W. Eichinger
Michael M. Lombardo
Dave Ulrich

Published by Lominger International: A Korn/Ferry Company
Minneapolis, MN